WOMEN IN HIGHER EDUCATION

WOMEN
IN
HIGHER
EDUCATION

Edited by
W. TODD FURNISS
PATRICIA ALBJERG GRAHAM

AMERICAN COUNCIL ON EDUCATION
WASHINGTON, D.C.

Library of Congress Cataloging in Publication Data
Main entry under title:
Women in higher education.

Papers presented at the 1972 annual meeting of the
American Council on Education held in Miami Beach,
Oct. 4–6, 1972.

Includes bibliographical references.

1. Higher education of women—United States—
Congresses. 2. Women as college teachers—United
States—Congresses. 3. Women college graduates—
United States—Congresses. I. Furniss, Warren Todd,
1921–   ed. II. Graham, Patricia Albjerg, ed.
III. American Council on Education.
LC1756.W66   376'.65   73-22230
Library of Congress Cataloging in Publication Data
ISBN 0-8268-1421-2

PRINTED IN THE UNITED STATES OF AMERICA

Contributors

JULIA T. APTER, Professor of Surgery, Rush Medical College, Chicago

HELEN S. ASTIN, Professor of Higher Education, University of California, Los Angeles; formerly Director of Research and Education, University Research Corporation, Washington, D.C.

CAROLYN SHAW BELL, Katharine Coman Professor of Economics, Wellesley College; Chairman, Committee on the Status of Women in the Economics Profession, American Economic Association

McGEORGE BUNDY, President, The Ford Foundation

JEAN W. CAMPBELL, Director, Center for Continuing Education of Women, University of Michigan

K. PATRICIA CROSS, Senior Research Psychologist, Educational Testing Service, Western Office; Research Educator, Center for Research and Development in Higher Education, University of California, Berkeley

BARBARA DEINHARDT, Class of 1973, Yale University

ROBBEN W. FLEMING, President, University of Michigan

ANN L. FULLER, formerly Assistant Professor of Mathematics, Oberlin College; Assistant Professor, Department of Educational Services, Brooklyn College

LISA GETMAN, Class of 1973, Yale University

MASON W. GROSS, President Emeritus, Rutgers University

PATRICIA ROBERTS HARRIS, Partner, Fried, Frank, Harris, Shriver & Kampelman

ROGER W. HEYNS, President, American Council on Education

KATHERINE L. JELLY, Graduate Student, Graduate School of Education, Harvard University

LEO KANOWITZ, Professor of Law, Hastings College of the Law, University of California

KATHERINE M. KLOTZBURGER, Special Assistant to the Chancellor, and Project Director, Chancellor's Advisory Committee on the Status of Women at the City University of New York

JUANITA M. KREPS, James B. Duke Professor of Economics, Duke University

THELMA Z. LAVINE, Elton Professor and Chairman, Department of Philosophy, George Washington University

JULIAN H. LEVI, Professor of Urban Studies, University of Chicago

ROSALIND LORING, Director, Department of Daytime Programs and Special Projects, University Extension, University of California, Los Angeles

JACQUELINE A. MATTFELD, Associate Provost and Dean of Academic Affairs, Brown University

ROBERT M. O'NEIL, Vice-President and Provost for Academic Affairs, University of Cincinnati

MARTHA E. PETERSON, President, Barnard College

MINA REES, President Emeritus, Graduate School and University Center, City University of New York

JOAN I. ROBERTS, Assistant Professor, Department of Educational Policy Studies, University of Wisconsin

GRISEL RODRIGUEZ, Student, Miami-Dade Junior College

MARTHA P. ROGERS, Special Assistant to the Vice-Chairman, U.S. Equal Employment Opportunity Commission

DOROTHY ROSS, Assistant Professor of History, Princeton University

MARGARET L. RUMBARGER, Associate Secretary, American Association of University Professors

BERNICE SANDLER, Executive Associate, and Director, Project on the Status and Education of Women, Association of American Colleges

BEVERLY SCHMALZRIED, Chairman, Human Development and Family Living, Stout State University

BARBARA SICHERMAN, Assistant Professor of History, Manhattanville College

HEATHER SIGWORTH, Attorney; formerly Project Coordinator, Project on Criminal Instructions, Committee on Uniform Jury Instructions of the Supreme Court of the State of Arizona

MABEL M. SMYTHE, Vice-President, Phelps-Stokes Fund

CATHARINE R. STIMPSON, Assistant Professor of English, and Acting Director, Women's Center, Barnard College

SHEILA TOBIAS, Associate Provost, Wesleyan University

ANNE THORSEN TRUAX, Director, Minnesota Women's Center, University of Minnesota

DAVID B. TRUMAN, President, Mount Holyoke College

Contents

Foreword

THE COUNCIL'S FIFTY-FIFTH ANNUAL MEETING, for which the papers in this volume were prepared, was held in the same week that the Office of Contract Compliance published the first official guidelines on affirmative action. Within the next several months, congressional legislation extended to still other federal agencies authority for enforcement of nondiscrimination in colleges and universities. In the same period, reduced rates of growth in higher education and their effects on employment, retention, and salary policies, potentially disproportionate for women, became realities and began to be felt nationally.

It was the purpose of the meeting, as its co-directors point out in their preface to this volume, "to establish a solid ideological base line for future change in the practices of colleges and universities, and provide the rationale for some new practices now established or being tested in several kinds of institutions." The soundness of that aim has been justified by subsequent events: The considerations of equity made inescapably clear in this book—by reason and anecdote more than by emotion—must be translated into operational terms.

The academic community has not yet resolved all the issues raised in this book. A number of them are being dealt with in formal hearings and judicial proceedings now in progress. Nevertheless, the fundamental positions set forth and illustrated here are, for the most part, accepted as the starting point for resolving the remaining problems.

For the American Council on Education, the Fifty-fifth Annual Meeting and the publication of this book are only two elements in a larger program designed to help colleges and universities provide full equity for women students, faculty, and staff, and to assist the agencies charged with administering the laws of the land. Much of this effort is focused in the Council's Office of Women in Higher Education, its Equal Employment Opportunity Task Force, and its Office of Leadership Development in Higher Education, but it is also the continuing concern of the Council's Board of Directors and all its principal offices.

ROGER W. HEYNS, *President*
American Council on Education

Preface

THEORISTS OF SOCIAL MOVEMENTS have long argued that it is a mark of progress when attention moves from ideological to technical issues.

Such signs of progress in resolving issues dealing with women in higher education were evident at the 1972 Annual Meeting of the American Council on Education as more than sixteen hundred registrants discussed aspects of the issues in twenty-two sessions. The present volume is designed to capture a moment in the history of colleges and universities when the shift from ideological to technical is sufficiently far along that action can be taken without the need to review yet again the fundamental principles on which it is based.

From the sixty-six papers presented to the meeting, we have selected a number which together establish the ideological bases of issues related to women as members of the academic community and suggest practical steps that can turn theory into practice. In addition, we have included papers which set the issues on campus in the contexts of other issues that are demanding equal attention from institutions, notably questions of accountability, institutional autonomy, and social justice.

The attentive reader will detect disagreement among the authors, quite as there was disagreement during the discussions at the Council's meeting. On two basic points, however, the authors and the registrants were agreed almost unanimously: Discrimination against women in higher education exists, is wrong, and should be eliminated; such discrimination is illegal, and those who practice it today are subject to stringent and costly legal sanctions, as they were not even a few years ago.

It is our hope that this book will establish a solid ideological base line for future change in the practices of colleges and universities, and provide the rationale for some new practices now established or being tested in several kinds of institutions. Much still needs to be done that will require leadership of the sort called for by Martha Peterson and Roger Heyns in the papers that open and close this book.

W.T.F.
P.A.G.

Acknowledgments

The Fifty-fifth Annual Meeting of the American Council on Education, held in Miami Beach, October 4–6, 1972, was planned by the editors of this volume with the generous help of Martha E. Peterson, Mina Rees, members of the Council's staff, and representatives of several higher education associations. We regret that space limitations make it impossible to include in this volume all the fine papers that were prepared for discussion and wish here to acknowledge the contributions of the following participants, some of whom have published their papers elsewhere: Suzanne S. Armacost, Margaret H. Arter, Mary Woods Bennett, Ruth C. Benson, Audrey C. Cohen, Thorndike Deland, Alvin C. Eurich, Konnilyn G. Feig, Marilyn Gittell, Barbara B. Green, George L. Hall, Elizabeth H. Kaynor, Miriam G. Keiffer, Catherine Kerr, Gerda Lerner, Elizabeth S. Lyman, J. Barry McGannon, Norma C. Noonan, Rosemary Park, Betti Pate, J. Stanley Pottinger, Geraldine Rickman, Lorene L. Rogers, Steven B. Sample, Gertrude J. Selznick, James S. Smoot, John E. Smylie, Sandra S. Tangri, M. Elizabeth Tidball, and Robert A. Wallhaus.

A rough estimate of the number of persons involved in the administration of the meeting and the editing of the book, at the Council, at Barnard College, and in the institutions and organizations represented by our contributors, is a staggering 200. We wish to thank all of them by recognizing as their representatives Council staff members Olive Mills, senior editor, Douglas F. Bodwell, staff associate, and Lilyan S. Kahn and Ruth C. Smith, administrative secretaries.

Part One

WOMEN IN HIGHER EDUCATION

MARTHA E. PETERSON

Women, Autonomy, and Accountability in Higher Education

WITHIN ONE YEAR'S TIME, some messages that are important and possibly historic have emerged from conventions held in Miami Beach. At a meeting of the Southern Association of Colleges and Schools in November 1971, Alan Pifer, president of the Carnegie Corporation of New York, spoke forthrightly on issues related to the neglect of women in higher education. In 1972, the Democrats met in Miami Beach in July, the Republicans in August, and the American Council in October, with at least one shared purpose—the final, resolute step in the liberation of women.

Unlikely as the setting is, and these organizations are for the honor, it is just possible that the Carnegie Corporation, the major political parties, and the Council have made Miami Beach the Seneca Falls of the twentieth century.

When I was invited to give this keynote address—"a summary of the interrelationships of the women's issues, autonomy, and accountability, the areas in which higher education is today most in trouble"—it occurred to me I should decline because I have other responsibilities on the program. But I quickly overcame any sense of obligation to forgo the opportunity, for I have something I want to say about higher education and women, and I want to say it to this particular audience.

The remarks will be somewhat personal, growing out of my thirty years' experience as a teacher and administrator in what I consider excellent, representative institutions of higher education: the University of Kansas, the University of Wisconsin, and Barnard College, and, through it, Columbia University. I shall be critical, although I am on the whole optimistic about the future of higher education if we can "get it all put together." Some may regard my comments as those of a female chauvinist, attacking the male of the academic species. That will be a false deduction for I regard

3

myself as one of those responsible for the current state of affairs. In fact, I consider each person here, male or female, newcomers or regulars, as culpable. The members of this particular audience would not be here if they did not have some influence on education. Therefore, the shortcomings I shall discuss are the responsibility of all of us; we are here to see if we can learn how to do something about them.

My comments fall into three categories: some observations on current conditions in higher education, with particular emphasis on the condition of leadership; a more detailed examination of the woman's issue as an example of current conditions; and some suggestions on what we might most appropriately do right now to bring about change.

The purpose of a keynote speech is to stimulate listeners to action at the meetings and thereafter. The planners of these sessions hope to bring about a rational examination of conditions in higher education, particularly as they affect women, autonomy, and accountability; they anticipate that change on campus will be a natural consequence of such an examination. I shall now try to get the process under way.

CURRENT CONDITIONS ON CAMPUS

College campuses these days are not exactly scenes of joy and rapture; nor do they seem to fit the former characterization either of complacent apathy or explosive radicalism. Perhaps the writer of a September 5, 1972, editorial in the *New York Times* on "The Education Issue" gave us the terms to describe current conditions when he observed, "Higher education is in a financial as well as emotional depression."

There is no question about the financial crisis in higher education, although "depression" may not entirely convey the always dynamic, sometimes unpredictable, ever frustrating challenges that are a part of all financial considerations these days.

Describing the current campus mood as one of "emotional depression" is more questionable. If we want a general characterization, it may be the best phrase. It could be argued that, in light of present realities, the student, faculty member, administrator, or trustee who is not somber, even depressed, is out of touch. And, on campus, everyone except the entering freshman can claim a right to exhaustion (a close ally of depression) from the emotional excesses of the recent years.

But there is danger in applying this or any other generally descriptive term, particularly now. The danger lies in the exceptions. Certainly no one would apply the term "emotionally depressed" to those women on campus who are aware of their claim to an equal share of the opportunities and who are vigorously pursuing that fair share. Nor are the law schools and the lawyers, currently in a position of high prestige, an example of exhaustion and resignation. And there are others with equally high morale on campus. We put ourselves in a trap if we agree on "emotional depression" as a fitting description of the campus mood, and then find it applies only to the administrative staff, the male tenured faculty, the losing football team, or the trustees. By a slip—Freudian or otherwise—we have revealed our rating of who is important as we describe the campus.

Let us turn, therefore, to the attitudes of those we know best, ourselves—the official and unofficial academic leadership. What is our current condition? I shall attempt by illustration and inference to convince you that we are not in very good shape and that, in our ineffectiveness in achieving real accountability, we—as we represent the colleges and universities—are forfeiting important claims for accountability.

Roger Heyns tells of a conversation with a nonacademic friend who recently asked him, "Where have you fellows been lately?", by which he presumably meant that nothing much has been heard recently from those persons who formerly could be counted on to speak out on important issues in higher education—to lead. Further, we haven't heard much in the public media, the professional journals, or on the speaking circuit. Yale apologizes for a smaller deficit than anticipated. But is that intellectual leadership? We may claim to be at home "tending the store," but then we are haunted by that September *Times* editorial, mentioned earlier, which observes: "The universities lack internal direction and external support." If that is true, we seem not to have been doing much to talk about. This accusation we have heard before.

Do you remember Daniel Patrick Moynihan, in St. Louis at the 1970 Council meeting, chiding leaders in higher education about their lack of interest in the new educational policies being developed in Washington?[1] He acknowledged that everyone had been busy with internal crises, but he wondered whether we would regret abdication of external responsibility to politicians and legislators.

WOMEN'S ISSUES

We thought then that Moynihan spoke only of the White House proposals to the Congress for changes in financing higher education, and we feared we might be being enticed to take sides in a partisan political battle. But how many persons have thought of Mr. Moynihan's advice in connection with affirmative action experiences? Is it not possible that failure to take positive and strong positions on campus in support of affirmative action has, of necessity, caused the U.S. Department of Health, Education, and Welfare to intervene in such a way that, on campus, ability to govern is eroded?

I shall speak of "affirmative action" as it applies to women because that aspect appears to be the volatile issue now. It is the one about which I know the most. We must remember, however, the term applies to all forms of discrimination that are based on any classification which excludes by reason of race, age, ethnic group, religion, or sex.

Let me digress now briefly to state what it is women are seeking. I do this as a background for "affirmative action," but I shall put the statement in broad terms because the sessions which follow will provide opportunities to investigate the practical consequences illustrated in such topics as women's studies, maternal and paternal leave, day care centers, nepotism, and part-time tenured positions.

What women are seeking is fairly easily stated and fairly easy to support, at least as a general premise. Women on campus— whether students, the staff, or faculty members—seek open access to the opportunities to which their abilities, their interests, and their willingness to work entitle them. They believe such equality of opportunity is their right and should be granted to them willingly, even with enthusiasm by those who make the decisions. The woman student asks for equal treatment with all other candidates

1. "On Universal Higher Education," in *Higher Education for Everybody?* ed. W. Todd Furniss (Washington: American Council on Education, 1971), pp. 233–54.

in admission, in selection of what she will study, in financial aid. She would like to see elimination of the "second sex" condescension she sometimes experiences in the classroom.

The young woman entering the academic world as a teacher, staff member, or employee asks to be hired on her qualifications and paid and promoted on the basis of the quality of her work. She knows that if she is married and has young children, the demands on her time may be different from those of a man or a single woman, but she believes these different demands need not inhibit her academic career provided quality of work, rather than predetermined stereotypes, is the criterion for evaluation. The woman who has established herself professionally in the academic world seeks the elimination of any barriers to promotion, pay, or other rewards of the academic world, such as committee service, honors, membership in policy-making bodies, and appointment to administrative posts. These barriers do exist because she is a woman, and she asks that they be removed both for herself and for the young women who wish to enter the academic world in increasingly larger numbers.

No one can really deny on a rational level the justice of these claims in the academic community on a rational level. Equal opportunity simply does not exist on the campus currently, and in a curious way colleges and universities seem less enthusiastic than almost any other major component of society in doing something about the inequities. With those observations I turn to affirmative action.

The disgrace of affirmative action is just what Alan Pifer pointed out a year ago at the Southern Association meeting: that HEW had to get into it at all. Through intransigence, unperceptiveness, or preoccupation with other issues, the higher education community seemed unable to recognize and to take action in correcting injustices until forced to do so by HEW—a dismal example of lack of internal leadership.

The second disgrace follows the first quite closely: the reaction of the academic community to HEW's requests for affirmative action programs. Many will recall our distress during the past two years over the lack of guidelines for affirmative action. In retrospect, we sounded a bit like the student who says, "Show me the rule that tells me I can't do what I have just done!" The intent of affirmative action was clear enough. We could have written our own set of policies and procedures for attaining its goals. But few institutions have done so, and the American Council got itself in the unfortunate position of asking HEW whether or not it would be helpful for the Council to write a set, only to be told to wait a bit inasmuch as a set would shortly be forthcoming. I can excuse institutions who were under threat and therefore sought the rules from the adversary. The rest of the institutions must have had priorities other than guidelines to which they gave attention.

Then there is the matter of retroactive pay. Of course budget conditions are tight and money must not be squandered. But once an institution knows it has an indefensible pay scale based on discrimination, it has no choice legally or morally except to right the inequities, including whatever back pay is deemed reasonable by an unbiased mediator. To do less is to abdicate leadership responsibilities. We have met other financial contingencies—natural disasters, an unexpected drop in enrollment, support of a program from which foundation or governmental support has been withdrawn. We probably can weather the additional cost of a reasonable amount of retroactive pay if we care enough.

We have expressed alarm that the representatives of HEW would obtain access to confidential records of employees. Only a few years ago we learned about confidentiality of records in another arena, and now we appear to use this new principle as an excuse to slow down progress toward the removal of barriers to equal access. It is true that we must safeguard the records of the individual, but legal protections are available and we would have done well to exhaust those avenues before expressing so much alarm.

We ask, Do affirmative action procedures apply to part-time as well as full-time jobs? We sigh that excellence must now be forgotten as a criterion in making academic appointments. We quibble about goals and quotas rather than reacting to requests to show good faith in eliminating past discrimination with positive vigorous leadership. Have we insisted to everyone on campus that the time has come to do, with as much good grace as we can muster, what we should have done long ago? We hesitate, look for loopholes, and appear persecuted.

Lest these remarks be seen as a defense of HEW's administration of Executive Order 11246, let me hasten to restate my first point. HEW did not belong in this business in the first place. It has invaded the right of autonomy of the campus and not always with great skill. But we made it possible.

There are other examples of loss of autonomy by failure to be accountable. Under the new Higher Education Act, the Commissioner of Education must certify the eligibility of institutions to receive aid. We, of course, have voluntary accrediting agencies which we like to believe would be a reasonable source for determining academic eligibility. But suppose we are asked, as we will be, What about the intent of the law to encourage the development of postsecondary educational opportunities for all? Do the establishment accrediting agencies encourage such development?

If we turn from the federal government to the states or to our own campuses, we can cite example after example of the need for effective leadership in a time of radical change. Perhaps there is no way for administrators to preserve autonomy through accountability in these explosive times, for the neglect has been neither benign nor willful. But the lack of a positive momentum is real, and the leaders—like it or not—are held responsible by those who have expectations for the academic community.

How to Bring about Change?

What of the future? What can higher education do to improve the present state of affairs? As I said earlier, I am optimistic about the future if we can "get it all together." What are the areas where change is possible, and what are the conditions of change?

It would help, I believe, if we could forget what was and come to terms with what is. The days of euphoric expansion are over, the days of more and more students, of increases in numbers of programs, departments, schools, and even colleges, of ever increasing funds for research, and unquestioning public support. The present and the immediate future are better described as times of a leveling-off of enrollments, redefinition and redirection of already established curricula, carefully evaluated research, and a time of critical public reactions. Postsecondary education need not stagnate under such careful scrutiny provided it accepts reality and works with it, not against it.

Most of us must face too the absolute necessity of interinstitutional cooperation through voluntary or regional or state or national organizations in which each institution sacrifices some of its institutional autonomy for the larger good. And in these organizations and consortia, we will become accustomed to supporting our accountability by hard data, not past reputation.

Further, educational institutions must attempt to recapture their sense of responsibility for intellectual leadership. We cannot afford another defensive reaction to public good like our reaction to the principles of affirmative action.

I could elaborate on these three concepts: the acceptance of reality, the need for cooperative effort, and the need to exert intellectual leadership. But many in this audience have already heard such discussions and all will hear them at every turn in the year ahead. Those concepts clearly summarize the direction in which we must lead on campus and, together, lead as a voice of higher education.

K. Patricia Cross has concluded her paper for this meeting, "The Woman Student," with these words: "The question of providing equal educational opportunity without regard to race, sex, age, or any other class identification is not one that is likely to go away if ignored. The options are really two—whether to lead with a bang or follow with a whimper."

In the true spirit of our predecessors in conventions at Miami Beach, may I suggest that we have followed with whimpers and our efforts have not been overly productive. Let's try leading with a bang.

PATRICIA ROBERTS HARRIS

Problems and Solutions
in Achieving Equality for Women

Most people in academic life are elitists. There is a deliberate search in academic life for "the best": the best student, the best teacher, the best performance. Therefore, the aspirant for admission to the groves of academe must be the best available, if the employing peers are to be satisfied. Because more men than women are encouraged to attend graduate school, present papers at meetings, and publish them, the standard of competence has been established by male performance. More men than women have been college teachers, and, therefore, the only test of performance is that of teachers who are already in the work place. The collegiate Mr. Chips and the Dr. Einsteins, tempered by Kingman Brewster types, are still the ideals. Since no "mother's preference" accompanies the application of the woman Ph.D. who took time out to have two healthy babies, and thereby learned self-discipline and responsibility in a way that is difficult for her preoccupied and dependent spouse, and because the assumption prevails that women will be mothers and wives before seriously indulging their intellectual interests, women tend to get short shrift in the academic selection process. No extra academic points are available to women being considered for appointment to an all-male sociology faculty examining a society in which 51 percent of the population is female; no sex points are available to a woman seeking appointment to a faculty teaching literature of the Brontës and George Sand or teaching biochemistry, with its need for gestalts and intuitive flashes. Although many women teaching assistants are coauthors of scientific papers with men, they seem not to show up later on university faculties.

There is an assumption by both male and female elitists that women are generally less well qualified than men for the higher ranks of the educational hierarchy. Women are penalized both by

11

raw sex prejudice and by relatively unimportant criteria such as "temperament," length of previous experience, and time in lower academic ranks. It is clear to me that the restrictions which limit women's participation in higher education are due largely to prejudiced assumptions about women and their roles and not to objective questions of competence.

WOMEN'S LIBERATION

As for higher education, women's liberation is the best thing that ever happened to it. The modern women's liberation movement began outside academe with Betty Friedan's *The Feminine Mystique*. This in itself is interesting. As the chief interpreters and molders of modern value systems, the university community apparently was unable to perceive the enormity of the problem of women in modern society or the nature of subjugation of women in the university community. If one places Gunnar Myrdal in the university community, it becomes clear that this myopia with respect to women's problems was quite different from the academic concern with problems of race in this country. Although many of us complain about the limited research on race in this country, the examination of racial concerns was exhaustive when compared with the analysis of the sociopolitical role of women.

Betty Friedan started the new public dialogue, but my impression was that academe heard and understood little of the debate raging in student dormitories, communes, and the kitchens of faculty wives. This situation continued throughout the decade of the sixties, with its turbulence and abrupt as well as subtle changes. The demonstration of dissatisfaction with institutions that used them but ignored them as persons led first black, and then white, college students to attack something they described as "the system" with all the weapons available to them. Significant change resulted even though not all of the change was within the parameters envisioned by the protesters.

Despite the agitation for change which marked the sixties, the essential role of women and the relationship of women to institutions of the society was little altered. Such alteration as took place was more apparent than real and related largely to the ability of young women to lead lives less restricted by sexual taboos than had been the lives of previous generations of women. However, even the emerging pattern of apparent female sexuality was not new. "Bohemian" women in the twenties, "political" women in the thirties, and "sophisticated" women in the forties had quietly chosen to enter into sexual relationships which did not necessarily result in marriage. The primary difference between the behavior of the Bohemians of the twenties and their successors of the sixties was that the Bohemian was less than candid about the extent of the extramarital sex in which she was engaged. My rather vague memory of flapper literature is that the flapper talked a lot about personal freedom but was sexually puritanical.

The verbalized demand of pre-sixties males for marriage to a chaste woman, whether serious or not, made it propitious for every woman to give the appearance of chastity. Although "nice" girls were exploited and intimidated by young men in their sexual relationships, there was general agreement between young men and women that, all things being equal, premarital sex gave the woman a claim upon the man that would eventuate in marriage between the two. However, the pervasive existentialism of the sixties made this unspoken agreement less and less acceptable to males, who had never been happy about it. The sixties girl was not permitted to retain even the appearance of chastity. Males insisted on the establishment of sexual relationships without any commitment to a continuing relationship, and made the establishment of such sexual relationship the sine qua non of the establishment of any relationship at all.

The "new sexual freedom" of women in the sixties was based on the continuing sexual exploitation of women by men.

At the same time, cooperative (or communal) patterns of living were revived, with the "newly free" women allowed the privilege of cooking and cleaning for the community. The first signs of true revolt by young women that came to my attention centered on the casual assignment of traditional roles to women in these allegedly radical living arrangements. Although the returning veterans of the forties had brought respectability to the idea that a man in college could be supported by his working wife who remained responsible for the household management, this combination of housewifery with employment was deemed to be temporary, to last only until the husband was employed. The communal housewife, who had no promise that she would be a wife, began to wonder why the new sexual freedom deprived her of the protection of wifehood, but spared her none of the chores of housewifery.

These women, usually college students or college dropouts, were getting another lesson in the reality that the exploitation of women is not limited to thoughtless, uneducated males, but is considered the perogative of the intellectual male as well as his brother, Archie Bunker.

WOMEN IN THE UNIVERSITY

In fact, the producer and refuge of the male intellectual, the university, turned out to be one of the most sexist institutions in this country. Although women have been present in college student bodies in significant numbers through most of this century, and even though the performance of women on tests of intellectual ability tends to be better than that of men, women are second-class citizens in higher education.

Despite the theory that coeducation changes men's attitudes toward women by convincing men that women are their intellectual equals, all of us who are the products of coeducation know that this is not the case. The university has managed to operate in semi-isolation from the reality of the world in which the men and women will operate when they leave the campus. In fact, the classroom has tended in its coeducation to operate in isolation from the very institution of which it is a part, because that institution almost invariably is run by men, classes are taught by male professors, and the message is given directly and indirectly that college is an interlude for women who seek intellectual equality and thus they had better cherish it in the classroom because they will not see it again. Male professors still mourn the fact that their brilliant female students are female because, they still say, these women will waste their education by getting married and having children. So certain are they of the role to be played by women that they seldom recommend women for fellowships and almost never invite them to return to teach in the department in which they showed great promise.

Both male and female students receive a clear message from the university that men will use their brains and women will waste theirs. The young man may well marry the smartest girl in the class and spend the rest of his life killing himself to prove that she was not wrong in marrying him, by working to become as rich and famous as he knows she would have become had she been born male. Acceptance of the fact that women may choose to assume roles that have traditionally been male roles—such as lawyer, college president, dean, newspaper publisher, hospital administrator, prime minister, judge—is still difficult for many men.

Much to my surprise, I have discovered that male academicians and academic administrators (they are not always identical) are among the most insecure men when confronted by the aspirations of women. Although they usually rationalize their insecurity in a generalization about wanting only "qualified women" on the faculty, many male faculty members of every rank react to the possibility of a faculty with a higher proportion of women with much the same emotion that legend assigns when an elephant is confronted by a mouse.

I suspect that soon Midge Decter will become the darling of such male intellectuals. Her assertions in *The New Chastity* that "the plain unvarnished fact is that every woman wants to marry," and that every sane woman "requires both in her nature and by virtue of what are her immediate practical needs ... the assurance that a single man has undertaken to love, cherish, and support her," express the conscious and unconscious assumption of intellectual males. Although I suspect that Mrs. Decter would deny it, her statements retain the conservative notion of the essential dependency of women on their roles as wives and deny the existence of a drive to succeed in a particular field. Women are found by Mrs. Decter to need marriage, while men only assent to it. Even when a girl is "adolescent, ... or a student committed to completing her education—a girl almost by instinct organizes her relations with the opposite sex around the principle of rehearsal for wifehood," say Mrs. Decter.[1]

MARRIAGE AND THE BLACK EXPERIENCE

Were these assertions a necessary consequence of female biology, the treatment of women in academic life would be justified. Without arguing the question of whether men assume a future with a continuing sex partner, with or without legal consequences, it is highly questionable whether many women would choose a

1. New York: Coward, McCann & Geoghegan, 1972.

secondary role as wife, deriving their status from their husband's work rather than their own, if other choices were real and socially acceptable. Women now take out the best insurance available against lack of status: acquisition of husbands who will provide alternatives to their own status as individuals. That certain women for whom such insurance has been limited have made a different choice is something generally overlooked by people such as Mrs. Decter, largely because this society can only see white role models.

One of the little appreciated results of the black experience has been an anticipation by a significant part of the black middle class of the life style now sought by white middle-class women in the women's liberation movement. Although both white females and white males treat the demands of white females for equality as a demand for a trip in uncharted wilds of human experience, there are among us some who are living in the closest approximation of male-female equality that I know about.

The urge to protect black women from domestic service and sexual intimidation and exploitation by whites led to special efforts by black families to educate the black girl. The availability of teaching positions for black women made this education a practical investment, but there was general acceptance by the black community that women would work, and that the better educated the woman, the less demeaning the work. Most of the educated black women became teachers, and they and women in other fields formed a significant proportion of the educated black community. Although some of these women married men who had less education than they, a large number married their fellow students. From these unions of educated black men and women was developed a familial life style which is indicative of what life will be like in a society that accepts the equality of men and women, that is, the life style of the middle-class professional black family. Cynthia Fuchs Epstein, in an excellent study, suggests that the black middle-class professional family is "one of the closest models to equality between the sexes we have in American society."[2]

Despite the sometimes derogatory picture painted of the Negro family in the United States, this statement by Mrs. Epstein is accurate. The negative picture of black family life painted by

2. *Woman's Place: Options and Limits in Professional Careers* (Berkeley and Los Angeles: University of California Press, 1971), p. 35.

Moynihan, and luridly broadcast and embroidered by overt and covert racists, is in fact the picture of the life of severely damaged black members of American society who were never permitted to achieve the middle-class status that is considered the birthright of most American whites. Almost nothing has been told of that tiny fraction of the black population that manages, in spite of the roadblocks placed in the path of all black Americans, to achieve middle-class professional status.

Middle-class black women married to middle-class black professionals are among the most attractive and the most accomplished women I know, and their husbands tend to be the most urbane and relaxed of the men I have met. Because these middle-class black families are seldom attached to major white academic institutions, they are virtually unknown to white scholars, or, when known, are discounted on the theory that they are exceptional. Let me describe a few of these families, all of them real and among my personal friends.

First, there is a woman psychiatrist married to a lawyer. They have two children and live in a small house in Washington, D.C. Each is in active professional practice, and they are delightful to be with. Despite racial discrimination, the husband is moving up in the legal field, and the wife is one of the most respected young psychiatrists in Washington. The husband feels secure about considering changing his present job because he knows the income from his wife's practice will enable them to continue to live comfortably. Their children are well mannered, highly verbal, and clearly well adjusted, with no probem of knowing who is Mama and who is Papa. She teaches part time at a medical school.

The second family is an older couple. The husband is a retired army colonel, whose wife and two daughters accompanied him on duty tours to Japan, France, and Germany. When they were stateside, she taught school, as she was trained to do. Today, he is employed in the field of his army expertise, and she is one of the most effective elementary school teachers in Washington. He retired from the army early because the pressure of looking to the next step in promotion, that of general officer, was more than either husband or wife wished to endure, and, financially, they did not need the additional money because their joint incomes, even with two college-age daughters, made it unnecessary for him to push himself psychically for a promotion against which the odds were great.

Then there is the internist and his wife, whom he met when he was on a special tour of duty as a teacher in a Midwestern medical school and she was earning a graduate degree in social work. He has always taught medicine, and she has been a practicing social worker. Years ago, she told me that her husband had had many opportunities to enter private practice with a lucrative income, but that he preferred teaching and institutional medicine. Her significant professional status and commensurate income enabled him to accept the lower income from his teaching position, a decision he might not have been able to make had he not had a wife who was professionally successful. Their two daughters, both in college, are well adjusted and happy. One expects to marry before she finishes her senior year, an indication that such an equality-based family does not discourage their children from marriage. She moves in and out of academic life, and has been a full-time member of a university faculty as well as an adjunct professor. Nepotism rules prevent her employment in her husband's institution.

Another such family is a chief executive of a major city and his educator wife, chief of a federal government bureau. Grandparents, their only daughter is married and working on her Ph.D. Grandma is taking care of the granddaughter, and, to the surprise of all their friends who had assumed that Grandma was the force in the family, it is revealed that the real politician and the strong personality was not Grandma, who had for years been in the limelight as one of the outstanding black professional women in the country but, instead, her husband, who turned out to be a major politician. She has been a college professor.

Last, there are our neighbors, a young black couple with two children. He was an executive with an international agency, and she is a highly paid educational consultant who serves on numerous boards. He left his position with the agency, it is rumored, because of his sense that there was no future for him. He now has a position in which he is engaged in an interesting experiment dealing with problems of poverty stricken communities. He will soon become an executive in a major corporation, a change that he might not have considered possible had it not been that his wife's employment gave him the security to leave a prestigious but unrewarding position in order to assess his goals for the future.

I could go on describing such couples, all with beautifully adjusted children and with pleasant and well-rounded social lives, who assume that both husband and wife will work at their highest professional capacity. Of course, the husbands sometimes complain, and the wives are often torn by the same guilts that afflict their white sisters who work. The difference is that it was always assumed that most middle-class black women would work, and we were "programmed" to do so because our parents were not wealthy and our chances of finding a wealthy black man to take care of us were even more limited than similar chances were for our white sisters. Therefore, the more secure the parents of a black girl, the more likely she was to have a profession; and the brighter she was, the more likely she was to be encouraged to maximize her employment opportunity.

White and black male supremacists have interpreted this role as the "black matriarch" attempting to castrate the black male. In truth, as the result of her training, the middle-class black woman has protected the dignity of the black male professional by aiding him, through her employment, in maintaining his professional status and by increasing the economic security of the family, including the children. The man is not considered his wife's inferior: they are equal contributors; each has a significant role to play. The children know who is Daddy and who is Mommy and they respect both. The black woman professional knows she is competent and that she is significant. The problems of the feminine mystique do not confront this woman. Black professional women have a life experience of equality with black men which ought to be emulated by white women and accepted as a goal by white men.

This acceptance of the reality of equality is doubtless what has made it easy for institutions seeking women of experience and training to find black women for widely varied roles. Although white women have recently cited the prominence of black women in situations from which women were previously excluded as examples of "reverse racism" (that is, an attempt to exclude white women by an appeal to blacks), the truth is that black women are both competent and secure in dealing with men as equals because they have been working seriously for so long.

EQUALITY IN COLLEGES AND UNIVERSITIES

The life style of equality demonstrated by black professional couples is the life style upon which higher education for men and women should be predicated. What a waste to impose differential calculus on one who is only going to measure the pabulum, and how unfair to limit her opportunities to working as assistant to the boy whom she helped to pass the course. It is equally unfair to deprive men of the support, emotional and otherwise, they can secure from women who will share all the responsibilities of life equally. Sexual inequality dies hard, even in a society committed to equality, as is demonstrated by the sight of Russian women sweeping the streets, and the lack of the sight of significant numbers of women at the Politburo level. It is the responsibility of the academic community to take leadership in ending sexual inequality.

Respect for a productive intellectual life for women and assurance of the opportunity for women to match performance to capacity are essential if higher education for women with men is to have any new meaning. The opportunity for free and meaningful choice of career can be provided for women, if men join in insisting on these rights. If education for women and men is to have any meaning in today's world, it must have the goal of providing real equality between its male and female students in college and after graduation. No longer can women accept the idea that they are educated for the purpose of providing their husbands and other dinner partners with sparkling conversationalists or for the purpose of producing educable male children. Faculty, administrators, and fellow students of the new woman student must accept the reality of women's demand that their education prepare them for the same kind of life for which men are prepared: a life as a productive citizen, only one of whose roles is that of producing and rearing children.

But like Midge Decter, women in academe are not yet sure they want to change the present dominance of males. For example, I am opposed to replacing women presidents of women's colleges with men so long as women are not considered for presidencies of coeducational colleges. I said this once to an extraordinarily able, strong-minded former woman president who was succeeded by a man. Her reply was that she wanted for her institution the best president possible, and that no woman was available who measured up to her successor. Although her successor is an able man, he does not match his predecessor in skill. What his selection really reflects is that we choose college presidents for reasons that have little to do with providing role models for women students (even though such considerations vis-à-vis men often do enter into presidential selections), and without concern for providing a sexual balance in the administration of academic life.

Women in academic life acquiesce in the elimination and exclusion of women from the top of academic life for several reasons. First, women rather like to have a father-lover figure in the chairs of responsibility and as associates, even if all are happily married to other people. Much as we dislike the idea, the sense of strangeness men have in dealing with women makes most women feel more comfortable with males. For this reason, in the past, the female assertion of the right to advancement in academe has been more individualistic than group oriented.

Even where there is female militancy, males are more comfortable with the idea of a male superior or a male colleague. I use the word "idea," because I find little resistance from men to the reality of leadership from a skillful woman. However, the expressed hostility of males to the idea and the reality of the preference of many women for male associates lead to acceptance of the notion that the appointment of a man is the best insurance against problems.

Despite the improvement in employment of women in higher education and the increase in the number of doctorates awarded to women during the last decade, the picture for the future is still bleak. Between 1960 and 1969, only 11.6 percent of all the doctorates in the country were awarded to women. And although a whopping 13.8 percent of the doctorates in the biological sciences went to women, women continue to hold a very small percentage of advanced degrees in scientific and technical fields. Save for home economics, in which women received 76.3 percent of the doctorates (God bless those males in the 23 percent), women exceeded 25 percent of the doctorates granted only in folklore, foreign languages, and library science. In most fields, fewer than 10 percent of the doctorates granted in the last decade were granted to women.

I am elitist enough to assume that most university and college teachers will come from the pool of doctorates. Obviously, even the best-intentioned institutions cannot secure more women Ph.D.'s for the faculty than exist. In addition, the women must want to be where the institution is at the time the institution needs them. Clearly, we must encourage women to use their talents in fields where there is still a need for teachers, and not in the fields that have recently seen overproduction of both men and women Ph.D.'s.

In the past, little sincere encouragement was given women Ph.D. candidates outside the traditional women's disciplines such as social work, education, English, and foreign languages. Such a bleak picture was painted of employment opportunities that it scarcely seemed worthwhile to get a Ph.D. This treatment was one of the few evidences of equality between black and white women considering the Ph.D.: they were treated the same way. Thus the pool of women Ph.D.'s has been kept at a minimum by discrimination against women Ph.D. candidates, without regard to race.

Even those women who had the support and motivation to secure the Ph.D. and moved on to a college faculty found the upper ranks difficult to attain. Many of the women were married to relatively successful men, and the assumption was that they did not need the extra money that accompanied higher rank. Or it was assumed that single women had fewer expenses than married men and therefore needed less money.

Equally important was the acceptance by women themselves of these and other assumptions about women's rights and roles. In voting on tenure and leadership roles such as department chairmen and deans, women have tended to be uncomfortable about moving into leadership positions themselves and about supporting women who were assertive, opinionated, and forceful. Often men with exactly the same characteristics were elected. In many instances, however, gentle, sensitive men were chosen, while women with such characteristics were vetoed because they were said to be not strong enough to perform the task. I have talked to many college presidents over the years, and, despite their experience with women as intellectual equals, almost all expressed the view that there are limitations on the extent to which women can staff the upper echelons of the university.

College and university administrators and their boards, after years of excluding women from the upper echelons of the university, now are searching for "a woman vice-president," no doubt to balance the "black vice-president." Although search committees may routinely write to women when seeking new administrators, I find that often the original suggestion has come from the students. And, while I have seen the appointment of black men as presidents of interracial institutions, there seems to be a shortage of women as presidents of coeducational colleges. In fact, as noted earlier, there seems to be a shortage of women as presidents of any kind of institution of higher learning, including women's colleges. As a commentator once said, the only way for a woman to become president of a college today is to get thee to a nunnery, because the Catholic women's colleges which were supported by women's orders appointed presidents from the order. Even that is no longer true. During the past year I have noted at least two such colleges that have male presidents.

The reality still is that women are excellent students at universities but are seldom teachers or administrators because of some vague sense of their unsuitability. Every man and many women with whom I discuss this problem insist that efforts are being made to change the picture. I believe this, but I also believe that the efforts are not wholehearted because cultural bias and vested interests are too strong.

REMEDIES

If there is to be a change in the attitude toward producing women Ph.D.'s and toward employing them once they receive their degrees, women must have recourse to significant remedies for the discrimination which substantially interferes with their ability to compete with males in academic life. All has been said that can be said about providing part-time employment and about promotion and tenure based on such employment. In addition, I believe there has been adequate discussion of the need to provide day care and auxiliary housekeeping facilities to free women from certain aspects of housewifery.

I wish to suggest some matters for consideration that have not been adequately discussed. The problems of eradicating the unconscious bias of everyone confronted with a woman student or candidate for employment are such that they must be met with strong, affirmative, corrective action. I urge the consideration of the following policies with respect to encouraging women to move into all parts of higher education:

- The assumption that women will be wives and that men will have tasks to perform should be eliminated from all policy considerations related to the education of men and women.
- Discussions of the consequences of women's role as mother should include, as rational alternatives for women, marriage with children, marriage without children, and single status.
- Strong remedies, including recovery of money, should be instituted to discourage intentional or accidental discrimination against women or assignment of unwanted roles because of sex.
- Women should be informed of all opportunities for education and for employment placement. All women students should be given access to scholarship aid and placement on the same bases as men.
- Steps should be taken to make individuals and institutions liable in money damages for failure to disclose to women students all educational opportunities available in all fields, on the same terms that such disclosure is made to men.
- All recruitment of faculty members should make manifest that the position to be filled is open to both men and women.
- Any department chairman or other officer failing to recommend women for appointment to available positions in proportion to their general availability in the area of employment should be required to explain, with particularity, why no women were recommended.
- Departments in which there are either no women or fewer women than would appear to be available in the particular discipline should be required to engage in special recruitment of women to correct any possibility of past discrimination, intentional or accidental.
- Nepotism rules prohibiting employment of both husband and wife should be eliminated.

- Institutions discriminating against women by reason of sex should be held liable for money damages caused by such discrimination, including salary that would have been paid had such discrimination not been present.
- Individuals using academic office to cause discrimination against women should be liable for money damages for such discrimination.
- Women candidates for academic employment should form organizations to inform institutions of the availability of women for employment in various fields, and secure foundation money to support such a short-term employment service.
- Individual women should be credited in employment evaluation with all relevant nonacademic experience, and should be paid accordingly.

The most important aspect of any remedy for discrimination is the provision of firm financial exposure of persons who might otherwise discriminate. In the discrimination area, the possibility of a money penalty is more likely to prevent discrimination than any other remedy. Although I recognize the massive financial problems of most institutions of higher learning, there appears to be no substitute for such a remedy. The use of a similar remedy by the federal government in the threat to withdraw contracts has led to some movement to end discrimination against women. However, the intervention of the government to set the standard of performance in the hiring of women should not be the only way to achieve change, and may, in fact, be the worst way, permitting deals and pressure of an ugly kind.

A direct relationship between claimant and institution will ensure a continuing pressure for improved performance, and will put the responsibility on persons capable of bearing it. I think that such individual responsibility is not too great for women holding the Ph.D. degree, and carefully drafted legislation, encouraging determination of facts by boards of review satisfactory to both sides, without the intervention of lawyers on either side, would encourage negotiation.

I accept the fact that such liability places a heavy burden on already burdened institutions, but I believe the existence of such a burden will speed solving the problem of sex discrimination. The increased concern of industrial firms to end racial discrimination when they face a financial exposure assures me that this approach is valid, and I am sure such financial exposure will make the more rational educational institutions willing to correct their misdeeds, both in training and hiring women.

To paraphrase Patrick Henry: If this be reverse discrimination, make the most of it. We women must catch up on opportunity, and if it takes action against the pocketbook to achieve it, and some momentary discrimination against men, so be it.

Part Two

THE WOMAN STUDENT

K. PATRICIA CROSS

The Woman Student

ALTHOUGH MOST EDUCATIONAL LEADERS are aware of inequality of opportunity for women in higher education, many find it hard to get excited about the matter. The Newman Task Force stated that "Our study found that discrimination against women, in contrast to that against minorities, is still overt and socially acceptable within the academic community."[1] In light of the present pressures for equality of educational opportunity, attitudes that prevent realization of the goal for women are difficult to understand.

The negative attitudes seem to stem from biases of knowledge and sensitivity. A few educators deny that discrimination against women exists. Some know it exists, but believe that women have distinctively female talents and roles and that educational opportunity may be differentially presented to men and women. Others maintain that higher education is less important or less useful for women. And still others have adopted a style of crisis administration that calls for attention and change only when the old way becomes more uncomfortable than a new alternative.

Equal educational opportunity for women presents some new problems that are both more and less difficult to resolve than those faced in the drive for minority rights. The relative distance from the presumably aggrieved parties affects the view held. Most men, after all, know some women well enough to feel that they understand their attitudes and feelings. If a wife, for example, finds ample satisfaction and fulfillment in her role as wife and mother, the husband (and many wives, too) may readily feel critical of, and even threatened by, women who want another way of life. Some people believe that the extremists of the women's liberation movement will deny women the right to choose to be wives and mothers without feeling guilty or unliberated. But that is not what the women's rights movement is about. It is about blatant or subtle discrimination that treats women as a class rather than as individuals.

1. Task Force, Frank Newman, Chairman, *Report on Higher Education*, U.S. Office of Education (Washington: Government Printing Office, 1971), p. 80.

To discriminate is to deny freedom of choice; it is to make decisions affecting the lives of individuals without their consent and frequently without their knowledge. Women are becoming sensitive to such restrictions. Those who do not want to follow the life pattern of their grandmothers are pressing for the right to choose. Women are asking for the right to pursue higher education on the basis of their interest and achievement instead of their sex. They do not now have that freedom of choice. Some are denied it by institutional practices that are consciously or unconsciously discriminatory. Some are denied it by social pressures that define acceptable behaviors for women. Some are denied it by their own social conditioning and attitudes regarding women's roles. Denial of the full development of individual potential is, or should be, of concern to educators everywhere.

This paper examines issues involved in granting equality of educational opportunity for women of all ages and at all levels of postsecondary education. Since the problems are somewhat different among undergraduates, graduate students, and adult women, each group will be discussed separately.

Undergraduate Women

Access to college is more difficult for women than for men, and the handicaps have a way of piling up. Women from poor families, for example, receive less parental encouragement to attend college than do their brothers,[2] and they also receive less in institutional financial aid than do men.[3] If they are not good students, they have less chance of being accepted than do men with equally poor records.[4] Add to these handicaps the fact that, despite better high school grades, women have less academic self-confidence than men[5] and more deterrents that can be classified as family responsibilities (illness in the home, care of younger children, and the like) and we can only admire the determination of the women from the lower socioeconomic levels who make it to college at all.

2. Joseph Froomkin, *Aspirations, Enrollments, and Resources,* U.S. Office of Education (Washington: Government Printing Office, 1970), p. 17.
3. Elizabeth W. Haven and Dwight H. Horch, *How College Students Finance Their Education* (New York: College Scholarship Service, College Entrance Examination Board, 1972), p. v.
4. E. Walster, T. A. Cleary, and M. M. Clifford, "The Effect of Race and Sex on College Admission," *Sociology of Education* 44 (1971): 237–44.
5. K. Patricia Cross, *The Undergraduate Woman,* Research Report No. 5 (Washington: American Association for Higher Education, 1971), p. 5.

Research shows that women are still underrepresented in the college-going population, with the national ratio of entering freshmen now standing at 54 men to 46 women. The bastions of male predominance at the undergraduate level are the private universities and the public community colleges, where the ratio is 60 men to 40 women among entering students.[6] It is notable that the greatest imbalance exists in the most selective and the least selective institutions.

Open door colleges

Open door colleges can hardly be accused of practicing discrimination in their admissions policies, but a closer look is necessary before concluding that community colleges can be absolved from considering the need for corrective action. Inasmuch as public community colleges were established explicitly to provide equality of educational opportunity for all, it is ironic that they, of all places, find themselves devoting more money and effort to the education of men than women. The reason: the community colleges serve large numbers of students from the lower socioeconomic levels, and in this conservative segment of society women's roles are clearly stereotyped. Mothers who have attended college express no significant difference in their desire for college education for sons and daughters: 98 percent want college for their sons, and 97 percent want it for their daughters. Mothers with a grade school education, however, are more likely to want college for their sons (73 percent) than for their daughters (60 percent).[7]

Not surprisingly, the largest reservoir of academically superior young people who are not now attending college consists of women from the lower socioeconomic levels. Whereas 25 percent of the high-ability (top quarter) males from the lowest socioeconomic quarter fail to enter college, 40 percent of their equally able sisters fail to continue their education.[8] Included in the low socioeconomic group are black women, but, as a group, they seem to be responding more rapidly to the new opportunities for further education

6. Staff of the Office of Research, *The American Freshman: National Norms for Fall 1971* (Washington: Office of Research, American Council on Education, 1971), p. 16.

7. Froomkin, *Aspirations*, p. 17.

8. K. Patricia Cross, *Beyond the Open Door: New Students to Higher Education* (San Francisco: Jossey-Bass, 1971), p. 7.

than are white women. Knoell studied the college-going rates of whites and blacks in urban areas and concluded that able white women constitute the group most neglected by college recruitment personnel. She found that, in some major cities in 1968, black women were attending college in larger numbers than their brothers, and that in some cases they were surpassing the percentage of white women of similar ability in going to college. As Knoell points out, she is not suggesting any lessened effort to recruit black women to higher education but is calling attention to the "reservoir of ability among the white women who are not yet attracted to college."[9] This message, of course, is addressed to selective as well as nonselective institutions.

Financial assistance

Inasmuch as the largest number of high-ability women not now in college are from families with limited financial resources, recruitment efforts must be combined with realistic financial assistance. A 1969–70 study of the finances of college sophomores found that, on the average, women, in comparison with men, received smaller grants and scholarships, took out larger loans, and, if they could find work, received less pay. Despite no significant differences in the socioeconomic backgrounds of the men and the women in the sample, institutionally administered grants averaged $671 for men and $515 for women. Although the parents of women contributed more money for educational costs than the parents of men, this is part of the problem and not part of the solution, since parents from the lower socioeconomic levels are less interested in sending a daughter than a son to college. Neither are the larger loans to women reported in the study a logical solution.[10] The "negative dowry" effect of taking out loans for a woman's education should, one would think, deter chauvinists from saddling women with larger loan amounts.

If any favoritism is to be shown, it would appear that colleges should make larger grants to women to compensate for fewer and lower paying jobs and the frequent requirement that women live in more expensive campus housing than men, who are permitted to

9. Dorothy M. Knoell, *People Who Need College* (Washington: American Association of Junior Colleges, 1970), p. 73.
10. Haven and Horch, *How College Students Finance Their Education*, p. 19.

cut costs by doing their own cooking in apartments off campus. "Contract" dining, which requires women to contract for board and room while men pay room only bills in campus housing, is another practice that is financially discriminatory.

Selective institutions

Let us now see how women fare in the male-dominated universities. Here the pool of potential students is quite different from that characterizing the enrollments in open door institutions.

The universities draw their students largely from high school graduates who rank in the upper half of their class academically and whose families are in the upper half of the socioeconomic range. Among this group, women enter college at the same rate as men. Eighty percent of the women and 80 percent of the men in this able and privileged group are now continuing their education beyond high school, most of them in four-year colleges and universities. The fact that advantaged men and women are equally likely to enter college does not necessarily mean freedom of choice, however. Women constitute 47 percent of the enrollment in state colleges, whereas they represent only 40 percent of the student body of private universities.

Historically, four-year colleges—public and private—have emphasized liberal arts and teacher education, curricula that have appealed to women. But with new career fields opening to women and with an oversupply of elementary and secondary school teachers, it is time to examine the sex distribution in institutions of postsecondary education. For example, how does a prestigious university that appeals to many women, able financially and academically to attend, maintain a 65-35 male-female ratio while selecting one in four applicants?

Quotas exist in many places on the campus, and when they are all collected in the admissions office, the total effect can be dramatic. It is, for example, still common practice to require on-campus housing for freshman women but not men. With campus housing limited, this practice leads to differential selection rates and to complaint by both men and women students on many selective campuses that the women are "too intellectual" for the men. Coed dorms have one major advantage: sex discrimination becomes painfully obvious. But it creeps into the curriculum in more subtle

ways. A university may have relatively more "spaces" for agriculture majors than for home economists, a practice that leads to
denial of admission to able women interested in home economics
but acceptance of less well qualified men into agriculture.

Even in these days of heightened consciousness about discrimination, it is not hard to find blatant examples of discrimination at the
undergraduate level where many people still insist it does not exist.
Table 1 was computed from information contained in the latest
College Handbook,[11] which serves to acquaint students, parents,

TABLE 1: *Percentages of Acceptances to a Selective Four-Year
Liberal Arts College*

Criterion	Percentage of Applicants Accepted[a]	
	Male	Female
High school class rank		
Top fifth	92	62
Second fifth	58	18
Third fifth and below	36	4
SAT score, Verbal		
700–800	92	93
600–699	87	75
500–599	73	32
Below 500	35	6
SAT score, Mathematical		
700–800	91	85
600–699	81	68
500–599	59	33
Below 500	19	11

a) Applications were received from 1,037 men and 1,097 women.
Overall rates of acceptance were 68 percent for men and 45 percent for
women.

and high school counselors with the admissions practices of more
than eight hundred colleges. Women who take the trouble to com-
pute their chances should certainly get the message that they must
be better qualified than men to gain admission to the selective
four-year liberal arts college illustrated.

Experimental studies[12] as well as field data[13] indicate that highly
able women are not as likely to suffer inequities as are their average

11. New York: College Entrance Examination Board, 1969.
12. Walster et al., "Effect of Race and Sex on College Admission"; L. Simp-
son, "A Myth Is Better than a Miss," *College and University Business* 48, no. 2:
72–73.
13. Cross, *Beyond the Open Door.*

or below-average sisters. But as the competition and the discrimination become stiffer—from undergraduate to graduate student to faculty member—women who persevere become increasingly aware of discrimination on the part of educational institutions.

Dual roles

Not all inequities are the result of discrimination. In general, women have been unable to pursue higher education with single-minded purpose. The typical college woman today is sensitive to the need to plan for both career and marriage. Part of her dilemma is how to keep open the options for both. The ambiguities of women's lives are apparent in group statistics. The largest proportion of women in college today (45 percent) hope to be married career women fifteen years hence, but a substantial number (35 percent) prefer the more traditional role of wife and mother.[14] The duality of women's concern with home and career is also confirmed when 65 percent of the young women entering college today say that raising a family is essential or very important to them, but almost as many (54 percent) are equally emphatic that being an authority in their field is important to them.[15]

Despite the swing toward serious preparation for careers among college women, they are probably still underestimating the importance of this aspect of their futures. Today, it is the typical rather than the atypical woman college graduate who is in the labor force. Furthermore, 40 percent of the female workers work because they must. They are single, widowed, separated, or divorced. Another 30 percent of the female labor force are married women whose husbands earn less than $7,000 per year.[16] The old argument that women will not use their education or that they suffer no economic hardship because of discrimination is surely belied by the facts. Whether the primary purpose of education is career training or liberation of the mind and the enrichment of life, it is hard to argue that the education of women is less important than that of men.

14. College Student Questionnaires (CSQ), *Comparative Data* (Princeton, N.J.: Institutional Research Program for Higher Education, Educational Testing Service, 1972).

15. *The American Freshman*, p. 36.

16. Women's Bureau, U.S. Department of Labor, *Underutilization of Women Workers* (Washington: Government Printing Office, 1971), pp. vi, 1.

Academic ability

Although I suspect most educators *know* that intellectual capacity is not a sex-linked characteristic, many still *feel* that it is somehow more satisfying to engage the "male mind" in disciplinary inquiry than the "female mind." Interestingly enough, many professors espousing this point of view are also staunch supporters of the validity of grades as a measure of intellectual competence. Just how they explain that, by their own judgment and standards, women are better *students* than men is something of a mystery. From grade school through college, women receive markedly better grades than men. Among all freshmen entering college in fall 1971, 41 percent of the women and 25 percent of the men reported high school grades of *B+* or better.[17] In college, the story is similar. In spring 1970, for example, 46 percent of freshman women at the University of California, Berkeley, made first semester averages of *B* or better, compared with 39 percent of the men; for seniors, the same proportions held, with 45 percent of senior women and 38 percent of senior men achieving spring semester averages of *B* or above.

On other measures of academic aptitude, men have a clear edge in scores on quantitative tests, whereas women score slightly better on tests of verbal abilities. Although rarely discussed in the literature, the use of test scores as admissions criteria helps men compensate for the better high school records of women. The College Board Commission on Tests tacitly accepts this use when they observe that tests "tend to reduce the advantage that girls enjoy in graded school work, since males and females have roughly the same mean scores on the SAT."[18] If the purpose of testing is to predict the college grade-point average (as it is in admissions testing programs), then men should be required to have higher test scores than women in order to achieve comparable success in college as measured by the GPA.[19]

Grades are coming increasingly under fire as a measure of academic prowess, however, and critics often point to a lack of intellectual excitement in the conscientious, conforming grade-getter,

17. *The American Freshman*, pp. 33, 25.
18. Commission on Tests, *Righting the Balance* (New York: College Entrance Examination Board, 1970), pp. 51–52.
19. R. L. Linn, "Fair Test Use in Selection," Paper presented at the City University of New York, 1972 (Mimeographed).

which is the frequent stereotype of high school and college women. Chauvinists of both sexes feel that men are better able to deal with big ideas and abstractions, whereas women handle day-to-day problems in a more practical manner. But research measuring the personality trait called "intellectuality" fails to support the stereotype. Evidence indicates that women are slightly more interested in esthetics and in working with ideas and abstractions, whereas men are more interested in theory and the use of the scientific method.[20] Although cultural expectations may push males and females toward emphases in academic choices and behavior, the research on academic interests, abilities, and personality characteristics indicates no important differences between men and women in their potential for academic accomplishment.

The greatest problem in reaching equity for women in higher education is getting them into college following high school graduation. Once in college, their graduation completion rate is about the same as that of men. As a matter of fact, in recent years, with the relatively large influx of low-achieving males (but not of low-achieving females, as yet) into the open door colleges, the four-year completion rate is slightly higher for women than for men.[21]

GRADUATE WOMEN

For women, graduate study poses problems that are different from those encountered at the undergraduate level and that sharpen the conflicts between traditional roles and alternative roles. The typical age for women in graduate school is also the age when society makes its greatest demands for traditional role behavior. Women between twenty-two and thirty both expect and are expected to be wives whose husbands are establishing their own careers and also to be mothers of preschool children. This traditional role frequently conflicts with the student and scholar role.

Further, graduate study is considered a commitment to a professional career, and hence the use made of the education becomes an issue. If a woman fails to use her *undergraduate* education in a career, one argument runs, she uses it, perhaps equally well, in raising her family, preserving the cultural heritage, contributing to her community, and furnishing appropriate companionship for her

---

20. Cross, *Beyond the Open Door*, pp. 141–42.
21. A. Ferriss, *Indicators of Trends in the Status of American Women* (New York: Russell Sage Foundation, 1971), p. 47.

college-educated husband. The case for liberal arts education for women has frequently been made on these grounds, although some of the career curricula most attractive to undergraduate women— nursing, elementary education, and home economics—are also considered highly appropriate for futures as homemakers and mothers. Their dual usefulness helps make them popular. But few would maintain that a master's degree in any field is necessary or even desirable for women who expect to live out their lives as wives and mothers, and many people would argue that a Ph.D. is a downright disadvantage. Thus graduate education for women is more controversial than college education. It is also much more difficult because the woman who embarks on this path runs into the barriers erected by the broader society as well as those erected by graduate and professional schools.

Societal barriers

Among the highly selected segment of the population that make it through four years of college, graduate school is a popular aspiration for both men and women. Of the 130,000 women who received the bachelor's degree in spring 1961, 72 percent expected to enter graduate school, and three years later 42 percent had actually done some graduate work. Many factors determined who did or did not go, among which the most important were marital and parental status. Fifty-nine percent of the single women went on to graduate study compared with 44 percent of the married women, but the percentage of mothers taking graduate courses dropped sharply, to 24 percent. When women aspiring to graduate study but not enrolled in graduate school in 1964 were asked what provisions would enable them to do so, the largest proportion (57 percent) said that child care facilities would be essential.[22]

Two 1970 studies of academic women at the Universities of Chicago and California, Berkeley, confirm earlier findings. At the University of Chicago, 33 percent of the men and 77 percent of the women with children said that care of their children interfered with academic work.[23]

At Berkeley the report of the Subcommittee on the Status of

22. National Institutes of Health, *Women and Graduate Study*, Report No. 13 (Washington: Government Printing Office, 1968), p. 93.
23. "Women in the University of Chicago" (Chicago: The University, 1970).

Academic Women concluded that "The largest single category of grievances or proposed changes was the need for high-quality child care facilities for members of the University community." An attitude often encountered in discussion of child care is that young mothers should be at home caring for their children. Illustrative is the testimony of a graduate student at the University of California, Berkeley: "In our department at least one professor cut off funds to a married student when she became pregnant, thus forcing her to TA and increasing the time it took her to finish. He said the reason for cutting off funds was that 'You should be home caring for your family.' "[24]

Women, too, voice sharp criticism of other women for "neglecting" their husbands and children. The research on this issue fails to support the arguments. Marmor cites research showing that the percentage of disturbed children in the homes of nonworking mothers was three times as high as in the homes of working mothers. He concludes that "there is no sound evidence that the mothers' working per se tends to create behavioral disturbances in children. It is the unhappy or disturbed mother whose children tend to be disturbed."[25] Thus, the establishment of child care centers can hardly be opposed on the grounds that women should be at home taking care of their children. Children may be far better off with people who choose to spend time with them rather than with those who resent the obligation.

The premise that women who stay home are less likely to neglect their husbands is also of dubious merit. An unhappy homebody may be more neglectful than a happy career or student wife. According to the reports of graduate women at the University of California in 1970, some professors have opposed advanced study for them on the grounds of protecting their marriages. One woman related the following incident: "I was asked . . . in a formal interview, with two other professors present, whether I felt that my husband and I were competing intellectually. I am sure he would not have asked such a personal question of a male student."[26]

24. "Report of the Subcommittee on the Status of Academic Women on the Berkeley Campus" (Berkeley: University of California, May 1970), p. 75.

25. J. Marmor, "Women at Work: A Study in Prejudice," in *Exploding the Myths*, Report of a Conference on Expanding Employment Opportunities for Career Women, held at the University of California Extension, Los Angeles, Women's Bureau, U.S. Department of Labor (Washington: Government Printing Office, December 1966), p. 55.

26. "Report on Status of Academic Women, Berkeley," p. 70.

No doubt some men feel threatened by what they see as intellectual competition from women. Astin found that 12 percent of the women who had received doctorates reported negative attitudes from their husbands,[27] but one suspects that at least as many husbands welcome the intellectual interests of their wives. In fact, many husband-wife teams find great satisfaction in intellectual collaboration despite the frequent institutional nepotism regulations that discourage it. Because marriage is a close personal relationship between two people, the educational community cannot devise general policies that will add to or detract from the satisfaction of the marriage. To oppose graduate education for a woman on the grounds that it is bad for her marriage, her chances of marriage, or her children is unwarranted and certainly an unacceptable role for the university.

Cost effectiveness

There is still another major criticism of increasing the opportunities for graduate study for women. Graduate study is expensive; it is designed as career training; and if it is not so used, then it is a waste of money and effort that would better be used for educating someone else for whom the expenditure is justifiable. Lewis succinctly presents the most frequently heard arguments.

> Many graduate and professional programs for which members of both sexes commonly apply tend to discriminate against women, and many authorities believe they have good reason. Women are poorer bets than men to finish such a program, and those who do are less likely to use their education productively. A university feels some obligation not only to educate individuals but also to be of benefit to society; thus, if an admissions committee must choose between a capable man and a capable woman for a place in its program, the choice can logically be made in favor of the man. The woman who is thereby rejected may, of course, be the exception who would have finished and who would have made a worthwhile contribution, but her more casual sisters have prejudiced the committee against her.[28]

Such arguments appeal to many rational men and women everywhere, and yet they are akin to "solving" discrimination against

27. Helen Astin, *The Woman Doctorate in America* (New York: Russell Sage Foundation, 1969), p. 102.

28. E. C. Lewis, *Developing Woman's Potential* (Ames: Iowa State University Press, 1968), p. 212.

blacks by observing that society has tolerated conditions that have resulted in few blacks completing graduate study and making professional contributions. The argument would then continue: they have not demonstrated professional productivity in the past; they seem poor bets for the future. There are, however, research reasons as well as moral reasons for not accepting the three major arguments summarized by Lewis at face value.

Differential admissions

Women cannot afford the luxury of indignation over the rejection of women who are *as* capable as the men who are accepted, at least until the problem of rejection of women with superior academic qualifications is solved. An increasingly popular method of dealing with discrimination against women is to base acceptances on the proportion of women applying. Thus at Berkeley, 31 percent of the applicants are women, and 29 percent of the acceptances are granted to women.[29] On the surface that doesn't look bad until one considers that women who apply for graduate study at Berkeley are highly self-selected. Under the equal rejection rate system, a department may be—and usually is—accepting men who hold poorer credentials than some of the rejected women.

On the whole, women would be better off if they were evaluated solely on the basis of their credentials rather than under quota systems. Lannholm's survey of admissions policies showed that most departments reported that they assign the greatest weight to the undergraduate record.[30] And women do have the edge on grades. In a national sample of enrolled graduate students, 51 percent of the women and 40 percent of the men reported undergraduate GPA's of *B+* or better.[31]

Completion rates

The second argument for differential acceptance rates to graduate school concerns the likelihood of the candidate's completing the degree. It is said that so many things can happen to interfere with

29. "Report on Status of Academic Women, Berkeley," p. 38.
30. G. V. Lannholm, *The Use of GRE Scores and Other Factors in Graduate School Admissions* (Princeton, N.J.: Graduate Record Examinations, Educational Testing Service, 1968), p. 17.
31. John A. Creager, *The American Graduate Student: A Normative Description* (Washington: Office of Research, American Council on Education, 1971), p. 45.

a woman's commitment to graduate study—marriage, pregnancy, moving away with her husband, and so on—that a man is a better bet for a long-range contribution to society. Although such practice seems unjust to the individual (since no one can predict which man or which woman will complete the degree), many regard it as a more responsible use of graduate training resources. Actually, little information is available on completion rates for men and women because longitudinal studies of graduate student progress are missing from the literature. Bits and pieces of data indicate some validity to the argument, however—at least on the surface. The ACE–Carnegie Commission report shows that women constituted approximately half of the graduate students aiming ultimately for the master's degree.[32]

If women are completing their studies on a par with men, they should receive roughly half of the master's degrees granted, but they do not; in 1968, they received 36 percent of the master's degrees granted.[33] At the doctoral level the trend is similar: more than one-fourth of the aspirants are women, but they receive only 13 percent of the degrees.

There is also evidence that women are relatively slow in getting their degrees. The Ferriss study found that the median time lapse from baccalaureate to doctorate was 7.9 years for men and 11.2 years for women.[34] These figures agree well with those of Astin, who reported that women took about twelve years to complete their degrees and were four years older than their male colleagues.[35]

As the Berkeley study points out, however, the fields in which women predominate—education, humanities, and languages—have lower and slower production rates than the sciences, where candidates tend to be full-time students. For example, 75 percent of the students in biosciences and 65 percent in mathematics and physical science are full time, compared with 25 percent of those in education and 52 percent in the arts and humanities.[36]

The University of Chicago study presents one of the few analyses of attrition rates of men and women within fields of study. For students in the biological sciences, it reports that 26 percent of the

32. Ibid., p. 17.
33. Ferriss, *Indicators of Trends*, p. 35.
34. Ibid., p. 43.
35. *The Woman Doctorate*, pp. 19, 21.
36. Creager, *The Graduate Student*, p. 111.

men and 33 percent of the women dropped out. Attrition rates in other fields were as follows: physical sciences, 16 percent for men, 20 percent for women; social sciences, 40 percent for men, 51 percent for women; and humanities, 24 percent for men, 19 percent for women.[37] This study, then, indicates that with the exception of the humanities, women are somewhat more prone to drop out than men. But how many return later or continue their study on a different campus? We need more evidence before we accept the common assumption that graduate training for women is wasteful.

Much can be done, of course, to protect our investment. The major obstacles to graduate study for women who entered graduate school and dropped out or who want to go but have yet to enter are financial limitations and family responsibilities.[38] The importance of child care has already been discussed as advantageous to graduate student parents, whether male or female. Financial aid also benefits both men and women, and there is no evidence of discrimination in the awarding of fellowships and assistantships. Among all graduate students, men are a little more likely to derive primary support from fellowships or assistantships, but the differences are not large, especially considering the higher levels of student assistance available in the sciences.[39] (A cynic might note Sharp's discovery of a high order of self-screening among graduate applicants for financial assistance. She reported that fewer than 3 percent of applicants for financial support were turned down— thus leaving little opportunity for discrimination against anyone.[40])

The real financial problems are not seen in the data collected from graduate students, however, because married women and divorced women with children who have limited resources probably do not get to graduate school. Most couples honor the custom which provides that if only one can go to graduate school, it should be the male. Although the popular press tends to sensationalize the sexual revolution, probably only a small proportion of young couples are experimenting with abolishing sex-typed behaviors.

37. "Women in the University of Chicago."
38. National Institutes of Health, *Women and Graduate Study*, p. 89.
39. Creager, *The Graduate Student*, p. 20.
40. L. M. Sharp, *Education and Employment: The Early Careers of College Graduates* (Baltimore, Md.: Johns Hopkins Press, 1970), p. 21.

Productivity

The third aspect of the rationale presented by Lewis is that even when women do get degrees, they are less productive than men. Those sympathetic to the scholarly aspirations of women view the presumed lack of productivity as a continuation of the role problems experienced in getting the degree, whereas those less sympathetic point to history and the lack of women Nobel laureates and listings in *Who's Who*. (History, of course, has a near perfect record of not rewarding or recognizing women for contributions outside the home and family.) Here again the arguments may be tested against research findings.

The charge that women doctorates do not use their advanced training is no longer true, if indeed it ever was, and the statistics indicate that the misconception may now be dropped as an argument deserving serious consideration. Astin found that 91 percent of the women who received doctorates in 1957 and 1958 were working in 1966—81 percent full time, and 79 percent of these women had never interrupted their careers.[41] Mitchell's study, reported by Robinson, found that an even more astounding 99 percent of women receiving doctorates from Oklahoma Ph.D.-granting institutions were at work, 98 percent full time.[42]

Evidence is not as clear on measures of scholarly production, but we are severely handicapped by a lack of studies that compare men and women in the same types of work. Women devote a greater proportion of their time to teaching than do men, who are more likely to hold research positions. This situation maintains within major research universities and also across national samples, inasmuch as women tend to hold jobs in teaching institutions rather than in research universities. Whether writing articles and books is more "productive" than teaching students is, of course, a moot question. Research based on self-reports of faculty indicates that women are more likely than men to express interest in teaching; they are less traditional in their teaching styles, and they are more eager for student criticism and evaluation.[43]

41. *The Woman Doctorate*, pp. 56, 58.
42. Lora H. Robinson, *The Status of Academic Women* (Washington: ERIC Clearinghouse on Higher Education, 1971), p. 2.
43. Unpublished data from Robert C. Wilson, Center for Research in Higher Education, University of California, Berkeley.

With the current emphasis on teaching, we would do well to adopt some new measures of "productivity." If, however, we accept the old definition of scholarly productivity and simply count the number of publications, then admittedly women in graduate school get off to a slow start. Among Ph.D. candidates, men are almost twice as likely as women to have published (21 percent, 12 percent), and they are also considerably more likely to be engaged in research that might lead to publication (61 percent of men, 44 percent of women).[44] But the rate of productivity varies enormously among fields of study, with majors in the sciences being the most likely to publish, and those in the humanities and education being the least likely to do so. Astin's work indicates that field of study rather than sex is probably the primary determiner of publication rate; 25 percent of the women receiving doctorates in the natural sciences were highly productive (eleven articles or more) compared with 7 percent of those in education.[45]

The questions regarding the productivity of women scholars have not been answered. Our present measures of productivity are woefully inadequate, and the results of research vary from showing no difference between the publication rates of men and women Ph.D.'s[46] to minor differences. In any event, the notion that it is wasteful to educate women at the level of the doctorate is an exaggeration, if it is valid at all.

In summary, the research fails to support the old arguments for preferential treatment of men for admission to graduate study. Conclusions regarding the alleged lower and slower rates of degree completion among women await further study which will take into consideration the field of specialization, completion at a later date, and so on. Once women do get their degrees, there is every evidence that they make good use of their education. It is the highly unusual Ph.D. recipient who does not work full time, making apparently good and productive use of her training.

ADULT WOMEN

The segment of the population with the greatest potential for enormous expansion into higher education consists of mature

44. Creager, The Graduate Student, p. 50.
45. The Woman Doctorate, p. 81.
46. R. Simon, S. Clark, and K. Galway, "The Woman Ph.D.: A Recent Profile," Social Problems 48 (1970): 72–73.

women. The typical woman today has sent her youngest child off to school by the time she is thirty-five, and she faces some thirty years of productive work life but reduced home responsibilities. The number of women who fill these years with work outside the home is increasing dramatically. Between 1940 and 1966, the number of women in the labor force more than doubled in the 35–44 age group, more than tripled among those 45–54, and more than quadrupled in the 55–64 age group.[47] The continuing invention of labor-saving devices for the home plus new career opportunities for women in the labor market plus concern about the population explosion plus the rising level of educational achievement in the population all combine to create new demands for career education as well as for general education. If the women's movement had not come along, someone would have had to invent it. Indeed, it solves more problems for society than it presents.

But higher education is not yet ready for the learner who does not fit the stereotype of the young, single, unemployed student who is ready to devote full time to pursuing a degree. With the possible exception of the community colleges, higher education has taken little note of the changing character of the student population. Mature women constitute a significant segment of that new population. Although one survey of 750 colleges and universities found that 95 percent claimed to offer opportunities for mature women to complete degrees,[48] Mattfeld's follow-up determined that only 49 percent made *any* concessions in rate of work, class hours, or other customary academic practices to meet the needs of mature women.[49]

Many graduate departments, for example, do not accept candidates over age 35, and others "discourage" older applicants. The prejudice in this instance is against age rather than sex, but women are more educationally disadvantaged by such attitudes because of their life patterns.

The discouragement of part-time study is another practice that is not directed against women but operates to their disadvantage.

47. *Exploding the Myths,* Report of a Conference on Expanding Employment Opportunities for Career Women, p. 3.

48. R. Oltman, *Campus 1970: Where Do Women Stand?* (Washington: American Association of University Women, December 1970), p. 14.

49. J. A. Mattfeld, "A Decade of Continuing Education: Dead End or Open Door" (Mimeographed; Bronxville, N.Y.: Sarah Lawrence College, 1971).

Almost three-fourths of the married women living near enough to the University of Illinois to participate in on-campus classes said that they could attend school only part time. One student confessed, "When I was single and a college undergraduate, I know that I took the privilege of attending college for granted; now I would give anything in the world to be able to go to school again. I can go only at night or on Saturdays."[50] Mothers of older children frequently prefer the customary class schedules so that they can attend while their children are in school. The point is, however, that part-time educational opportunities are essential for the majority of adult women.

The mobility of women, or—more accurately—the timing of the move, is another problem that we have yet to face in providing education to an increasingly mobile population. The notion that it is "normal" for a student—even a young student—to graduate from college four years after entrance to that same college is a quaint relic of an earlier era. We have yet to deal realistically with the "portability" of credits. This problem is exaggerated for women who move generally, not at their convenience, but when husbands have completed a given segment of education. Shelden and Hembrough found that most (69 percent) married women students and student wives expected to leave the university area in three years or less—not enough time to add up to a University of Illinois degree, especially when part-time student status is a necessity for most of them. And yet 71 percent of women without a bachelor's degree expressed the desire to obtain one.[51] They will need better mechanisms for transfer of credits, and many will need better methods for evaluating credits that have "aged" while they were totally engaged with a young family. The rapidly growing opportunities to receive credit by examination will certainly be a boon to women who had to leave school at times unpropitious for their educational careers.

Incidentally, a little-touted advantage of the credit-by-examination movement is the psychological boost it gives older women in being able to compare their performance with that of "regular"

50. M. A. Shelden and B. L. Hembrough, *The Student Wife and the Married Student: Their Educational Needs, Desires, and Backgrounds* (Urbana: Office of the Dean of Women, University of Illinois, September 1964), p. 49.

51. Ibid., p. 32, 13.

college students. One of the messages that the women's movement may get across is that women have egos too, and there is an understandable reluctance among adult women to reenter a classroom in competition with youth who have been idolized in the popular press as the brightest, best-educated generation ever. Home study, with validation by examination, may help to bridge the confidence gap.

The usual way of easing the transition for women returning to college, however, is through counseling and group support. Among the programs for mature women, some of the oldest and most effective consist primarily of counseling services that bolster self-confidence and help women surmount the obstacles placed in their way largely by history and tradition.

Related to the old-fashioned notion that education is reserved for the young who can spend full time at it are a host of practices and requirements that are grounded more in tradition than in logic. Why should scholarship and loan aid be so commonly restricted to full-time students? Do residency requirements and regulations that call for continuous enrollment serve a purpose so valuable that we are justified in shutting out students whose life circumstances prohibit meeting them? Why must an individual's academic load be determined by the institution rather than by the learner?

One of the great unsolved problems of education is the transfer of our excessive concern with procedures to more realistic concerns about purposes and outcomes. We have a way of defining education in terms of the pathways traversed rather than in terms of the ends reached. Most of the problems of women students—and of many men as well—could be solved if we permitted them to reach defined goals via open-ended but interconnected pathways that suit their life style rather than restrict them—through some preconceived notion of conformity—to the procedures that will bestow the proper credentials on those who follow them faithfully.

In the final analysis, the barriers to individual development through education will come down when we as a society decide that educational opportunity depends not on class stereotypes based on the color or shape of one's skin,[52] but upon individual

52. The phrase is from Bernice Sandler, "What Constitutes Equity for Women in Higher Education," in *The Expanded Campus*, ed. Dyckman W. Vermilye (San Francisco: Jossey-Bass, 1972).

needs, desires, and potential for contribution. Once we recognize that women as well as men can be doctors, lawyers, scientists, businessmen, politicians, and important writers and artists, we will find the ways to prepare them for their new roles.

RECOMMENDATIONS

1. Recruitment efforts by selective and nonselective colleges among women of lower socioeconomic status must be increased. We need not resign ourselves to wait for society to free lower SES women from limiting, stereotyped roles. Our experience with the active recruitment of ethnic minorities to higher education proves that it takes hard work and that progress is frequently slow, but it can be done with long-range benefits to society.

2. Financial aid must be realistically combined with recruitment efforts and must be impartially administered. On-campus employment for both undergraduate and graduate students should be studied for equality of opportunity in terms of the relative number of jobs available for men and women and for equity in pay scales. Housing and dining requirements must be examined for discriminatory practices.

3. Admissions and enrollment statistics for undergraduates and graduate students must be examined year by year to disclose intentional and unintentional discriminatory practices. Affirmative action programs should be instituted wherever needed.

4. Fact-finding committees operating with strict deadlines should be appointed to assess local problems and needs. The committees should be charged with looking into the feasibility of nationally recognized needs such as child care centers, part-time study options, and adequate educational and career counseling for women of all ages. But they should also give special attention to the full spectrum of local problems.

5. Resources of the institution must be allocated to reflect the value commitment to equality of opportunity.

6. The appointment of women to positions where their counsel will contribute a natural and continuous input to decision making will be an important improvement over the black-out of women's participation or the practice of seeking advice only when it becomes necessary or convenient. In addition, exposure to talented

female scholars is a vital educational experience for young men as well as young women.

The question of providing equal educational opportunity without regard to race, sex, age, or any other class identification is not one that is likely to go away if ignored. The options are really two—whether to lead with a bang or to follow with a whimper.

Women's Right to Choose, or Men's Right to Dominate

JOAN I. ROBERTS

IF THE AIM of education is the full development of human potential, then educators have substantially failed one-half of humanity. Patricia Cross has detailed the facts of that failure in "The Woman Student." Although her analysis is expressed in institutional terms, the responsibility for failure belongs to individuals or, more specifically, to men, since it is they who control almost all aspects of organizational life in colleges and universities.

The ignorance of some male administrators about even the most basic statistical facts of female existence, such as those Cross presents, is matched only by their arrogance in dealing with women. Some administrators simply do not know the facts of sex discrimination. Some, although grasping rudiments of the problem, do not care enough to place a high priority on resolution. Others, as Cross indicates, display a crisis mentality; they raise a few salaries and hire a handful of token women to meet the minimum demands of federal investigators. It is probable that within another year, a mirage of minor changes will be created to make the public feel that the problems of women on campus are resolved. For university women who are working to improve the status of women, the problems are most assuredly not yet resolved, nor will they be in the next months or even, possibly, in the next few years.

Paradoxically, within the crisis context, many faculty members have not yet realized the full extent of women's dismay and determination; a state of bewildered denial, complete disregard, or remote disdain seems to prevail. A few of our male colleagues are catching on and throwing occasional paragraphs into articles or recasting research reports to make it appear that they are cognizant of, if not concerned with, the problem. Fortunately, some colleagues are genuinely sympathetic, increasingly knowledgeable, and often helpful.

Releasing women from sex-stereotyped restrictions so as to give them the right to choose is no simple matter to be overcome with superficial administrative ploys or a few faddish intellectual sops. The breadth of the problem should be evident from Dr. Cross's analyses of women students in terms of female statistics. The depth of the issue may not be so readily apparent. Therefore, let me expand on Dr. Cross's discussion of barriers to educational attainment by describing the woman student as she experiences herself in relation to male faculty and administrators.

Women live with two existential facts that differentiate them from their male counterparts. The first fact is physical vulnerability. Every woman lives out her life with the realization that she is the victim in the con game of men "protecting" her from other men. In our culture, this eventuates in the woman student as a sex object. In recent hearings conducted with women students, in research interviews with women students, in discussions with individual women and groups of women, and in their responses to questionnaires, they accused some male faculty members of subtle and even blatant sexism, ranging from verbal to physical, sometimes with put-out or get-out connotations. Verbally, a professor aggresses, saying, "Your sweater looks big enough for both of us." Or he may invade the woman's personal space, by touching a pin or her blouse while commenting on its ostensible beauty. (I sometimes wonder what the male professor would do if the woman student made equally personal gestures in public.) Or he may, as in one case reported, make sexual overtures, which, when rebuffed, lead him to fail the woman student on her doctoral examination. The same man was later overheard telling a colleague that he did not bother to read her exam. Fortunately, this kind of overt unprofessionalism is infrequently reported. Women have traditionally been silent on such matters. "Nice girls" did not tell what happened to them. They might share the social ostracism that so often has been directed toward women. But now, many nice women students are no longer protecting male faculty members with their silence.

The second existential fact for women students is that they are not taken seriously. Unlike vulnerability, this problem does not derive from biology, but from culture. The state of imposed "non-seriousness" forces the woman who wants to do important work into constant battle to prove she is worthy of consideration. The dropout rate which Cross notes can, in my estimation, be traced directly to the attitudes of men and even some women faculty members toward women as serious students. The women students in the research study referred to above overwhelmingly indicated that this denigration was a major problem in their careers. Derogatory and sexually disparaging comments were common experiences. In a Medical School class which included women students, the professor stated, "Women ought to be sterilized before being admitted to Medical School." In the School of Education, a professor told his class, "What the women will want next is a Ph.D. for having a baby."

Repeatedly, women reported, professors assumed careers would come second and duties as wife and mother, first. The chairman of one department stated publicly that women should not have careers; they should get married, have babies, and stay home. Again and again, there is the assumption that women are not serious about careers, and if they are serious, they should not be. One woman reported being refused admission to a department on the grounds that they preferred men to women because men are more stable and some women in the past had quit the program. The self-fulfilling nature of the prophecy is obvious, and the reactions of women to it are devastating. One woman reports:

> I was told that women are too great a risk to be accepted in this department, despite [the] admission that my qualifications were equal to or above those of the average candidate. They recommended that I go back to literature where I belonged. Namely, where women belong! These same professors were responsible for the termination of my fellowship after one year, allegedly on the grounds that I was not "serious." The charge was unjustified from every consideration and the episode has made me extremely bitter.

The combined states of imposed nonseriousness and vulnerability become most evident in sexually defined interaction patterns in the classroom. The belief that women are incapable of the same serious work that men do comes out in sexist comments in class, such as: "What was the question, dearie?" One woman stated:

> In classes, I experienced myself as a person to be taken lightly. In one seminar I was never allowed to finish a sentence; there seemed to be a tacit understanding that I never had anything significant to say. Invariably, I was called by my first name while everyone else was called Mr. ——. All in all, I was scared, depressed, "not living up to the competitive atmosphere."

The self-sacrifice of many a woman whose own life is secondary to the needs of others is in direct conflict with the competitive ego trips of some male faculty members and students. Worse than this, self-blame, combined with their isolation from each other, may lead women to believe they are probably wrong in any intellectual or personal confrontation. Furthermore, their proclivity toward co-operation often means that others use their work without reference to the source of ideas. Finally, although women are considered to be talkative, their training to withdraw into silence, rather than make a man look foolish by destroying his argument, leads to constant underestimation of their real knowledge.

Current job demands place heavy emphasis on the trained intellect of the specialist who can operate as a good technician on sharply limited problems. This kind of intellectual development is incompatible with the traditional training of a woman to become the "all-American girl," a generalist of the first order. When traditional training is joined with the socialization of women to become competent synthesizers on the basis of careful readings of complex interpersonal relations, then women act out the traditional harmonizer role. Finally, women's direct experience of daily reality runs counter to the sometimes incomplete and simplistic abstractions propounded by male scholars who may have little grounding in the human experiences they seek to predict.

Even if the intellectual styles of men and women were congruent, or even complementary, the woman student has further problems with institutionalized intellect. The history of her sex is all but obliterated; her psychology is interpreted, usually erroneously, by men; her physiology is a mystery to her. Practically everything she reads comes from a male perspective. Who, then, were the women before her? Who, then, is she now?

Where can she go for help? Too often, because she is surrounded by male professors and administrators, she goes to them, and they do what men have done for centuries. They tell her who she is and what she should do. Frequently, what they tell her is shot through with sex bias, particularly as the woman comes closer and closer to the power base of men. The woman student may come to see no role that is acceptable. Sex prejudice is directed toward single women who are not under the protection of men and who, therefore, become fair game, sexually. It is directed against single women who plan to marry, for they may, in fact, marry. It is directed against single women who do *not* want to marry, because "something must be wrong with them"; they must be lesbians. It is directed against young married women because they may have a baby. It is directed against young women with babies because there are no child care facilities and surely they must "stay home and take care of the kids." It is directed, most ironically, against those women who do what society says: stay home and take care of children; then when they return to the academic world, they are regarded as "too old" and presumed to be out of touch with their fields.

As a result of all this, women move, as Cross notes, into the so-called women's professions in which they supposedly can find compatible role arrangements. They do so knowing even beforehand or finding out subsequently that they are not intellectually attracted to such fields. The compromise eventually leads to dissatisfaction in the profession or to a shifting pattern of career aspirations. Many young women have come to my office during their senior year or their M.A. work and said, "I am in training to be a teacher, but I really *don't want* to be a teacher," or "I am trained to be a social worker, but I really *don't want* to be a social worker."

Women students come to realize that they pay a high price for moving, not according to their intellectual proclivities, but rather according to societal channels. The greater length of time that many women graduate students take to complete their degrees is not, therefore, simply a product of child-bearing and child-rearing responsibilities; it is more likely a product of the interrupted and inconsistent career patterns that result when the women realize that they do not want to be what society demands they become.

There is now the feeling among at least some women students that they can go, without losing that elusive quality of "femininity," into law, medicine, or other areas of intellectual endeavor. Many, however, are still confused about their possibilities. One of the most startling characteristics of graduate women is that they do not have a clear sense that they will actually become what they are training to be. Male students do not experience this sense of unreality; to men, it is an assured thing that they will, in fact, take on a distinct occupational status. For the women, such intellectual and occupational definition is often lacking. And this very uncertainty may make the opening of other disciplinary roles even more difficult for women, even assuming the options are in fact available.

Women students are in the throes of severe disequilibrium in matters of role definition. They are searching politically for a means of significantly altering the vertical hierarchical structures that males have bestowed on all of us. They are seeking a consciousness of self that precludes the "female" definitions previously imposed on them. Their alienation from the male-dominated institution is doubled; in contrast to even the dissatisfied men students, the women students are even more discontented. The cynicism of one woman student is reflected thus:

> If a male decides to drop out because he does not like graduate school, he does not become the same sort of statistic as a female who does likewise. She becomes a part of that statistic of women following their "natural instinct" and heading for home—demonstrating again just what "bad investments" women really are.

Women students are *not* heading for home. They are courageously demanding equality. They look to women faculty members, when they can find any, to help them. In presenting their personal struggle as an extension of the factual profile drawn by Dr. Cross, I hope that I, as a faculty woman, have done just that: helped them, just as they have so often helped me.

DAVID B. TRUMAN

The Women's Movement
and the Women's College

IN RAISING THE QUESTION of the future of the independent women's college, we are dealing with a single point in a fluid and highly unstable situation in the whole world of higher education. To say where, what, even whether that single point will be in the future requires premonitory endowments that I cannot claim. Almost any other single point in higher education would present comparable difficulties, but foreseeing the future of the independent women's college is particularly complicated because one's forecast depends heavily and directly on changes in the society, over which neither the women's colleges nor the higher education system has any significant control. In almost equal degree, the future of independent women's colleges will depend on actions that these colleges themselves take. On this point I can suggest fairly clearly what should and can be done. The uncertainty enters when one attempts to predict whether these things will be done and what the exchange pattern will be between developments in the society and what is attempted, or neglected, by the independent women's college.

These are the two points to which I shall address myself: First, what likely changes and persistent patterns in the society will directly affect the women's colleges? Second, what can and should these colleges do within this context? I am, of course, a biased witness. A year ago my institution, Mount Holyoke, recommitted itself to being a women's college. I supported and favored that recommitment. Since I would not knowingly lead the college to disaster, I am inescapably biased on the side of a positive future for it and for its sisters.

PATTERNS AND CHANGES

I start from the conviction that the current women's movement is a fact and a persisting one, not a passing fashion. It is a genuine

56

social movement responsive to real factors in the society, and it will persist indefinitely. Discounting some of its more colorful and ludicrous features (the necessary accompaniments of any major effort), the women's movement is directed at the wastefulness as well as the injustice in traditional family and manpower utilization practices. The waste is probably more important than the injustice, for a society can, and many do, perpetuate injustice, even recognized injustice, as long as it is in some sense socially useful. Many developments—including changes in the size and character of the nuclear family, in a traditional division of labor between male and female such as that on a family farm, and in the period of full dependence of children upon parents—have exposed the waste and the social nonutility in the misuse and underuse of talent among women. This exposure and the associated injustice give the women's movement its current force and momentum.

As I view the movement—and I cannot pose as an authority on either its present or its past—the assault on male monopolies is not new, though it is stronger and more effective than it was in the 1920s and earlier. The comparatively new pressure, if I see it right, is for a wider range of options, for a more varied combination of possibilities than the social system normally encourages or than would be easily forthcoming merely from permitting women to do anything that men do.

This element is new, I suspect, partly because the movement in the 1920s bore a peculiar stamp, symbolized by the peace movement of that day. The women's peace effort rested in no small measure on the assumption that women are morally better than men, a not unnatural premise in the circumstances, but one that was a curious mirror-image of the Victorian myth that put women on a pedestal and also kept them out of the larger challenges in the world's work. Whether that premise is valid or not, it seems no longer to be controlling. The new feature that I detect is aimed not so much at displacing men because women are better, but rather at giving women a wider range and combination of opportunities because they are people with talents and incidentally females of the species.

If these wider options are not merely to appear but, more important, are to be exercised in significant measure, more, far more, will be required than the reduction or elimination of overt discrimination in careers and employment. To make these options completely real, we shall have to see a total change in the child-rearing practices, especially in the early years, now characteristic of the American family. Concretely, when one can walk into any family with children under the age of five and know confidently in advance that parents, grandparents, uncles, aunts, and friends are as likely to ask the little girl what she wants to be when she grows up as they are to ask that question of the little boy, the change will have occurred. But it will not come soon, because these practices are not accessible to legislation or even to fashion, as are such consciously controlled matters as when to begin toilet training. Their roots are far deeper, their effects more subtle, and their causes, therefore, more intractable.

But no valid evidence will show that talent, especially intellectual talent, is unevenly distributed between the sexes. And every indication suggests that the adolescent female is quite capable of suspecting or discovering her talent. What she does then is critical for her future. All too often she feels cruel cross-pressures, real enough but essentially false, between being an accomplished person and being a female. If she denies her potential, the waste has begun. But if she pursues the call of her talent, she also all too often unconsciously feels a sense of guilt and of unworthiness that surely lies at the root of that fear of success which research—for example, that of Matina S. Horner—has explored.

The Women's College Role

The existence of cross-pressures, real but false, provides a significant place for a college that is dedicated to assisting the young woman to reassess herself and the forces working upon her. That college—the independent women's college—cannot alter the child-rearing practices that society has followed and has reinforced through most of her life. But it can help to correct their effects, and that is not simply a declaration of faith.

To fill this place, the women's college must consciously and actively concentrate on its role, its new challenge—the second major point I wish to make. In making this assertion, I do not intend to detract from what has been done by these colleges in earlier years. What was done is not sufficient today, but to say that the women's colleges should have done what now is clearly both necessary and possible is to ignore the context in which their work was carried on. Such Monday-morning quarterbacking often has delights, but it is almost always bad history. The independent women's colleges, as the evidence developed by Dr. Elizabeth Tidball demonstrates, have always done a disproportionate share in producing women of talent and accomplishment.

To continue that disproportionate contribution, the women's college must deliberately and aggressively develop its distinctive advantages. The most important of these is, quite simply, its ability to specialize. Concentrating the total energies of an institution on the new issues of women's education promises far more impressive results than treating them as one of a number of sidelines. Setting up a new counseling and advising service, desirable as that may be in the circumstances of a coeducational college, is not the equivalent of an exclusive institutional concern. That concern is not met, however, simply by having a student body that is wholly or predominantly women. To realize on the advantages of specialization means, among other things, that the college, and especially the faculty, must become consciously aware of the special problems and challenges in women's education—no easy matter. The college must, in consequence, address the vexing questions of whether, when, and how one teaches women differently. I am not referring to differences in standards of accomplishment or differences in content. What I mean is pedagogical method related to the psychological problems characteristic of late-adolescent women in our society.

Most faculty, for reasons that are not entirely clear to me, shy away from serious, systematic examination of pedagogy. To the extent that this reluctance reflects an objection to the displacement of content by method, it is reasonable. The concern I wish to emphasize is basic, but it is aimed at support, not displacement, of content, and it certainly does not envisage turning an educational institution into some sort of out-patient clinic. It is nonetheless true that unless faculties self-consciously consider how pedagogical technique may frustrate or contribute to the woman student's goal of reassessment, the college may miss the most important advantage of specialization.

Course or curriculum content is a less important aspect of the advantage of specialization, but it is not negligible. Much more can and should be done in new and modified courses to assist the young woman to examine intellectually the role of women, especially in other times and cultures. That road leads more readily to lasting insight and reassessment than any kind of direct attempt at consciousness-raising. At the same time, I am unalterably opposed in this context to programs or departments of women's studies. That expedient may be desirable in a coeducational institution, especially a large one, but it is, at best, out of place in the women's college. Among other things, it implicitly indulges the conceit, which we know but seldom acknowledge, that the course and the class are dominant and independent influences on development rather than one element in a total institutional environment that may either reinforce the classroom or put it on the sidelines. The creation and maintenance of a supportive and complementary environment is a major aspect of the specializing advantage of the women's college. If that is accomplished, a program of women's studies becomes at best a negligible contrivance.

The importance of the total institutional environment points to a supplementary but significant advantage of the women's colleges —size. All of them have small or medium-sized enrollments, which make it feasible consciously to create an identifiable educational community. In these days of radical individualism, only the smaller college can hope to maintain an institutional environment that is distinctive and predictably consistent with its educational goals. Without such an environment the woman student's necessary reassessment of herself and her options is likely to be largely a matter of chance.

Finally, lest my purposes be seriously misunderstood, let me emphasize that it is not my intent that the women's college should be a base or bastion for women's liberation or for any other social movement. Our concern is not with movements but with the development of individuals of talent, individuals who in the present and prospective circumstances of the society are most likely to find their talents wasted, their potential unfulfilled unless their college years assist them in reassessing and revaluing themselves and their opportunities. That, as I see it, is the mission of the women's college, its challenging future.

Is anyone out there listening?

Undergraduates View
the Coeducational Campus

Coeducation: One Student's View

KATHERINE L. JELLY

I FIND COEDUCATION more difficult to discuss now than I could have imagined a year or even six months ago. Since I am no longer an undergraduate at Yale, a newly "coeducated" college, no longer working in the Coeducation Office there, as I did for a year after graduating, I feel quite removed from the topic of coeducation. That coeducation was, and still is, a "topic" at all almost annoys me. Living and working in a coeducated society, I tend to consider that one's education should be coeducational. Yet looking back at my four undergraduate years and at my year in administrative work, I realize, sadly, that coeducation still needs discussing, that certain of my assumptions seem not so obvious to others as I, in my somewhat removed state, would expect.

As a high school senior, I applied to six colleges, four of them coeducational and two, coordinate. Because I expected coordinate education to be no different from coeducation, I chose Pembroke, the women's college in Brown University. It turned out not to be coeducational. There is no need to pursue what I saw as the problems of Brown and Pembroke except to say that I consider the subsequent decision to merge the two as a wise and necessary determination. I am led to believe that, since my time, life there—both social and academic—has greatly improved.

My principal reasons for transferring to Yale University after my sophomore year were related to wanting to attend a coeducational school. It seemed to me that the experimental nature of Yale's coeducation would be both challenging, in that I would be helping to shape and direct the venture, and supportive, in that I would be among many other transfers. (Other reasons also entered into my decision to choose Yale, including its strong academic offerings and its superb history department.)

I asked, then, of Yale that it be a natural, open environment in which the sexes shared fully and easily both their social and academic lives. As one could reasonably expect, I found a place self-conscious about coeducation, a place where women would be, for a time at least, a novelty. I found an old guard of men who were not receptive to my presence; I found many others who were. I found a group of women whom I liked and looked forward to knowing better.

It was exciting for me to be at Yale then. Feeling as strongly as I did about the artificial ways men and women relate to one another, about the unequal academic terms on which they meet, about the limited and limiting roles they are forced by society to play, I was glad to have a part in creating an atmosphere in which men and women were people, in which they worked and played together as human beings. I was glad to have a part in beginning to break down old, stilted social systems, in demonstrating to men that they need not be intimidated by my intellectual challenge.

Yet on looking back, I see not only the excitement and challenge of attending a newly coeducated school, but the difficulties as well. During my first year, the ratio of men to women was eight to one. Such a ratio does not provide for a comfortable or natural atmosphere. Men were intimidated by the numbers; women found little time to give one another and found too few other women from whom to select female friends. I did not realize then the extent to which I lost sight of myself as a woman and found myself drowned in a male ethos.

Only later were these essentially negative processes turned to good advantage, only later, through losing a sense of myself as a woman, did I come to consider womanhood all the more thoughtfully. By trampling on my self-image, Yale forced me to assert my femaleness, to discover myself as a whole human being. Having been poured into certain male molds, I emerged a stronger woman.

Life, then, at a newly coeducated college is not comfortable for either sex. Often it is difficult indeed, sometimes even destructive. Yet the problem lies not with coeducation but with the lack of it. Coeducation does not mean the education of the opposite sexes at the same institution on unequal terms. Hence my feeling is that Yale and probably most other schools that claim to be coed are not yet coeducational. Institutions that admit women under a quota system which results in the rejection of qualified women in favor of men with lower qualifications, institutions whose tenured faculty is 99 percent men, institutions where the majority of administrative positions are filled by men, these institutions are not yet coeducational. Becoming so will take time and effort. Becoming so is absolutely necessary to the well-being not only of the men and women directly involved but also of the society.

From Conestoga to Career

LISA GETMAN

As THE FIRST WOMEN arrived at Yale, I remember thinking that we should have been pulling up in Conestoga wagons instead of Chevrolets. We were all very earnest and thought of ourselves as the architects of a "City Upon a Hill," dedicated to equal access for women to the best educational resources in the country, to be erected on top of the layers of tradition that we all knew was Yale. The pioneer excitement soon dissipated, and we found ourselves in the deepest doldrums, the tonnage of tradition resting on our necks.

We were a minority. In the dining room, in the classroom, in the living room, we were blatantly outnumbered. There were 800 of us and 4,000 of them. The male students were largely responsible for the "us-them" split. We were an anomaly, laboratory specimens closely watched for our reactions under the stress of tokenism. Generalization about our psyches was rampant: the girls are too serious, the girls are always in the library, the girls are prima donnas. During the first year no one ventured to look beneath the surface to find out what the actual situation was with the women students. For the women themselves, realization was a slow but steady process. We came to understand that we were over-represented at the library because only there could we find privacy. Perhaps one of the most unfortunate effects of the ratio was that we were so sought after that we had neither the time nor energy to explore our own insides. We were comfort-suppliers and ego-boosters, receiving no reassurance in return except in terms of our subjective desirability as mere females. We increasingly felt that we had been brought to Yale for the edification of the male students and that we weren't iconoclasts at all but merely appendages to make the traditions more decorative. We went to Mory's only with an escort and received our stingers on sufferance.

In the midst of all the pampering and publicity, a strange deterioration of will took place. I was a poet when I came to Yale—I had won a national competition and felt sure that I wanted to continue writing. One of my roommates was a dancer and another an artist. As we were getting acquainted, we proudly performed for each other and supplied admiration and encouragement. When the telephone began ringing thirty times a day and there was a constant knocking at the door, Allison stopped painting, Jamie stopped dancing, and I stopped writing. Instead of saving secret time for self-cultivation, we doled out our time to the curious, and became tourist attractions to our male classmates. Giving hours and evenings instead of autographs took a definite toll on our individuality and development as people.

The first women at Yale were scattered in their living situations, and this dispersion contributed to our sense of resignation to the role of social butterfly. I could walk for blocks at night without seeing another woman's face. A woman dreaded being the only female in a seminar, and some of my friends dropped courses rather than deal with this extra burden. The lone woman couldn't ignore the situation that her papers would be singled out and read in a different light. I was the only woman in a course in Victorian history where one of my classmates felt it his responsibility to come over after every session and repeat the important points of the lecture to me. Will this, I wonder, also happen in law school and then in the courtroom? Must I always be babied and checked?

The first time I went swimming at the gym, a man yelled to me from the side of the pool, "You swim like a girl! You should keep your head down and take longer strokes." I started to apologize and then the realization hit me that I was being derogated for being myself. I had been able to ignore instances when I was not taken seriously intellectually, but it was simply outrageous that I be attacked when I was not even threatening any male's ego.

During the second year of coeducation at Yale, the introduction of women's studies courses into the curriculum marked a new blossoming of consciousness for us. A woman professor, women classmates, and the presence of a male minority combined to open up dialogue that had been repressed. Proponents of the courses continually had to justify themselves—a very radicalizing experience. The women's suffrage movement had never been taught at length in any Yale history course, and it was gratifying to see my male peers conduct research on the Grimke sisters.

Also during the second year, a program of career planning seminars for women was initiated. Accomplished women from many of the professions came to the campus to discuss their careers with women students. This valuable program helped to make up for the extreme dearth of women role models at Yale. There are simply not enough women in the faculty or administration. Although it is unfortunate that we have had to import women to emulate, they have overwhelmingly been supportive and have encouraged continued contact between themselves and interested students.

My roommates have both taken leaves of absence in an attempt to regain a sense of self-confidence. We accept the fact that there will always be sexual politics, but we will not permit it to be an obstruction to us in the competitive avenues that still lie ahead. I was struck by a friend's musing, "I wonder how many men I can sleep with before marriage until I become a whore?" I don't think that my male peers have such considerations. Until coeducation at Yale progresses from a policy statement into reality, until students are admitted and faculty hired on the basis of qualification without regard to sex, the women will bear the brunt of the nebulous implications of the present "coeducation." At baccalaureate, when the graduates are exhorted to be successful contributors to society, we are not quite sure whether the exhortation will be meant to include us. We still have the feeling that at Yale, in graduate school, in a challenging job, we are there on sufferance and must prove ourselves worthy of the benevolence that put us there.

When I filled out the Yale application, one of the spaces inquired about the field I intended to pursue after graduation. I thought, "This doesn't apply to me; they didn't have time to modify the applications for women," because I had never really thought about my future as a field to be pursued. I am grateful to that application, and to my entire Yale experience, for shocking me into finding concrete, serious answers to that question.

Yale is a conduit to careers for its women students. The pressure toward professionalism is both socially and personally derived. I do not see this pressure as a negative by-product of a newly co-educated Yale, but rather as a firm shaking to bring us out of our lethargy of easy alternatives such as housewifery and the traditional female occupations.

We want to be economically and therefore psychologically independent entities. We will buy our own stingers, write our own books, and swim as we please. We do not want to be phenomena, just merely good at something. We want to be as good as we can be, and to enjoy the recognition that that achievement alone deserves.

"Mother of Men"?

BARBARA DEINHARDT

MANY TIMES I have been asked, "Why did you come to Yale?" Looking back, I find it difficult to ignore what I know now and try to uncover those original reasons. Several, however, I remember: the quality of academic life, flexibility of the academic structure, the resources available, the faculty, the libraries. I must admit that, having gone to a private women's high school the previous two years, the prospect of having so many men around also attracted me. And the very idea of being at Yale was exciting. All these reasons could also have applied to my other college choices, Radcliffe and Stanford. It seems that the overriding, almost indisputable reason was, How could I turn it down? Although I had applied somewhat on a whim and under considerable parental pressure, when the mail brought the thick envelope instead of the thin one, I suddenly asked myself, as my classmates asked of me, "How can you turn it down?" So I didn't. I arrived in September, naïve, hopeful, and terrified.

Like the other new women, I had read the *New York Times Magazine* article on the Yale Super Woman, and I was sure that I was the only one who hadn't built a submarine in my back yard or who had not been in the Bolshoi Ballet for ten years or whatever. The paranoia which had followed me for many years struck again. Now I will be found out, I thought. It must have been a mistake that I was admitted as I certainly was not as exceptional as the other incoming students, and Yale, with its professed tradition of producing a thousand male leaders a year, would soon find out that I was not its kind. Yet accompanying this fear and paranoia was the great hopefulness, the great excitement, the great pioneer spirit that Ms. Getman has described. I had taken seriously Yale's commitment to offering its high-quality education equally to women. I knew this commitment would be hard to meet, and I was ready to help. I thought that Yale would want to make it work, and I would help them do so. Looking back, that sounds not only presumptuous but also very naïve.

My first year I was occupied with other things. The normal adjustments to college took all my energy. I struggled through classes, I had a whirlwind romance, the May Day strike came and went, and then it was summer. That summer I realized that something had been missing, something that I had grown accustomed to in high school and missed at Yale. Although that "something" was vague, I recognized it had many components. I missed having women friends, having informal contacts with teachers and counselors, and feeling a part of the institution. It was more than the transition of going from a small school where I was a big star to a big school where I was no star at all. It was a feeling of alienation from the students and the faculty, from the buildings and the content of the course work, from everything. I began to feel like a somewhat superfluous addendum to the already established Yale pattern. I realized that I had come to Yale for many different reasons, but that Yale had brought me here for totally different ones. I grew skeptical of that original commitment I thought Yale had made to women. I doubted that they really wanted to make that commitment work, and thus they certainly didn't want me to try to help them do so. In short, I felt betrayed. I had energy, I had ideas, I had things I wanted to do; and yet all of these seemed to be rejected by the forces I had hoped would be accepting.

Many things happened during my second year at Yale. I moved off campus and helped organize an undergraduate women's liberation group called "the Sisterhood." This group accomplished many things in its early days. We worked with the Yale Ad Hoc Committee to End Sex Discrimination in connection with the affirmative action investigation of the U.S. Department of Health, Education, and Welfare, and we helped organize many women's studies courses. More important perhaps, we formed a small community of women in the larger Yale community. Its meetings provided a short respite from the constant flow of male faces in male surroundings. It provided a mechanism for making friends and a way to react with people without the self-protective hostility often felt by many of the women students toward each other, and without the need to be mother, lover, sister, confidante, as demanded by many of the men. But something happened, and the pressures of the greater Yale community caused the group to deteriorate slowly. We felt hostility from the administration toward our work with the HEW investigation; we felt hostility from faculty members in our attempts to set up women's courses; and we felt hostility from the men we might have been involved with who demanded all our time. With that avenue seeming no longer open to me, I reached out to the New Haven community where the women's liberation movement was very strong. Since then, my work in the women's movement has been divided between work with New Haven women's liberation and work within the Yale structure. By necessity, the latter has been done individually rather than with a group.

The summer after my sophomore year I worked with a group of Yale undergraduate women in the Coeducation Office on a number of different projects. We put together *SHE*, a book of information for women at Yale containing lists of women faculty members and women administrators, resources at the Health Department and the Athletic Department, lists of women's studies courses, women's organizations, and so forth. We collected and edited many of the papers that had been written that year in women's courses. We compiled a bibliography of books on women's issues for the library, and we worked on setting up a Women's Center to be used not only by Yale women but also New Haven women to try to overcome the division between the two groups. The summer collective worked well; yet, again, when school started, pressures seemed to break and we dissolved. I took a leave of absence for the second semester of 1971–72 and am now administrative assistant to the special assistant to the president on the education of women.

At this point, I have conflicting emotions about Yale. My years at Yale have been rewarding in many ways. I still feel that the quality of education is high, that the flexibility of the academic program that is available is good, and that many of the people here as students, faculty, and administrators are good people. I feel, however, that I have spent too much time banging my head against walls that would have been nonexistent had Yale been sincere in its commitment to women. Changes have been made, but I feel we are coming to a standstill. The major obstacle now is numbers. There simply are not enough women students, simply not enough women on the faculty, simply not enough participation of women in the decision-making process on all levels. The problem of numbers manifests itself in many areas: in the classroom, in the residential colleges, in career counseling, as well as in the more subjective area of wanting to be part of this community, wanting to be accepted as a significant member of this institution. Yale is a good place to be, but not good enough.

Coeds View an Undergraduate Campus

GRISEL RODRIGUEZ

I AM A RELATIVE STRANGER to coeducation. Most of my schooling has been in private girls-only institutions. Having been in so many sheltered institutions, I decided to test my abilities against those of men and the public school group. I also felt that my vocational indecision would not be resolved by continuing in elitist schools. I was not eager to face the competition characteristic in such institutions because I feel it is demeaning to those who get along well in most situations but are shattered by the demands of competition. In summary, my reasons for attending Miami-Dade Junior College, a two-year institution in my home town, are: to test my talents, to make a career choice, and to get away from overachievers.

I had expectations of being the conventional commuter student. I wanted to become immersed in my books and sit on the sidelines for a year. Instead I found myself caught up in a group of student activists. The enthusiasm and stick-to-it-iveness of this tightly knit group is uncanny in a commuter college. My talents were in de-

mand; these people made room for me. I haven't had to compete
fiercely or lose my femininity to become an editor or noted around
campus. The adjustment I had to make from a competitive atmosphere to a casual working relationship has taken a year to accomplish. I haven't had occasion to hide my female role; it hasn't gotten
in the way of my relationships with men. I've never had to forsake
my sexuality to succeed.

In my academic career, I have gone from the competitive atmosphere to a more relaxed attitude toward my studies. There is
competition to be in the top tenth of the class, and the average
necessary is a 3.91 or better. The competition is just as keen here
as in an achievement-oriented elitist institution. The stress, however, is on personal enlightenment, not grade-point averages. Also,
students may schedule their classes to study under professors whose
teaching style they find congenial.

Most of the women I have met at Miami-Dade are highly
motivated, bright women who are finishing their aborted college
careers. They are strong enough to pursue the tremendous paper-
work tangles that confront those not accustomed to the system.
Other women sometimes flounder because they don't know where
to turn for help. These students usually last until the end of the
semester and then drop out, discouraged because no one knew of
their problems.

Because I chose to become as involved in extracurricular activities as in my academic career, I have not had the grade-point
average I am capable of. Two years ago failure to make top grades
would have upset me. Today I can state that I have grown as much
in overall knowledge as the coed who got the 4.00 average, and I
have had a better time doing it, too. This evaluation characterizes
a major difference in the attitudes found in achievement-oriented
institutions.

I have discovered that my confidence as a woman has been
enhanced since my areas of interests have broadened. I have learned
that I can hold my own with a Pakistani man, a KKK member,
irate Young Republicans, administrators, and ex-Weathermen, and
somehow that confidence is more reassuring than knowing I can
outsmart anyone else in class.

Coeducational institutions are not meeting the needs of the
increasing numbers of coeds they are attracting. In many quarters

there are remnants of objectionable attitudes toward coeds. Men as well as women need to explore the role possibilities for women in today's world. In-service seminars should be planned for students and faculty to explore their attitudes.

Vocational counseling for women must be stepped up to help them make the most of their talents and to start funneling them into more areas than teaching and the social sciences.

Department faculties should reflect the proportions of men and women among their students in departments that usually attract one sex or the other, in order give both men and women a chance to be able to relate to their professors.

An effort must be made to find women who are capable of serving as administrators and in other positions of consequence.

A conscious effort must be made to facilitate the change in life style for older women who come back to pursue their educational-vocational goals. Carefully planned orientation programs and a thorough grounding in college procedures would help women who might otherwise become lost. A semester-long seminar of this kind, I believe, would benefit many women who have said to me they dropped out because the institution offered no such added counseling.

Women students with children should be able to place their children under supervision while attending classes. If there are no day care centers available on the campus, funds should be allocated in the form of financial aid to help coeds finance the cost of a private day care center.

Part Three

THE WOMAN PROFESSIONAL
IN HIGHER EDUCATION

JUANITA M. KREPS

The Woman Professional
in Higher Education

Academic women constitute a different population, statistically speaking, from academic men. In the world of academic women, career patterns develop along different lines. Women tend to serve in institutions which emphasize different functions, and they themselves are attracted to different kinds of functions. Further, they tend to be in areas which are not in strategic positions in the academic market place and which are not as productive as the areas that attract men.

JESSIE BERNARD, Academic Women, 1964

SEX DIFFERENCES IN ACADEMIC CAREER PATTERNS, analyzed by Professor Bernard nearly a decade ago, have recently caught the attention of many scholars, whose subsequent work has provided new information on rank, tenure, and salary differential.[1] In addition, study has focused attention on the extent to which the lower status of women is explained by discrimination,[2] despite Executive orders

1. See Alan E. Bayer and Helen S. Astin, "Sex Differences in Academic Rank and Salary among Science Doctorates in Teaching," *Journal of Human Resources* 3 (1968): 191–200; Jessie Bernard, *Academic Women* (University Park: Pennsylvania State University Press, 1964), and *Careers of Ph.D.'s, Academic v. Nonacademic: Second Report on Follow-ups of Doctorate Cohorts, 1935–60* (Washington: National Academy of Sciences, 1968); Helen S. Astin, *The Woman Doctorate in America: Origins, Career, and Family* (New York: Russell Sage Foundation, 1969); Ann S. Harris, "The Second Sex in Academe," *AAUP Bulletin* 56 (1970): 283–95; Patricia A. Graham, "Women in Academe," *Science* 169 (1970): 1284–90; Helen S. Astin and Alan E. Bayer, "Sex Discrimination in Academe," *Educational Record* 53 (1972): 101–18; Burton G. and Judith A. Malkiel, "Male-Female Differentials in Professional Employment," Working Paper No. 35 (Princeton, N.J.: Industrial Relations Section, 1972); Michael A. LaSorte, "Sex Differences in Salary among Academic Sociology Teachers," *American Sociologist*, November 1972. See also Alice Rossi, ed., *Academic Women on the Move* (New York: Russell Sage Foundation, forthcoming); the publications listed in Helen S. Astin, Nancy Suniewick, and Susan Dweck, *Women: A Bibliography on Their Education and Careers* (Washington: Human Service Press, University Research Corporation, 1971); and John C. McKinney, "Women in the Academic Labor Force" (Duke University) *Graduate School Report* 3 (1972).
2. See especially Astin and Bayer, "Sex Discrimination."

which prohibit differences based on race, color, religion, sex, or national origin, on projects under federal contracts.[3]

Institutions now under compliance review are expected not only to correct personnel practices which fail to treat men and women equally, but also to increase the numbers of women employed, particularly at the higher levels. The difficulties of accomplishing the latter result without violating the former principle have not gone unnoticed. At a recent meeting of the American Association of University Professors, some delegates viewed with alarm the beginnings of reverse discrimination.[4] Nevertheless, the overall thrust of the regulations should result in the hiring of greater numbers of women and the upgrading of others. A quick appraisal indicates that the status of academic women will gradually be moved toward equality with that of males.

Important questions persist. The first set is contained in the issue Jessie Bernard raises: To what extent do the career patterns of academic women differ from those of men? Do the differences reflect divergent preferences of men and women, or do they merely indicate that each sex is fulfilling its expected role? Can it be argued that academic women are "a different population, statistically speaking, from academic men"—in brief, that the two are noncompeting groups? A second set of questions concerns the rate at which institutions will be able to accomplish the goal of sex equality, particularly in numbers of women hired. How long will it take for improved incentives of higher rank and pay to produce substantial increases in the numbers of women who complete doctorates and then go on to become productive scholars? Given the constraints on the geographical mobility of married women, will the opportunities afforded women scholars not remain below those of similarly qualified men? Finally, there is the problem of disentangling market forces from institutional bias. If the number of additional professors required to staff universities and colleges in the 1970s is small, the probability of improving the lot of academic women is much lower than could occur in a high-growth period such as the 1960s, even if sex discrimination were discontinued.

3. Executive Order 11246, as amended by Executive Order 11375. The latter contains the specific prohibition of discrimination against women.
4. Query: Why is discrimination "reverse" when it is against men?

FEMALE EDUCATORS: A NONCOMPETING GROUP?

Examination of the differences between the men and women now staffing institutions of higher learning gives no basis for immediate optimism. Appendix A shows that women faculty members have Ph.D.'s or Ed.D.'s less than half as often as men, and that women are heavily concentrated in the humanities and education, whereas men are dispersed throughout the disciplines. The data further reveal marked differences in rank, salary, and type of appointment. Present market conditions clearly operate to the disadvantage of women faculty members; until there are substantial changes in the characteristics of women academicians, or until there are shifts in the kinds of academic talent demanded, significant salary differentials are likely to remain. Specifically, current demand and supply conditions indicate a need for women in higher education

· To enter the physical sciences, engineering, and some of the social sciences in larger numbers, and
· To choose education and the humanities less frequently;
· To complete their doctorates more frequently than they have in the past;
· To invest more time in research, leaving men to give greater emphasis to teaching, and
· To move from colleges into universities, where salaries tend to be higher and research potential greater;
· To move far more often from one institution to another;
· To request administrative posts provided they do not preclude the research and writing necessary to ensure full professorships.

Thus it can be argued that if women gain their doctorates in a broader range of disciplines, if they are prepared to place a heavier emphasis on research and writing, and if they are willing to move to the universities offering the best opportunities for advancement, they can achieve academic status comparable with that of men. Even if these shifts begin to take place, progress will be slow; the changes will occur primarily at the lowest ranks, where careers are in their infancy. Only after the new cohorts of women have moved up through the professorial ranks will there begin to be equal representation of the two sexes at the various levels of teaching, research, and administration.

THE SLOW PROCESS OF CHANGE

But there are prior questions of whether women's *preferences* mesh with the demands of the academic market; whether the reward system operates in the same manner for the two sexes—are the *incentives* for women sufficiently strong to induce them to make heavier expenditures in human capital?—and finally, whether the *constraints* that impede their career development will allow women to accommodate to market demand.

The question of preference

If women are to be represented in all fields of higher education, they need to make much greater inroads into certain disciplines and functions, and to contribute much smaller supply increments to other subject areas. Women, though they are currently strongly attracted to the humanities and some of the social sciences and are finding acceptance there, have produced relatively few scientists, engineers, economists, lawyers, physicians, and dentists. Despite the higher salaries in the latter fields, women have persisted in going (or have been allowed to go) into the more crowded disciplines where the number of job applicants has tended to outstrip demand.

We need to know a great deal about the woman's selection of major in college, and particularly about her decision to pursue the chosen subject to graduate school. What we do know about preferences tells us that they are the product of a lifetime of socialization: women are expected to have some types of intellectual interests and capacities, but not others. The rare woman who elects engineering or physics has constantly to explain her choice, whereas a woman Ph.D. in Romance languages seems to be quite "normal." In the same manner, women are expected to be teachers of children; college teaching is considered an extension of this function. But scientific research is thought to be somewhat out of character for females. University administration has similarly been a male calling (except in cases of deans of women), in part because male administrators usually have wives who are also fully employed, although without pay.

For women who have strong preferences for the humanities, who want to teach instead of research or administer, the academic policies that need to be reexamined are those dealing with the relative worth imputed to teaching, research, and administration, and also the policies that affect interdiscipline salary differentials. But those women who are discouraged from competing for university posts that at present hold the promise of higher pay and prestige— because women are not accepted as scholars, or because teaching is considered a more womanly role—are having their potential contributions stifled. The result is a poor allocation of talent that subverts the academy's supposed search for excellence. What appears to have happened in the past is perhaps the worst set of circumstances: women have chosen their desciplines and their functions within the perceived role expectations, going into teaching (most often in colleges) in those areas in which they faced the least competition from men. Having made this commitment, women have then spent their time teaching and counseling, and as a result have failed to advance in rank and salary because they were "unproductive."

Many exceptions to this career pattern can be found among women, of course; similarly, men who follow this path face much the same promotional hazards as women. What we do not know is whether, once all disciplines and academic functions become equally acceptable for both men and women, there will any longer be sex-related preferences. We may discover that research and administration are much more appealing to women, teaching more attractive to men. Given a freedom of choice no longer obscured by stereotypes, academic rank and salary in the various disciplines will come to reflect the preferences of both sexes. By contrast, the traditional pattern has encouraged women to restrict their choice to a narrow range of subjects, and the excess supply of women entering these fields has held down salaries.

In order to increase substantially the total supply of women Ph.D.'s (to the point where universities could be expected to hire approximately the same numbers of both sexes), some pervasive changes in attitudes must occur. Further necessary shifts fall under the headings of *incentives* to professional achievement, and *constraints* on that achievement.

The question of incentives

Heavy investments in human capital are required for full-time entry into university teaching and research. This investment consists of expenditures for tuition, living expenses, books—most of all, forgone earnings during one's educational stint. The woman who would go into the academic profession must be willing to forgo earnings for a number of years, and both she and society must make significant educational outlays in the hope that a satisfactory rate of return (financial as well as psychic) will ensue.

Investments in a man's education are seldom questioned;[5] barring premature death, his lifetime earnings are likely to compensate him handsomely for his educational expenses.[6] But for a woman, earnings have been far less predictable. If she marries and has children, she may face interruptions in earnings, possibly for several years, and encounter need for reeducation before she returns to her profession. In some disciplines knowledge erodes rapidly, leaving the value of an advanced degree dependent largely on when the degree was earned.

Under these circumstances, the reluctance of women to invest in themselves is readily understandable. Certainly understandable is the societal attitude that investments in the male's education should be favored: such investments bear a more certain return, on the average.[7] The wonder is not that we produce so few women who

5. Duncan Bailey and Charles Schotta conclude, however, that whereas "the private and social return to undergraduate education in general is in excess of 6 percent ... the social rate of return to graduate education in general is either zero or less than 1 percent" (in "The Returns to Graduate Education: Pecuniary or Psychic?" Paper presented at the 1970 meeting of the Western Economic Association). Their study does not differentiate between returns to the sexes, but it does note that the fields whose supply might well be reduced are the humanities, education, and some of the social sciences, where the rates of return are particularly low.

6. See Juanita M. Kreps, *Sex in the Marketplace: American Women at Work* (Baltimore: Johns Hopkins Press, 1971), pp. 58–59.

7. Appendix B shows the methods of calculating lifetime earnings and the relation of these earnings to investments in education. Such procedures are of particular significance in discussions of differences in expenditures for the education of women and of men, and the relation of such expenditures to earning through the life course of the two sexes. Because the work-life expectancy of a college-age woman is shorter than a man's, expected lifetime earnings of females are smaller. Hence, the return on investment in a woman's education may be lower than the return on the same investment in a man's education, even when annual earnings of the two are equal.

make the investment, but that we produce so many. The fact that the supply of women aspiring to academic careers has increased during the past decade (as shown by their increased proportion of doctorates, from 10.5 percent in 1960–61 to 13.3 percent in 1969–70)[8] is perhaps due to a scarcity of attractive alternatives. Or stated positively, college teaching apparently offers one of the best combinations of salary, working hours and conditions, and intellectual challenge open to women.

If the supply of women doctorates is to increase even more rapidly, the academic marketplace must reward women more generously than in the past. The improved remuneration must persist over time, and it must be widely understood by women. Similar remuneration to the two sexes would help induce similar investments in human capital. In short, when lifetime earnings of the female approach those of the male with the same education, women are likely to respond much more enthusiastically to the financial incentive. Annual returns to women doctorates are lower on the average than those to males. Although it is sometimes alleged that women tend to discount too heavily their stream of future earnings, research might reveal that they were, instead, quite realistic in their estimates.

In general, the inability of women to pursue careers as systematically as men (because of the uncertainties and interruptions surrounding marriage and child rearing, or lack of mobility in job placement after marriage) leads them to settle for much less career preparation than men. When a high level of formal education is the primary prerequisite for a job, women tend to be shut out of the competition at the entry level, or permitted only temporary or part-time status in the profession. In higher education, much of the introductory-level instruction is done by women, who are usually poorly compensated instructors and who will have little upward mobility in the profession. The final blow to ambition is dealt them when they meet the requirements of degree and scholarly output only to find that the rank and salary rewards are not commensurate with those conferred on their male colleagues.

8. *A Fact Book on Higher Education* (Washington: American Council on Education, 1971), Fourth issue, p. 71.193. Includes in addition to the Ph.D. such degrees as Ed.D., S.T.D., and Sc.D.; excludes honorary doctorates and first professional degrees.

The question of constraints

The reward system will surely become less sex-related, with men and women of similar abilities moving much closer to equality in academic placements. Yet married women face serious impediments to acquiring academic credentials, and removal of these barriers is a slow process. In particular, married women face greater problems than men in job mobility and family responsibilities. And although improved transportation eases the geographical limitation, and better household technology and smaller families relax the time limitation, women's restricted freedom of job choice now inevitably prevents them from attaining the ranks and salaries reached by men of comparable competence.

Specific proposals have been made to reduce the barriers further: removal of nepotism rules will allow wives and husbands to hold posts in the same institution (or the same department); part-time teaching permits women to continue their profession without interruption; day care proposals abound. There are few cases, nevertheless, in which the woman's career is likely to develop at the same rate as her husband's, even in the absence of children, since he is usually considered the primary worker and his job choice determines geographical location. In recent years some young academic couples have followed a team approach, with equal weight being given to both careers in the final selection of jobs. And there are doubtless many instances in which the husband's job choice was heavily influenced by the availability of opportunities for his wife.

The geographical mobility disadvantage may even grow, for the proportion of young married academic women has risen. While urban settings that offer access to more than one educational institution are not rare, a single location rarely allows both persons to take their best job offers. Some professional sacrifice will be required whenever the mobility of either partner is impeded or whenever his or her bargaining strength is reduced because of the need to find two jobs. The degree of sacrifice ranges all the way from a minor salary differential to forgoing a job altogether.

Academic women who have children are likely to find the triple demands of teaching, research, and child care extraordinarily demanding, despite the best possible domestic arrangements. Earlier description of the issues has pointed up the problems that face both the woman and her family, and the possible repercussions on the children. But the accounts are balanced by children's reassuring comments such as the following: "She kept explaining until we were bored to death with the subject just why she had to work. We couldn't have cared less. It just meant that we had more freedom than other children whose mothers were always butting into our affairs."[9]

American women's attitudes toward combining career and family have shifted significantly in the past few decades; the academic woman is no exception. The woman who took her doctoral degree in the World War II era was likely to devote a substantial portion of her time to hearth and home, and sometimes apologize for having a career at all. In the 1950s, too, the woman scholar was both rare and subdued. Not until the decade of the sixties did women evidence strong career drives and a greatly increased interest in higher education. In that decade alone women's proportion of all Ph.D.'s increased by almost one-third.

To these younger women in higher education, career is likely to be the dominant theme. Home responsibilities and child care are taken seriously, but they are not all-consuming. Rather than fitting her job into those hours of the day left free of family obligations, the younger academic woman expects to be able to manage the household with a minimum of time, leaving her major energies for research and teaching. Not only does she expect to have a career, but she also expects her family to cooperate fully with her career aspirations.

The contrast between the woman college graduate of the 1940s who was going to marry and have six children, and the graduate of the 1970s who talks more of law or graduate school, should tell us something of the future academic marketplace. It is not an altogether reliable predictor, of course. Just as we found we had to flee the suburbs for jobs in the grimy, glamorous city (there was such a thing, we discovered, as too much fresh air), so, too, women graduates of the seventies may choose to redefine their priorities. We did not do precisely what we planned to do, and there is no reason to expect our daughters to do so.

But there is at least one critical difference. That difference lies

9. Bernard, *Academic Women*, p. 225.

not just in women's expectations of themselves, significant as that factor is; it emerges also from society's expectations of women. In particular, society has decreed that women have equal job opportunities; that when qualified and hired, they receive equal pay; that their sex does not disqualify them for any academic post; in brief, that when their performance in the workplace matches that of men, their rewards, too, shall be equivalent.

These are bold new declarations. We have not yet had time to witness their impact on the aspirations and performance of the new generation of academic women.

THE ACADEMIC MARKET, NOW AND IN THE FUTURE

The evidence emerging on the supply side of the academic market indicates the probability of a growing proportion of women in that market and a heavier investment in education on the part of women. Unless these trends are counterbalanced by decreased job mobility or greater concentrations in the oversupplied disciplines, women's better preparation and larger numbers should gradually change the sex composition of all levels of the academic labor force.

The pace of this change will turn in large part, however, on the demand for academic talent. In the immediate future, job prospects appear bleak. In contrast to the market of the past two decades, when the demand for college teachers seemed insatiable, projections now indicate that the supply of teachers will exceed the demand throughout the 1970s, at least.

Projections of the supply and utilization of doctorates, made by the National Science Foundation,[10] show a significant oversupply for the future. Specifically, the 315,000–336,000 doctoral scientists and engineers available in 1980 exceeds the expected demand for 270,000–297,000 by a wider margin than was earlier estimated. The most extreme imbalance is expected in engineering (where, in 1969, awards constituted 15 percent of existing doctorates). In physical sciences, the 1980 supply and demand are expected to be roughly

---

10. *1969 and 1980 Science and Engineering Doctorate Supply and Utilization,* NSF 71-20 (Washington: Government Printing Office, 1971), pp. 5–6, 16. The report notes: "Nonscience and nonengineering doctorates (e.g., Ed.D., M.D., L.L.B., D.B.A., Ph.D., in arts, humanities, history) . . . are outside the scope of this study. However, the term doctorate, as used in this study, includes the newer science and engineering doctoral programs (e.g., Doctor of Arts) as well as the more traditional Doctor of Philosophy (Ph.D.)" (p. 1).

in balance, but in the social sciences, where the rate of doctoral output is growing, an excess supply of 20 percent is anticipated. Life sciences will see a smaller oversupply of 9 percent, and mathematics, an excess of 10 percent.

Not all the doctorates in these fields will seek jobs in academia: in 1980, about 60 percent of the doctorates are expected to be in academic institutions. Yet the projected decline in college-age population and enrollments suggests that the academic market demand will decline significantly during this decade. Moreover, the disciplines under consideration are the ones which have traditionally provided the best opportunities within higher education and the broadest range of nonacademic alternatives. It seems unlikely that other fields will fare better.

Much larger numbers of Ph.D.'s would be absorbed in academic posts if society felt it could afford higher quality higher education or afford higher education for a larger proportion of the potential undergraduate population. A decline in the number of college-age youth need not signal a decline in the numbers of professors employed. If the teacher-student ratio and the proportion of youth attending college remain at their present levels, however, the market for college teachers, male and female, will be poor indeed. Placements of both women and men in teaching posts will then be slowed at a time when the numbers of persons available for such jobs are rapidly increasing.

Will such an imbalance in the supply and utilization of academic talent affect the status of women more adversely than that of men? A declining demand could reveal some sex-related differences in hiring policy that do not appear in a tight market.[11] When the job market is expanding, employers are prompted to reach further down the labor queue, hiring workers in the order of their attractiveness. Which potential employee is attractive depends on the mind-set of the employer as well as the characteristics of the persons waiting to be hired. The sex of the applicant is an important characteristic, so important for some jobs and to some employers that only one sex is acceptable. Members of the other sex are then so far down the line that they have little chance of being employed in that job; in effect, they constitute a different queue altogether.

11. Kreps, *Sex in the Marketplace*, pp. 61–62.

The great advantage of a tight labor market is the forced erosion of preconceptions and the acceptance of formerly unacceptable persons, who thenceforth can be considered on the basis of individual competence. For women, major breakthroughs have occurred during such tight markets as World War II, when employers "resorted" to hiring them for jobs only men had previously held. Once employed in the new jobs, women have generally not retreated to the second line.

Since World War II, women have not faced a serious downturn in demand for the jobs they typically perform. For the most part, declines have been in blue-collar jobs held by men, while the white-collar and service jobs in which women have been concentrated have expanded.[12] Primary and secondary school teaching has only recently suffered a downturn. What happens to the male-female mix of professors if the market for higher education personnel continues to soften? Have women applicants for academic posts advanced in the queue to the point where they compete with their male colleagues on the basis of their individual capabilities?

The short-run market

At present, two offsetting factors are exerting major influences on the demand for academic women: the slowed rate of hiring additional personnel, occasioned by reduced enrollments and budgetary cutbacks; and a counterpressure to increase the numbers of women on college faculties, brought about by the overall thrust for equality of treatment. The aggregate demand for professorial talent has thus leveled off, but a larger portion of the total appears to be earmarked for women. So whereas finding a job for a new woman Ph.D. may be easier than finding one for a man of similar ability, the problem comes in finding a job at all.

One of the new sources of demand for teachers is that coming from junior and community colleges, whose growth rate in enrollments is extremely high—threefold in less than a decade. These institutions, now staffed largely with nondoctorates, emphasize teaching rather than research. The teaching aspects, plus possible locational advantages, may make these positions appealing to women. It is not clear, however, whether the women going into junior and community college teaching will be drawn primarily

12. See Valerie Oppenheimer, *The Female Labor Force in the United States,* Population Monograph Series, No. 5 (Berkeley: University of California, 1970)

from the ranks of the doctorates or come from the oversupply of secondary teachers who, finding no jobs in the high schools, undertake to prepare themselves for college teaching. In either case, one possible outcome would be a substantial movement of women into this field, with the gradual effect of having women dominate community college teaching as they have secondary education. Since community colleges do not offer the career potential that universities afford, such a shift would increase sex differentials in higher education. Alternatively, women who move out of secondary education into the necessary graduate study, then on to community college teaching, will improve their status.

The disadvantage in having only women teach in any area lies in the tendency of female-dominated occupations to be poorly paid and to lack status. When men have entered a field in sufficient numbers, they have forced up the rewards. Individual preferences for different academic functions will be better met, moreover, if junior and community colleges employ both sexes, leaving the four-year colleges and universities to do the same. Sex differentials and interinstitutional differences would then be minimized, for men and women would be free to enter the academic market at whatever level their abilities permitted.

Competition for academic appointments is likely to become keener in the next few years as the supply of new doctorates grows and the demand for their services slows. At the moment, most institutions are acutely aware of the small numbers of women on their faculties, and women's opportunities for appointments are at least as good as those of men with similar backgrounds. It is probably inevitable that the shortage of academic jobs will come to be interpreted as a battle of the sexes, although similar competition among males has always been applauded, on the assumption that such competition resulted in improved selection. Educational institutions are under pressure, not just from women but from governmental agencies as well, to see that the competitive process is free of sex bias, and to observe this rule even when the shortage of jobs means that men as well as women go unemployed.

Some long-run considerations

Assuming that discriminatory practices are removed, what will be the sex composition of the academic labor force in the future? If women and men are hired on the basis of their qualifications, will the proportion of women in all ranks, functions, and disciplines begin to approach that of men? Or will the job specifications be so formulated that men will continue to excel in institutions of higher education? Earlier arguments that women are attracted to institutions and functions that differ from those which appeal to men must now be cast in the light of a current plea for reexamination of the academic reward system. Astin and Bayer question whether the system is not dysfunctional to higher education, in giving primary emphasis to administration, research, and publications rather than teaching.[13]

Questions of the appropriate balance between teaching and research, publications and student counseling, administration and committee work, highly important in their own right, are also central to the resolution of women's status in higher education. For some time to come, the traditional division of labor in academe is likely to be made along sex lines, with those women whose career patterns are already established continuing to be "unproductive," or teaching-oriented. The question of how well these women will be rewarded inevitably raises the basic issue of how the role of the university is to be defined. Is research to be more handsomely rewarded than teaching, on the assumption that the generation of knowledge calls for a more valuable (or at any rate, scarcer) talent than the transmission of knowledge? Should colleges and universities continue to give scholarly publications more weight than teaching quality in promotion decisions?

Current solutions to issues of this breadth and age often end in a plea for options. As long as students and faculty may choose between a teaching-oriented college and a research-minded university, a faculty reward system that serves both types of institutions is considered fair. The demand for space in universities has tended to be stronger; to a student, there are apparently compelling inducements to enroll there, and to a faculty member, to seek a post there. Severe criticisms of teaching quality notwithstanding, universities seem likely to continue to foster research and to reward faculty largely on that basis. Indeed, there will be very little change in the reward system until both men and women faculty opt for a reorientation of academic goals. And although teaching

13. "Sex Discrimination," pp. 101, 117.

quality is surely a more central issue than it was a decade ago, new doctorates have at least as great a thirst for research as the older faculty, and their expectations are shaped in traditional mold.

One set of questions not yet adequately researched has to do with the motivation for choosing an academic career. Is the choice prompted by a desire to teach? Or is the basis of decision the appeal of the subject and the promise of time for further explorations of that subject? When it is the latter, the research drive is paramount, whether or not the reward system favors publication; it may not be necessary, in fact, to reward the researcher more generously than the teacher. The faculty member who possesses both talents is perhaps not as rare as the dichotomy suggests, but there can be little doubt that his promotions are more often earned by journal articles than by teaching ability. The question of whether universities will reverse these priorities depends to a large extent on the importance faculty members themselves attach to the two functions.

A further research question pertains to the relative significance of research opportunities to younger women doctorates, and the extent to which these women's preferences differ from those of male doctorates of the same age. We may find that among the faculty members who were awarded the doctorate in the last decade, there is much less sex difference in research interest, choice of institution and discipline, and continuity of academic career than there is among the total doctorate population. If so, the system of academic rewards, though still an important issue for higher education, will harbor less sex bias in the future.

In the meantime

In the meantime, colleges and universities can set about correcting for salary and rank differentials that are clearly the result of sex discrimination rather than bona fide differences in academic qualifications. Institutions can further guarantee that women candidates for positions receive the same consideration given men with similar credentials; the practice of discounting young women's future productivity for reasons of possible marriage or child rearing or other frivolous pursuits can surely be discontinued.

But the obligation does not end there. If the quality of higher education is to be enriched and made more effective through a fuller utilization of women educators, Roger Heyns has argued, institutions have the further responsibility to set in motion new patterns of student selection, advisory services, curriculum flexibility, resumed education programs, part-time study and teaching arrangements, maternity leave and day care facilities. "There are enormous potentials of strength and performance in the women of the nation," he concludes. "Creating the conditions under which these potentials are likely to be realized is a necessary, honorable, and rewarding assignment."[14]

14. "Sex Discrimination and Contract Compliance: Beyond the Legal Requirements," *A.C.E. Special Report* (Washington: American Council on Education, April 20, 1972), p. 2.

APPENDIX A

TABLE A1: *Selected Demographic and Academic Activity Characteristics of College Faculty Members, by Sex and Type of Institution, 1969*

Characteristic	Percentage Distribution[a] in:							
	All Institutions		Universities		4-Year Colleges		2-Year Colleges	
	Men	Women	Men	Women	Men	Women	Men	Women
Highest degree held								
Bachelor's or less........	6.3	8.6	4.2	6.2	5.8	7.3	17.2	16.9
Master's................	30.1	53.3	18.3	48.9	36.9	51.5	63.0	67.7
Ph.D. or Ed.D...........	46.1	21.7	57.5	25.5	42.2	26.0	6.1	2.2
Rank								
Professor...............	24.5	9.4	30.1	9.9	22.0	11.2	7.1	3.6
Associate professor......	21.9	15.7	23.8	15.1	23.3	17.1	10.1	13.4
Assistant professor......	28.2	28.7	29.4	30.7	30.8	31.6	15.2	17.0
Instructor..............	16.3	34.8	11.5	35.7	5.8	29.6	38.7	45.6
Lecturer...............	3.3	4.6	2.7	4.0	5.2	6.5	.8	1.3
No rank designated......	3.4	3.3	.3	.3	1.4	1.4	23.1	14.6
Other..................	2.3	3.5	2.2	4.2	1.4	2.5	5.0	4.6
Salary (Academic Year)								
Below $7,000...........	6.2	17.0	5.3	16.2	6.0	17.8	10.9	16.6
$7,000–$9,999..........	21.7	45.6	13.1	38.8	30.0	48.8	35.7	52.7
$10,000–$11,999........	20.6	17.6	17.9	20.7	24.1	15.7	22.2	15.4
$12,000–$13,999........	17.4	9.9	18.1	11.3	15.9	8.8	18.8	9.8
$14,000–$16,999........	15.5	6.1	18.6	7.4	12.5	5.5	10.5	4.6
$17,000–$19,999........	9.1	2.0	12.7	3.2	6.3	1.8	1.2	.1
$20,000–$24,999........	6.3	1.2	9.3	2.0	3.7	1.0	.4	.1
$25,000+..............	3.1	.5	4.9	.3	1.5	.6	.2	.7
Teaching hours per week								
None...................	7.9	7.6	11.5	11.4	4.0	5.6	3.3	4.1
1–4....................	16.2	11.9	22.0	15.4	10.8	10.8	7.3	7.0
5–8....................	26.8	17.7	34.3	22.8	21.8	16.6	8.7	9.2
9–12...................	28.3	32.8	21.7	29.4	42.5	40.4	16.2	21.7
13+....................	20.7	29.9	10.5	21.0	21.0	26.4	64.4	58.0
Type of appointment								
Regular with tenure......	48.8	37.5	52.3	34.7	44.3	38.4	47.2	41.5
Regular without tenure...	46.7	57.6	43.3	60.5	50.8	55.4	49.5	56.3
Acting.................	1.9	2.9	1.8	2.5	2.0	3.7	2.1	2.0
Visiting...............	2.5	2.0	2.6	2.3	2.8	2.4	1.1	.2
Major field								
Business, commerce, and								
management..........	4.2	2.5	3.7	1.4	4.7	1.6	4.7	7.2
Education..............	9.6	16.1	7.3	15.4	10.6	16.6	17.2	16.5
Biological sciences.......	8.6	4.0	11.8	5.1	5.1	3.4	4.3	3.3
Physical sciences.........	12.6	5.0	12.4	4.0	13.8	6.1	9.5	4.8
Engineering.............	7.7	.3	9.5	.4	6.4	.2	3.2	.1
Social sciences...........	12.1	7.6	13.0	7.3	12.4	9.1	7.6	4.8
Fine arts...............	6.0	7.6	4.8	6.7	7.7	9.1	6.8	5.7
Humanities..............	15.4	20.6	12.6	17.4	19.6	23.9	15.2	19.6
Health fields............	4.9	6.7	8.5	11.8	.9	2.7	.6	5.2
Other professions........	2.9	4.5	3.3	6.9	2.6	3.5	2.0	1.7
All other fields...........	1.1	4.6	.9	8.6	1.1	2.4	1.7	1.3
None..................	15.0	20.3	12.1	14.9	15.0	21.3	27.1	29.9

Source: Alan E. Bayer, *College and University Faculty: A Statistical Description* (Washington: Office of Research, American Council on Education, 1970), pp. 13–14.

a) Based on 60,028 responses from faculty members of academic departments and professiona[l] schools. See Source, pp. 3–7, for sampling design and weighting procedure.

APPENDIX B

Investments in Education and Life Cycle Earnings: The Models

In analyses of human capital, investment in education or training is considered a primary explanation of observed differences in income.

The first models of this type relate formal training to earnings and income levels after training. The length of training is the crucial variable that raises productivity; but this training also postpones the receipt of income. Consequently, rational decision making requires that the future income stream be sufficient at least to cover the cost of training. An unsophisticated model holds the cost of training to be forgone earnings only; the actual cost of training (for example, tuition) and interest that would accrue to this investment are not considered.[15]

A second type of model includes experience and postschool investments as arguments in a general earnings function.[16] These models generally take the form:

$$E_{ji} = X_{ji} + \sum_{t=0}^{j-1} r_{ti}C_{ti} \quad \text{(Gross form)}$$

or

$$Y_{ji} = X_{ji} + \sum_{t=0}^{j-1} r_{ti}C_{ti} - C_{ji} \quad \text{(Net form)},$$

where

$i \equiv$ individual,
$j \equiv$ period,
$C_{ji} \equiv$ net investment costs for individual i in the jth period,
$X_{ji} \equiv$ raw earnings stream without investment for individual i in the jth period,
$r_{ti} \equiv$ market discount rate (for the individual over time t).

Generally, the life cycle earnings profile is upward sloping as a result of human capital investment at young ages. Becker attributes this to the following incentives: (1) Since lifetimes are finite, the later the investment, the shorter the period over which returns can accumulate, with the result that the later the investment is made, the smaller the total benefits; (2) When human capital investment is profitable, the later the investment, the smaller the present value of net gains; (3) Generally, as age increases, the opportunity cost of time also increases; hence, later investments involve a necessarily higher opportunity cost. Optimality arguments have concentrated on the additions made to human capital Q via a production function whose arguments are human

15. See, for example, Jacob Mincer, "A Study of Personal Income Distribution" (Ph.D. diss., Columbia University, 1957); or Mincer, "Investment in Human Capital and Personal Income Distribution," *Journal of Political Economy* 66, no. 4 (1958).
16. See Gary Becker, *Human Capital* (New York: Columbia University Press, 1964).

capital H, time T, and other market resources R, so that $Q = f(H,T,R)$. A graphical representation is presented in Fig. 1.

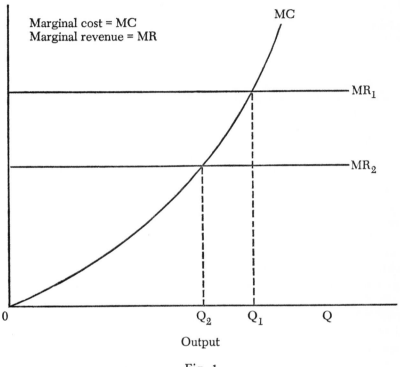

Fig. 1

The MC curve is upward sloping, inasmuch as costs will increase with the velocity of output. The MR is the discounted value of expected increases in earning power which result from the addition of Q. Since the benefits stream falls with age, it follows that the MR falls with age, (MR_1 to MR_2), and as a result, investment falls with age. It has been suggested that the MC curve will shift to the left with age to reflect greater opportunity costs, thereby causing an accelerated decline in investment.[17]

Ben-Porath has also shown, however, that investment may increase in the early stages of the life cycle and then fall. Nonetheless, it is normally thought that investment declines continually with age.

17. Yoram Ben-Porath, "The Production of Human Capital and the Life-Cycle of Earnings," *Journal of Political Economy* 75, no. 4, pt. I (1967).

Finally, this discrete model has been converted to the continuous case[18] so that

$$E(t,b) = B(t,b) + \int_0^t R(y,b)K(y,b)E(y,b)dy,$$

where

$t \equiv$ age in terms of years from the date of the investment decision,

$b \equiv$ vector of personal characteristics,

$E(t,b) \equiv$ the individual's earning capacity at age t,

$B(t,b) \equiv$ base earnings of individual with characteristics b at age t,

$R(t,b) \equiv$ return to a unit human investment in individual with characteristics b at age t,

$K(t,b) \equiv$ fraction of earning capacity invested at age t for an individual with characteristics b,

$y \equiv$ time of implementation of the investment decision.

It is clear that Ph.D.'s may not represent the normal declining life cycle investment pattern. As regards female Ph.D.'s, the following tentative statements can be made:

1. It can be expected that a woman will receive total benefits (or the rate of return on investment) which will be less than that of a man with equal annual earnings, since she will likely be absent from the labor force for certain periods.

2. The cost of training represented by forgone earnings may be smaller for women because of sex differences in salary. As a result, for identical life cycle income streams, it could be expected that human capital investment in women would be more profitable than that in men.

3. Since the opportunity cost of time is generally less for women than for men (even though both opportunity costs rise with age), profitable investment in women's education may be made at a later point in their life cycle than for men.

Clearly, the variables affecting returns to women are sometimes offsetting. The key question for research is the determination of the relative weights of the different factors. The optimal life cycle investment pattern for women, particularly for female Ph.D.'s, may be significantly different from that for men. This promising area of research has not yet been explored.

18. Thomas Johnson, "Returns from Investment in Human Capital," *American Economic Review* 60, no. 4 (1970).

The Talent Pool

Where Are All the Talented Women?

HELEN S. ASTIN

SINCE THE START of efforts by the U.S. Department of Health, Education, and Welfare for contract compliance in colleges and universities and the subsequent pressures put on noncomplying institutions to develop affirmative action plans, we have witnessed a considerable effort being made by institutions of higher education to identify and recruit women for their faculties.

An actual situation will illustrate some of the problems inherent in the present system of identifying and recruiting professionally trained women, and also suggest some procedures that potential employers might use in their efforts to recruit and hire women.

As chairperson of the American Psychological Association's (APA) Task Force on the Status of Women in Psychology, I receive many requests, averaging two per week, to suggest women candidates for various positions. Usually a search committee or an academic administrator identifies and describes a position and then requests the Task Force to publicize the position among individual women psychologists or among other groups concerned with the status of women. Sometimes the Task Force is asked to supply a list of names of potential candidates.

At first, we would suggest the names of a few women whom we knew personally. Occasionally, we would also search the biographical *Directory* of the American Psychological Association to provide the recruiters with a list of appropriate names. We would also mail a copy of the position description to the Association for Women Psychologists (AWP)—a caucus of women psychologists—which would in turn publicize the position to its list of members.

Over time, however, we began to see that these efforts might not do justice to the women who were less visible or who were not members of special groups such as the AWP. Thus, the Task Force moved to develop a roster of all women members of the American Psychological Association in order to facilitate the recruiting efforts of colleagues by providing them with a larger pool of names. The roster was compiled in January 1972 and has been distributed to about 400 people who requested it. The information was gathered by means of a one-page questionnaire which was mailed to over 7,000 women members of APA, 70 percent of whom responded. The names are listed alphabetically by professional subspecialties, such as child psychologist and physiological psychologist, together with each woman's degree, year of degree, and two primary work activities (research, teaching, administration, clinical practice, and so forth).

In the early fall of 1972 we surveyed a 10 percent random sample of persons who requested the roster. The few returns received thus far indicate that most of the recipients had not asked for it for recruiting purposes. Rather, they used it to become better acquainted with the available pool of women psychologists, and plan to use it as a reference source. Among the persons who indicated an interest in the roster for recruitment purposes, quite a few had difficulty in interpreting the codes for professional activities and degrees, which were adopted in the interest of brevity and economy. The potential users also expressed an interest in a more detailed entry for each person. To my knowledge, only one group has thus far used the roster for its intended purpose: they carried out an exhaustive search to recruit a woman for a research post. They mailed a letter and job description to each name listed under "Research Psychologist." The letter was personalized, and the request to send a vita was inviting indeed.

I have outlined the Task Force's effort to assist in the identification of "woman-talent" in order to illustrate the need for more programmatic efforts to increase the participation of women in professional activities and also to demonstrate some of the problems involved in developing a workable system. However, I personally am concerned more about the *underemployment* of professionally trained women than about their participation or nonparticipation in the labor force. Recent data indicate that highly trained women do indeed stay in the labor force. Contrary to the folklore that training women is a waste of time and money, we find that 91 percent of women doctorates are still in the labor force eight years after completing their degrees.[1] Thus, it is not a question of

1. Helen S. Astin, *The Woman Doctorate in America: Origins, Career, and Family* (New York: Russell Sage Foundation, 1969), p. 57.

whether woman-talent is "utilized," if utilization means being in the labor force, but rather *how* this talent is utilized, especially since it is in short supply. Are women indeed making the best possible contributions? Are they permitted to influence policy? Are they in jobs commensurate with their training and ability?

In responding to these questions, we cannot help but say no. Women are not in positions where policy is being made and where decisions for the direction of higher education and research are taken. They are not in high level academic administrative posts, they are on review committees, and they are not on educational boards and commissions. Moreover, they do not hold the professorial ranks or receive the salaries they deserve on the basis of their training, experience, and accomplishments. Apter has carefully documented the poor representation of women on review committees, and Bayer and I have reported on the low status of academic women.[2]

Despite the ample evidence of discrimination, many skeptics still insist that there is no discrimination and assert simply that "There are no qualified women to be found, and even if there were they would not be willing to move." Let me first address briefly the issue of availability and then move to the question of mobility. Of the pool of women who hold doctorates, we find about 31,000 between the ages of thirty-seven and fifty-seven (that is, women who received doctorates from 1950 through 1970). If this figure is corrected for about 300 deaths and for a certain proportion who never worked, about 400, we have approximately 30,000 women doctorates in the age span. I am not denying that this is a meager supply compared to about 244,000 men who received the doctorate between 1950 and 1970.[3] I am indeed concerned and depressed that over the last five decades, after a sharp decline from 1920 (a peak year for women doctorates), the growth in proportion of women

2. See Julia T. Apter, "Increasing the Professional Visibility of Women in Academia: A Case Study," in the present volume, and Helen S. Astin and Alan E. Bayer, "Sex Discrimination in Academe," *Educational Record*, 53 (1972): 101–18.

3. Sources of doctorate recipients: *Doctorate Production in United States Universities, 1920–1962*, NAS-NRC Publication 1142 (Washington: National Academy of Sciences, 1963); *Doctorate Recipients from United States Universities, 1958–1966*, Publication 1489 (Washington: National Academy of Sciences, 1967); annual *Summary Report: Doctorate Recipients from United States Universities* for 1967, 1968, 1969, 1970 (Washington: Office of Scientific Personnel, National Research Council). Statistics for median age, expected deaths, and proportion of women doctorates who never worked are derived from findings in Astin, *The Woman Doctorate in America*.

doctorates has been slow, for example, from 11 percent in 1960 to 13.5 percent in 1970. We all ought to share in the responsibility of encouraging and assisting young women to raise their aspirations and to achieve what they are capable of. Although the proportion of highly trained women is small as compared with men, these women represent an exceptionally bright and highly motivated group. There is ample empirical evidence, for example, that women doctorates are highly able and committed to their fields and careers; yet they have not been allowed to make contributions consistent with their abilities and commitments. Thus, it behooves all of us to devote our efforts to developing and implementing concrete plans for utilizing these women to their full potential.

The second question, or barrier, that is often raised by the skeptics is that of mobility. Male recruiters have often been skeptical about recruiting a woman, assuming that she will not be interested in the job or be able to make a move "because of her family commitments." This assumption is, of course, in part correct since the woman in our culture has been socialized to follow her husband, letting him make his own career decisions first. The fact remains, however, that the occupational and geographic mobility of women doctorates follows a pattern similar to that of men doctorates.

> Of the 1957 and 1958 women doctorates . . . 45 percent had been with the same employer since receiving the doctorate, and an additional 30 percent had changed jobs only once. These figures are comparable with the rates for men reported by Harmon . . . , who found that 52 percent of the men in the 1955 doctoral cohort had stayed on the same job for 5 years, and an additional 33 percent had changed jobs only once.[4]

I would also like to point out that in recent years, particularly among the younger generations of doctorate recipients, decisions about job changes do not necessarily rest with the husband alone. Such decisions are being made by husband and wife together, and frequently the husband may decide to look for a job after the wife has made a decision to relocate.

I should like to propose, then, certain recommendations which, if implemented, should permit *all* professionally trained and talented

4. Astin, *The Woman Doctorate*, p. 67.

women to compete more equitably for current and future opportunities.

- A national roster of woman-talent shall be developed. Based on
  the experience of the APA Task Force with the roster of women
  psychologists, any national roster should provide enough information about each woman's accomplishments and special interests to make it useful to people who want to identify women
  for jobs as well as for advisory posts.
- Employers should advertise their jobs openly and publicly, and
  they should specifically invite women to apply.
- In recruiting women, potential employers should show enthusiasm, a willingness to accomodate and to wait when necessary,
  and an excitement about adding the talents of a woman to the
  staff.

A Modest Beginning and a Modest Proposal

DOROTHY ROSS

MY EXPERIENCE in developing a talent pool of women professionals represents the modest effort of a middling-sized professional organization to achieve the maximum impact in the hiring of
women, at the least possible expense. The American Historical
Association membership numbers about 19,000 people. Because its
automated membership list uses only first initials, how many of
these are women is not known, though the number is probably
around 2,000. The total number of women historians may be half
again as large.

Thanks to the efforts of women historians who brought pressure
on the association to recognize the problem of sex discrimination,
and thanks to the enlightened support of a number of men on its
governing council, the AHA agreed to appoint, first, an ad hoc
committee and, then, a standing committee to initiate and oversee
substantial efforts to eliminate sex discrimination in the profession,
and, further, to hire a woman historian to serve on the staff full
time as special assistant to the standing committee to carry out its
program. Since the AHA has only two other professional his-

torians who work full time on association affairs, that position represented a substantial commitment of slender resources. I served as special assistant to the committee during the 1971–72 academic year. For 1972–73, the position is held by Dr. Charlotte Quinn, a specialist in African history. Thus, despite the reputed conservatism of historians, and despite the reluctance and opposition which still exists in large parts of the profession, the AHA has found itself taking real initiatives on behalf of women historians.

When the committee began its work in the fall of 1971, it decided to give priority to developing a roster of women historians which could be used to help them find positions. It was not at all clear whether this could be done. One problem was the legality of any roster of women. Fortunately, in advance of the last amendment to the Equal Employment Opportunity Commission (EEOC) charter, I was able to obtain a verbal opinion from its office of legal counsel that a roster was legal so long as it operated, not as a full-fledged employment agency, but as an information service to assist in affirmative action. I gather that this question is now clouded, and that the EEOC is willing to say only that such an operation may be legal, and that organizations with rosters ought to avoid a court test by enrolling any man who wishes to sign up. The AHA has been careful to state the purpose of our roster—to assist in affirmative action—in all communications, and the operation has been carefully limited to a "job information service": we notify qualified women of openings, and we notify departments concerning women who appear to be qualified for their openings, but we leave it to the woman herself to communicate with the department if she wishes to be considered for the position. Thus far we have had only one letter of complaint about the roster operation, and we shall continue in the hope that the roster will prove to be legal.

During the year, the AHA staff became concerned about the possibility of another legal problem concerning the tax status of the Association, a problem shared with many other disciplinary organizations. The AHA is, for tax purposes, a "charitable and educational" organization, rather than a "professional or trade association," both for historic reasons and because charitable organizations receive the more favorable tax treatment. Such a charitable organization cannot, however, devote a "substantial" portion of its resources to services to its own members. Unofficial legal estimates of "substantial" have varied from 5 percent to 30 percent. The AHA was concerned that the roster, as a service to women members, along with the other professional services which members are now increasingly demanding, would endanger the AHA tax status. Fortunately, the IRS has ruled that an organization providing nonpolitical services to women to help combat sex discrimination—for example, legal, employment, and consultation services—is performing a charitable service. To maintain the "charitable" classification, however, we must be careful to offer help and open the roster to all women in the profession, not merely those who are AHA members.

The practical problems we faced were speed and expenses: how to get women enrolled and job information flowing back and forth in time to affect conditions that year, and cheaply enough for the AHA to agree to it. We wrote up a brief vita form to serve as the basis for an alphabetical file for the roster, distributed it in December 1971 at our annual meeting to all women who registered, and in this way enrolled 600 women. The information on these forms was then typed onto McBee sort cards, an inexpensive, manual-sorting system which would permit us to find women in broad or in very refined fields of historical specialization.

In January 1972, we sent a form letter announcing our service to the 1,200 history department chairmen throughout the country. Thereafter, when a letter describing an opening came in, I duplicated it and sent it to all women whose cards indicated they were qualified for the position. I then duplicated the cards of the qualified women (three to a page) and sent the material, along with a request for detailed follow-up information, to the department. Meanwhile, we enclosed a roster form and return envelope in an issue of the AHA *Newsletter*, which goes to all members, and our women's caucus included it in its newsletter. The 800 additional roster forms that were returned were put into the system by May. Thus, on an expenditure of about $1,500—most of it for extra typing help, printing, and postage—we had by May 1972 a working roster of 1,400 women, a substantial portion of all women historians.

What was the result of all this activity? As of June 1, 1972, we had received notices of about 100 positions. For a variety of reasons, it was inappropriate to advertise some of these positions, so we sent out notices of 90 openings, nine of them in administration and the remaining 81 in teaching. In all, over 700 notices of these positions went out to women. As of June 1, we had definite information for 18 of the 90 jobs we processed. In ten of these, women were hired from our lists; in several other instances, the departments testified to the usefulness of our lists in their search, although they had hired other women whom they themselves had found. Considering the size of the problem, ten jobs may seem few, but considering the newness of the service and the substantial educational function performed, the number is impressive.

The educational side effects of the system were in many ways most important. Many women who were not actively seeking jobs, or not seriously thinking of moving to a better position, suddenly found themselves informed of opportunities all over the country. I know from letters we received that, for the first time, many women began to think in terms of job and geographic mobility. In addition, women who had not participated in the movement to improve the status of women historians saw the benefits of our activities and tendered their support. Indeed, though we were not astute enough to predict it, our service has greatly enlarged our constituency in the profession and created a demand for continued AHA services to women. Most important, a great many men historians, as some have written us, were forced to consider the large number of able women available in the profession. Our chief problem is the many departments who did not notify us of their openings. The response might have been much greater had we been operational early in the year, when their search procedures started. Others obviously need to be pushed. One effective method has been to notify the college's equal employment officer or the college women's group—where they exist—that we have received no word on openings from the chairman of the history department.

But despite these benefits, we probably shall not operate in quite the same way next year or thereafter. Two new factors will affect our planning. First, there is a growing and justified demand within the historical profession, as in many others, that all jobs, for men and women, be advertised openly, so that any persons who think themselves qualified can apply. In the long run, women and minority groups seem the most likely to gain from an open-listing system. Because of pressure brought on the association in the past year by the deteriorating job market, the AHA is making a real effort this year to institute an open-listing system. The committee has decided to support the AHA effort wholeheartedly and to use our roster service as an auxiliary to, rather than a substitute for, this professional service. All departments that open-list jobs will receive a copy of that portion of the roster applicable to their opening, and women historians will have to consult the association's *Employment Information Bulletin* to learn of opportunities. However, when job descriptions are either unusually vague or specific, or when time pressures require quick action, we shall continue to provide a specialized job information service; and, of course, we shall continue to use the roster for placements to committees, fellowships, and conferences, and to answer many other professional requests.

We are uncertain that the open-listing system will in fact enlist the support of anything approaching the whole profession, and we may need to return to a full notification system. The cost will be high. Our roster will easily reach 2,000 names by fall 1972, and, we estimate, will require a half-time assistant to keep it up to date and operate it on a basis auxiliary to the open-listing system. Expansion of the service would require the attention of one full-time person. A computerized roster would be a great advantage, but, given the uncertain legal situation and the cost, the association has thus far been unwilling to support such a program.

All these considerations bear, too, on the second element in our immediate future—the proposed A.C.E. roster. Because the pattern of hiring in professions is largely intradisciplinary, and likely to remain so, the bank of information collected for any super-roster must be usable within each profession for intradisciplinary functions. This function is especially important inasmuch as most professional organizations appear to lack resources or the will to develop their own roster, and cannot each, separately, command foundation support. If the A.C.E. roster will consult each professional organization about the basic career data needed for hiring, and supply each profession each year with an updated printout of the roster for its discipline, the A.C.E. could be assured that the widest possible use will be made of its talent pool of women professionals.

A host of problems remain to be solved, and in the interim we can only continue with our makeshift efforts.

Increasing the Professional Visibility of Women in Academe: A Case Study

JULIA T. APTER

WOMEN WHO LOOK FOR academic opportunities to achieve their career goals meet almost insurmountable obstacles. Promotions and jobs that women deserve and expect are awarded, instead, to men. In the scientific fields, a scrutiny of the names of their successful competitors often identifies men who sit on scientific advisory panels of the many granting agencies in Washington. Indeed, the successful woman competitor is likely to be one of the very few women who sit on such panels. Furthermore, panel members are the most likely to get funds for their own contracts, research, or training projects, even though the men were selected, not always for merit, but rather because they happened to "know the right people" at the granting agency. This selection system has led to the virtual exclusion of women from such panels (see Table 1) and from the fringe benefits of panel membership, including improvement from second-class status at her home institution.

TABLE 1: *Representation of Women on Scientific Advisory Panels of Federally Supported Granting Agencies, July 1971*

Granting Agency	Number of Scientists on Review Panels	
	Total	Women
Listed in *American Men and Women of Science*..	147,000	20,000
1. National Science Foundation...............	377	7
2. National Research Council–National Academy of Sciences.....................	4,593	53
3. Space Science Board (National Academy of Sciences).............................	128	0
4. National Institutes of Health...............	1,953	28[a]

Source: Prepared by Dr. Julia T. Apter from: (1) *National Science Foundation Annual Report 1970* (Washington: Government Printing Office, 1971); (2 and 3) *Organization and Members, 1970–1971*, National Academy of Sciences, National Academy of Engineering, National Research Council (Washington: November 1970); (4) *NIH Public Advisory Groups: Authority, Structure, Functions, Members*, Department of Health, Education, and Welfare # (NIH) 73-10 (Washington: July 1, 1972).

[a] In addition, 98 women are represented among nurses, technicians, physiotherapists, administrators, volunteers.

Some initially unsuccessful approaches made to the National Aeronautics and Space Administration and the National Academy of Sciences demonstrated that the virtual exclusion of women could not be rectified through action taken by any one person or organization. What was needed was a coalition of women's groups, including scientists and, in addition, lawyers and the lay public. A coalition—the Coalition of Professional Women's Organizations—evolved over a period of only several weeks. This rapid and effective evolution showed that the women's groups were then not only ready for unified action, but also—largely because of Executive orders and pending legislation (the Equal Rights Amendment)—promised a good chance for successful action.

The coalition appealed, first, on September 23, 1971, to Secretary of Health, Education, and Welfare Elliot L. Richardson, through Senator Charles Percy of Illinois. This approach was chosen because, on the basis of the directive issued by Secretary Richardson, HEW had given leadership to other institutions. An interview was arranged between representatives of the coalition, Richard Mastrangelo, director of special projects in HEW, and Dr. Robert Q. Marston, director of the National Institutes of Health. The women asked me to speak for them at the hour and a half conference held on November 15, 1971, as scheduled.

At this point, let me review the structure of the NIH public advisory groups as I have obtained it from NIH publications. There are ten institutes as well as several divisions. Each institute has a National Advisory Council, a Board of Scientific Counselors, and various advisory committees, members of which are appointed by the Secretary of HEW and his assistants. In addition, within each institute are applications committees and training committees, which review training grant proposals. The Division of Research Grants has study sections, which review research grant proposals. Both the training committees and the study sections are referred to as "initial peer review groups," with members nominated by staff executive secretaries to serve four-year terms according to the guidelines set forth in the "Handbook for Executive Secretaries." The handbook contains the only written NIH guidelines for the 150 review panels supervised by executive secretaries and gives directions about eligibility for the initial peer review panels; in particular, (1) reappointments are specifically discouraged, and (2) employees of private industry are not eligible for membership.

Despite these rules, the women's group found that at least 34 percent of current panel members were serving their second, third, fourth, or even fifth four-year term. What is more, a large percentage of the men panelists claimed an association with an engineering school or department and, therefore, also probably had a substantial connection with private industry. Thus, at least 40 percent of the 2,000 panel members were in violation of the handbook. It was our intention to ask that these violators resign if, at our November 15 conference, we found fewer than 500 panel vacancies were available for our women candidates.

We asked for, and obtained, a freeze on "about 500" vacancies available in 1972. We asked for, but did not get, a commitment to put two women from our group on Dr. Marston's own Director's Committee. (We learned that two women had been appointed that very morning.) We also pointed out that it was reasonable to expect reimbursement for our expenses in helping NIH in this affirmative action program. In particular, we pointed out that funds recently assigned to the NIH to study "whether there has been discrimination against women in the review process in the past" would be better spent in *eliminating* discrimination against women in this part of the review process. We were told that a search for funds to reimburse us would be made and that the job descriptions would reach us in four to six weeks. Our recommendations were to be sent back by February 1.

We were given data on the current distribution of women on panels and on the currently available 1972 vacancies. We were also given assurances of good will. The data showed, however, that only about 350, not "about 500," vacancies were actually open to women to compete for. We immediately lost some confidence in the "good will" expressed and lost even more a month later when correspondence began to reach us denying any promises of reimbursement, denying any efforts to get reimbursement, denying any commitments about "500" vacancies. As of March 1972, Secretary Richardson was reporting that 207 women had been appointed in the previous six month period, but NIH officials could supply us with only 131 names; Secretary Richardson was promising that 319 women would be appointed during the first six months of 1972, but only 60 have been appointed.

What had we done to identify women who would meet the qualifications for the vacancies on NIH public advisory groups? We found the names of all women listed in the 1971 directories of the Federation of American Societies for Experimental Biology, the Institute of Electrical and Electronics Engineers, and the Biophysical Society; all women listed in *American Men of Science*; all women listed in the *Directory of Medical Specialists* and the *Directory of Hospital Administrators*; all women listed as *authors* in the last five years in *Index Medicus*. The names so obtained constituted the set for our first run. In addition, we sent each person whose term on an NIH panel was scheduled to end in 1972 (496 of them) a form requesting the names, degrees, and addresses of women coauthors and collaborators. In all, we identified more than 1,000 women who were willing to serve, as well as about 100 women who had already served on NIH panels or had recently been asked to serve.[1]

I shall inject here our compassion for two women who responded that they preferred selection by the ordinary procedures on the basis of their scientific qualifications alone. One might expect that women scientists would note that often the men being selected for panel membership were of lesser distinction as scientists than the women. Could the women, therefore, not deduce that something besides scientific qualifications was responsible for panel appointments? To be sure, the women scientists on the panels have been good scientists. However, among the 2,000 NIH panel members of January 1971, only 28 may be classed as women scientists; the other women are paramedical personnel.

The number and quality of the vitae and résumés that poured in were more than sufficient to make the filling of vacancies on NIH panels a relatively easy task. (Although the women who were with us at the November 15 conference were not included in our lists, five have been appointed to panels since our original letter to Secretary Richardson.) We have three women available for almost every job and as many as twenty women for some of the jobs; not one job is left vacant for want of recommendations. But now

1. *Registry of Women of Achievement*, c/o Dr. Julia T. Apter, Rush Medical College, 1753 West Congress Parkway, Chicago, Illinois 60612.

we must get women actually appointed for the 363 panel jobs; we must have our expenses repaid; and we must have the remaining panel openings made available to us.

What else can our coalition accomplish? Let us consider the NIH retrospective study of discrimination against women in the review process. At the AAAS Symposium on Women in Academia, we heard of many university studies unable to detect discrimination even when it surely existed. Can we not say that we have, somewhere along the way, already had the "study to end all such studies"? Someone must recognize that it is *impossible to detect past discrimination against women.* We must point out the relevance of our data for an adequate evaluation of the situation. Our data show the size of the pool, areas of competence, and levels of competence. There is no reason why women should not be put on panels at rates commensurate with their accomplishments and their potential for accomplishment. When that has been done, the problem of maintaining the representation of women at the level of one woman for every two men, as desired by Secretary Richardson will be a small one.

Let us consider another statement. A speaker at another meeting stated in an educational television interview that women will be likely to have fewer children "now that they have found something more satisfying to do," implying that jobs will replace childbearing. Can he not see that women are responding to a basic human need by having children and raising them, and that this need does not necessarily preclude realization of their full potential? We are not demanding a decision-making and advisory role in academic society because it is more satisfying. We want these jobs because we have something valuable to contribute to our professions and because the fringe benefits will help improve our present second-class status. These reasons hardly conflict with our biological drive to bear the children and to share in their rearing. In fact, the help we get in child rearing from current technology makes it possible for women to have fully productive professional careers as well. To be sure, in our culture women need to be educated in methods for managing dual or multiple roles. Women need to be educated in standing alone. Women need to know that they usually require the help of a man only ex officio and not because of his viewpoint.

We have pressured the National Academy of Sciences, NASA, the National Science Foundation, and the National Research Council. There are thousands of men on advisory panels, but practically no women. The granting agencies pay lip service to efforts to find women but they can usually hide behind the statements about the supposed low or poor supply of competent women professionals. Such statements now have a libelous character; they certainly cannot be made in the face of *any* effort to find such women, certainly not in the face of our registry.

What else can HEW do for women? HEW might create special fellowships for women who want to continue or update their education even though responding to our culture by spending several years in professional hibernation during the childhood of their offspring. Experience shows that such fellowships provide substantial assistance and yield substantial rewards. The women work extremely well during the fellowship period and give full return for their investment afterwards. In our culture women *need* such fellowships; men do not.

The Biophysical Society has assumed responsibility for reimbursing the costs for compiling the registry and has also subsidized enlargement of the registry to include 851 women who are currently funded by 947 research grants from the National Institutes of Health.

Our registry of qualified women is now available and has been distributed to academic, governmental, and industrial institutions that promise a degree of accountability in considering the listed women for openings. We expect, for example, that the agency will reimburse expenses and moderate professional fees. We expect the agency to give us a list of people eventually chosen by the agency so that we can add those women to our registry or can compare the men selected with women suggested by our registry. We expect our registry to be a nucleus for much larger registries of the some 50,000 women scholars in this country.

HEATHER SIGWORTH

Issues in Nepotism Rules

I have written elsewhere about the legal issues raised by the enforcement of antinepotism policies in educational institutions.[1] I will first summarize and update this material before going on to discuss briefly some of the larger social and educational problems raised when competent married women are rendered incompetent to pursue their professions for reasons of institutional administrative convenience.

Legal Issues: Public Institutions

Some people argue that most antinepotism rules are not subject to legal attack because they exclude spouses or relatives generally, not just wives, and therefore cannot constitute sex discrimination. This formulation misses an important legal point which will be brought out later, but let us assume for the moment that no sex discrimination will be recognized. Even on such an assumption, "nepotism" regulations, at least as enforced by public institutions, should be declared invalid. The United States Supreme Court long ago held that the federal Constitution guaranteed a right to pursue a lawful livelihood which the state could abridge only on the strongest showing of purpose.[2] Although the Supreme Court has not invoked this guarantee for some time, and although it no longer carries its original purpose of protecting employers from state labor legislation, it has been used recently to protect individual civil rights. Both the California Supreme Court and the federal first circuit have invalidated state laws conditioning this employment right because the state could not show a compelling state interest in imposing the condition. If a court testing an antinepotism rule reinvoked this employment right, a public educational institu-

1. Heather Sigworth, "The Legal Status of Antinepotism Regulations," *AAUP Bulletin* 58 (1972): 31–34.
2. Legal citations supporting the propositions stated in this paper are given in the article cited in fn. 1.

tion would have to show it had a compelling interest in enforcing its antinepotism policy against the individual. This is a difficult burden to carry, and considerations of economy and administrative convenience are not sufficient to counterbalance the federally secured individual right.

A right more frequently upheld in recent years is that of personal, familial, and marital privacy. It has been used to void state laws ranging from miscegenation prohibitions to hair-length regulations, to improve the status of illegitimate children, and to prevent the firing, or force the hiring, of nudists, adulterers, and writers of obscene private letters. Of these variations, the marital privacy right probably has the strongest legal authority behind it. But even if a court recognized such a right in an antinepotism challenge, the authorities indicate that a public education institution would probably not have to show a compelling interest. In such cases, the court looks on the problems of educational institutions as special, and regards some incursion on privacy rights as justifiable. Instead of a compelling interest, the court requires only an interest sufficiently substantial and clearly related to educational purposes to overbalance the harm done to the individual. At stake in the enforcement of antinepotism rules is a substantial professional career representing years of expensive education, as against an apparent purpose to avert only a potential danger that could better be averted by a clear conflict of interest rule. One cannot predict with certainty the outcome of undecided cases, but the institution's apparent countervailing interest does not appear to me to be either substantial enough or sufficiently related to educational purposes to pass the constitutional test.[3]

3. Purposes for antinepotism rules other than prevention of conflict of interest can, of course, be elicited or conceived. However, these are all outdated, out-argued, trivial, or illegal. Some regulations were originally passed to prevent pressure to hire incompetents with influential connections, but they are now used almost exclusively to exclude women; see Simon, Clark, and Tifft, "Of Nepotism, Marriage and the Pursuit of an Academic Career," *Sociology of Education* 39 (1966): 357. Some academics find that married couples working nearby and near to each other are embarrassing; however, some writers consider that "tandem teams" are a good example for students; see R. and R. Rapoport, *Dual Career Families* (Baltimore, Md.: Penguin Books, 1970); Salzman, "Discrimination at U. Mass: Woman Scientist Fights Back," *Science for the People*, April 1971. Some administrators worry about embarrassment, too, if they have to turn down one spouse while hiring the other unless they have a rule to explain their actions or, worse, if they have to offer a position, a raise, or a promotion to a wife and not to her husband; see "Report of the University of Arizona Chapter of the

Besides these substantive legal objections to antinepotism rules, many such rules are subject to attack on due process grounds as being overly vague and inconsistently administered. For example, at one institution I attended, the rule prohibited "employment of relatives at any of the three state institutions," which was interpreted in practice (most, but not all of the time) to mean "employment of faculty wives, except in clerical, nonprofessional librarian, continuing education, part-time, unpaid, or some temporary positions, unless both spouses had tenure when they married, and applicable only within any one of the three state institutions." Another university also had a prohibition against the hiring of "relatives," but within the third degree only and excluding civil service employees. This degree of specificity was not much help, however, for it was interpreted to mean: Faculty wives should not be hired, but if a department head really wants to, he can, knowing that other people don't pay attention to the rule either. This resulted in some department heads conscientiously refusing to hire faculty wives for any academic purpose whatsoever, and others giving tenure to spouses within the same department. As shown in my article already cited, such vagueness and inconsistency affecting a substantial interest, such as employment, violates federal due process.

RECENT LEGAL ACTIONS: PUBLIC AND PRIVATE INSTITUTIONS

Even in the months since that article was written, however, these legal considerations have probably become of less practical

---

AAUP's Committee on the Arizona Board of Regents' So-called 'Anti-nepotism' Rule" (May 1970; duplicated copy on file in Washington, D.C., office of the AAUP); University of Chicago, Committee of the Council of the University Senate, "Women in the University of Chicago: Report of the Committee on University Women" (Chicago: The University, 1970). These worries appear to me both trivial and, in the light of the legal considerations given above and below on sex discrimination, illegal. Another reason, fear of the formation of husband-wife power blocs, is both trivial (doesn't a university run on more or less permanent power coalitions of far more than two people?) and misinformed about the nature of academic marriages. Finally, I have frequently heard of, and have documented by two letters in my possession (which cannot be identified for obvious reasons), a convenient, but clearly illegal, justification for one common type of "antinepotism" rule. These rules prevent the hiring of faculty spouses full time, or with job security, or above the instructor level. Such rules are for the sometimes avowed purpose of maintaining a "pool" of qualified people to hire in case of last minute shortages, illnesses, no-shows, etc. Since these people are invariably women, the rule would come within the strictures against sex discrimination discussed below.

importance. In that time. statutory prohibitions against sex discrimination in educational employment have multiplied, documentation that antinepotism rules constitute de facto sex discrimination has multiplied, and justification for the proposition that de facto discrimination is discrimination in law has increased.

Executive Order 11264, as amended by E.O. 11375, which prohibits sex discrimination by federal government contractors, has been in effect since 1968, and for some time it was the only federal legal inhibition against sex discrimination in employment at institutions of higher education.[4] The Department of Health, Education, and Welfare has interpreted de facto discrimination resulting from nepotism rules to be within the meaning of the order.[5] However, title VII of the Civil Rights Act, which formerly excluded educational institutions,[6] has now been amended to give the Equal Employment Opportunity Commission (EEOC) jurisdiction over such institutions.[7] The EEOC has not yet ruled on the issue of academic nepotism policies as sex discrimination, but if such policies constitute de facto discrimination for the purpose of the Executive order, it is difficult to see why they should not be discriminatory under title VII. Moreover, a consistent line of both EEOC and court decisions has held that, for title VII purposes, neither intent nor verbalization of discriminatory purpose is necessary; the test is whether or not an employment policy in fact discriminates.[8] It is probably not important that discrimination caused

4. Some states, however, have equal employment opportunity provisions applicable to challenge sex discrimination in educational employment and specifically to challenge "antinepotism" regulations. The *Colorado Civil Rights Commission Sex Discrimination Guidelines*, § 3 (n.d.), cover educational institutions and prohibit the exclusion of qualified women because of restrictions on the employment of relatives. The Massachusetts Civil Rights Commission has been willing to interpret its state law as prohibiting discriminatory application of "nepotism" rules; see Salzman, "Discrimination at U. Mass" and subsequent correspondence in my possession. See also the new Constitution of Illinois, art. 1, § 17 (1970) and the recent amendments to the Indiana Civil Rights Act, Ind. Acts (1971) P.L. 357.

5. Letter from HEW Office for Civil Rights, Senior Compliance Specialist, Dec. 22, 1971. Cf. that Office's *Sex Discrimination Guidelines*, § 60-20-3(d). See also *Science* 170 (1970): 834.

6. 42 U.S.C. § 2000 (e)(1) (1964) (amended March 24, 1972).

7. P.L. 92–261, 86 Stat. 103, § 702 (approved and effective March 24, 1972).

8. See, e.g., Griggs v. Duke Power Co., 401 U.S. 424 (1971)—U.S. Supreme Court approval of EEOC policy; Quarles v. Phillip Morris, Inc., 279 F. Supp. 505 (E.D. Va. 1966)—leading case. See also Chance v. Bd. of Exam., 51 F.R.D. 156 (S.D.N.Y. 1971)—same test adopted on constitutional grounds in an educational employment situation; *accord*, 329 F. Supp. 1340 (E.D. La. 1971); and cases cited in my *AAUP Bulletin* article (see fn. 1).

by nepotism rules is based not on sex alone, but on sex plus marital status, since the Supreme Court has held that such "sex plus" classifications at least shift the burden of proving a substantial employment purpose for discriminatory policies to the employer,[9] and lower courts have held them to be all but forbidden.[10]

The Education Amendments of 1972 (effective June 30, 1972) now also prohibit sex discrimination, including employment discrimination, in all[11] federally assisted education programs, and extend coverage of the Equal Pay Act of 1963 to executive, administrative, and professional employees, including all faculty.[12] Since the general employment provisions are presumably enforced by HEW,[13] de facto discriminatory "nepotism" policies should be regarded as sex discrimination, as they are for Executive Order 11375 purposes. The Equal Pay provisions do not require that jobs be identical but only "substantially similar"[14] and thus may well apply even in the absence of a formal or informal "nepotism" policy, where faculty wives are hired at lower pay or unfairly lower rank because of their relative immobility and easy availability.

Finally, besides the constitutional due process argument outlined at the beginning of this paper, there is a developing constitutional argument that *is* based on sex discrimination. The United States

9. Phillips v. Martin Marietta Corp., 400 U.S. 542 (1971).

10. Sprogis v. United Air Lines, Inc., 308 F. Supp. 959 (N.D. Ill. 1970), *aff'd*, 444 F.2d 1194 (7th Cir. 1971), *cert. denied*, 92 S. Ct. 536 (1971). See also Rosenfeld v. Southern Pacific Co., 444 F.2d 1219 (9th Cir. 1971); Oldham, "Questions of Exclusion and Exception Under Title VII, 'Sex-Plus' and the B.F.O.Q.," *Hastings Law Journal* 23 (1971): 55; Comment, "Sex-Plus: The Failure of the Attempt to Subvert the Sex Provision of the Civil Rights Act of 1964," *Gonzaga Law Review* 7 (1971): 83.

11. P.L. 92–318, 86 Stat. 235, 92d Congress, S. 659, tit. ix, § 901 (approved June 23, 1972). Military schools and some religious institutions are exempt. Rules on admissions are different.

12. Id. § 906(b). For a summary of these provisions, see Project on the Status and Education of Women, Association of American Colleges, "Sex Discrimination Provisions Concerning Students and Employees as Contained in the Higher Education Act of 1972" (June 1972), and *U.S. Code Congressional and Administrative News*, July 20, 1972, p. 2249 (the numbering and organization does not reflect that of the act as passed).

13. P.L. 92–318, 92d Congress, S. 659, tit. ix, § 902.

14. See, e.g., Hodgson v. Robert Hall Clothes, Inc., 326 F. Supp. 1264 (D. Del. 1971); Krumbeck v. John Oster Mfg. Co., 313 F. Supp. 257 (E.D. Wis. 1970); Shultz v. Brookhaven General Hospital, 305 F. Supp. 424 (N.D. Tex. 1969).

Supreme Court has traditionally refused to find that sex discrimination is a violation of the equal protection clause.[15] However, two cases decided in the 1971 term cast some doubt on the traditional approach, although their exact significance cannot yet be assessed.[16] Possibly more important, several state and lower federal court decisions have gone further, and have begun to treat "sex" as a "protected classification," similar to "race." This latter approach means that a state where such a decision has been made cannot discriminate by sex for just any reason, but must have a substantial or even a "compelling" reason for doing so.[17] And again, analogizing with "race" as with the statutory discrimination cases, if a state policy in effect discriminates, the fact that such a purpose is neither intended nor explicit would be constitutionally irrelevant.[18] If the Equal Rights Amendment is ratified, most of the above discussions will be moot, although it is not entirely a foregone conclusion how nonexplicit de facto discrimination, the issue in most "nepotism" cases, would be treated under the amendment.[19]

THE LARGER ISSUES

Given the now multileveled executive and legislative prohibitions of sex discrimination in employment by educational institutions, both public and private, and consistent interpretation of such provisions as prohibiting de facto discrimination, the only real *legal* issue now is whether or not antinepotism policies in fact discrimi-

15. See, e.g., Hoyt v. Florida, 368 U.S. 57 (1961); Goesaert v. Cleary, 335 U.S. 464 (1948).

16. Reed v. Reed, 92 S. Ct. 251 (1971); Stanley v. Illinois, 92 S. Ct. 1208 (1972).

17. See cases cited in Brown et al., "The Equal Rights Amendment: A Constitutional Basis for Equal Rights for Women," *Yale Law Journal* 80 (1971): 871, and discussion and cases cited in Sigworth, "The Legal Status of Antinepotism Regulations," p. 33.

18. See, e.g., Carmichal v. Craven, 451 F.2d 399 (9th Cir. 1971); Chance v. Bd. of Exam., 51 F.R.D. 156 (S.D.N.Y. 1971); Penn. v. Stumpf, 308 F. Supp. 1238 (N.D. Cal. 1970); Arrington v. Mass. Bay Transp. Auth., 306 F. Supp. 1355 (D. Mass. 1970). Cf. Griggs v. Duke Power Co., 401 U.S. 424 (1971). See also, Cirino v. Walsh, 66 Misc. 2d 450, 321 N.Y.S. 2d 493 (Sup. Ct. 1971)—principle applied both as to race and as to sex, but under state law.

19. The most extensive article written to date assumes that it *is* a foregone conclusion that the amendment would prohibit de facto sex discrimination (Brown et al., "The Equal Rights Amendment"). Needless to say, a constitutional prohibition would affect only public institutions.

nate. Evidence that they do may be found in a well-documented report from the University of California, which illustrates the almost uniform application of "nepotism" rules against wives.[20] Many other reports of investigations over the last few years show that "nepotism" policies, some of them informal, keep qualified women out (or down).[21]

At hearings before the House Subcommittee on Education, Alice Rossi showed the relationship between "nepotism" regulations and sex discrimination.[22] Either in response to charges of sex discrimination within the institution or under pressure of court action or HEW, numerous institutions have moved or are moving to modify "nepotism" policies.[23] And, finally, the increasing documentation of widespread sex discrimination in higher education institutions suggests that the sex discrimination resulting from nepotism rules

20. University of California, Committee on Senate Policy, "Report of the Subcommittee on the Status of Academic Women on the Berkeley Campus" (Berkeley: The University, May 1970).

21. Greenfield, "Women in Engineering Education," *Contemporary Education* 43 (1972): 224; Dahl, "Report on Women at the University of Delaware" (Washington: ERIC Clearinghouse on Higher Education [hereafter noted as ERIC], 1971); University of Minnesota, "Report of Subcommittee on Equal Opportunities for Faculty and Student Women" (ERIC, 1971); Indiana University, AAUP Committee on the Status of Women, "Study of the Status of Women Faculty at Indiana University, Bloomington Campus" (ERIC, 1971)—informal policy; University of Pennsylvania, Committee on the Status of Women, "Women Faculty in the University of Pennsylvania" (ERIC, 1971); Dunkle and Simmons, "Anti-nepotism Policies and Practices" (1972)—report prepared for Tufts University; "Report of the University of Arizona Chapter of the AAUP's Committee on the ...'Anti-nepotism' Rule"; "A Report on Women Faculty" [at Stanford], as reported in *Stanford Observer*, November 1971, p. 7, col. 1.

22. "Discrimination and Demography Restrict Opportunities for Academic Women," in *Discrimination Against Women: Hearings Before the Special Subcommittee on Education of the Committee on Education and Labor*, House of Representatives, 91st Congress, 2d Sess., on § 805, H.R. 16098, Pt. 2 (Washington: Government Printing Office, 1971), p. 925.

23. This statement is difficult to document precisely because most universities that have formulated affirmative action plans do not make the details public. However, my correspondence from women faculty members at affected universities indicates that rules have been abolished or modified to take account only of arguably legitimate conflict of interest at the following institutions: Ohio State University, Miami University (Ohio), University of Wisconsin (in response to a ruling by the Equal Rights Division of the state Department of Industry, Labor and Human Relations), University of Michigan, Harvard (apparent policy change), the Arizona universities under the State Board of Regents (cf. Sigworth et al. v. Board of Regents, Pima County Super. Ct. (1970), State University of New York (a variety of external and internal pressures seem to have been involved), University of Illinois, University of Maryland, University of North Dakota.

is not simply de facto, but at least partly caused by a more general-
ized bias.[24]

The extent of discrimination resulting from "nepotism" policies
is not trivial. In 1959–60, the American Association of University
Women found that 18.2 percent of institutions surveyed had informal antinepotism regulations, and 26.3 percent had formal ones.
However, the regulations had more restrictive effects than the
percentages indicate. The larger and more prestigious the institution, the more likely it is to have a restrictive "nepotism" rule.[25]
Of the 42 land-grant colleges replying (out of 63) to a survey
undertaken by an AAUP chapter in 1970, 74 percent had written
policies restricting the employment of relatives, and of these, two-
thirds were phrased in terms of restricting access of faculty relatives to faculty positions. Of these, 80 percent prohibit only employment within the same department; on the other hand, a few
of those permitting extradepartmental employment will do so only
in emergencies and 32 percent of those with written policies deny
tenure to relatives. Of *all* the replying institutions, 52 percent ex-

24. For some recent studies showing discrimination in this area, see Loeb and
Ferber, "Sex as Predictive of Salary and Status on a University Faculty" (Uni-
versity of Illinois), *Journal of Educational Management* 8 (1971): 235; American
Historical Association, "Final Report, Ad Hoc Committee on the Status of
Women in the Historical Profession, 1971" (Duplicated; Washington: The Asso-
ciation, 1971), presented to the AHA on June 5, 1971, summarized in *AHA
Newsletter* 9, no. 4 (September 1971): 16–22; Virginia public colleges, "Women
in Virginia Higher Education" (ERIC, 1971); University of Wisconsin, Madison,
"Final Report on the Status of Academic Women" (ERIC, 1971); National
Organization for Women, "A Preliminary Report on the Status of Women at
Princeton University" (ERIC, 1971); "Report on the Status of Women Employed
in the Library of the University of California, Berkeley" (University Council-
American Federation of Teachers, 1971); Van Fleet, "Salaries of Males and
Females: A Sample of Conditions at the University of Akron" (ERIC, 1970);
Weitzman et al., "Women on the Yale Faculty" (ERIC, 1971); "A Compilation
of Data on Faculty Women and Women Enrolled at Michigan State University"
(ERIC, 1970); Position Paper of New York State Board of Regents, as reported
in Association of American Colleges *Newsletter*, June 1972, p. 7. See also Folger,
Astin, and Bayer, *Human Resources and Higher Education* (New York: Russell
Sage Foundation, 1970), pp. 288–304; *Careers of Ph.D.'s, Academic and Non-
Academic: A Second Report on Follow-ups of Doctorate Cohorts, 1935–60*
(Washington: National Academy of Sciences, 1968); Simon, Clark, and Galway,
"The Woman Ph.D.: A Recent Profile," *Social Problems* 15 (1967): 221; Harmon,
High School Ability Patterns: A Backward Look from the Doctorate, Science
Manpower Report no. 6 (Washington: National Academy of Science-National
Research Council, 1965).

25. Cited in "Report of the Subcommittee on the Status of Academic Women
on the Berkeley Campus," p. 15.

cluded relatives within the same department.[26] The limitations presented even by a "within the same department" regulation are apparent when Helen S. Astin's figures are considered: of the women doctorates she surveyed, 61 percent in physical sciences and 45 percent in the biological sciences were married to men in the same or a very closely related field.[27] At Berkeley, two-thirds of the wives affected by the antinepotism regulation were in the same field as their husbands (96 percent where the wife had a doctorate).[28] And, finally, from a legal point of view, if only one qualified woman were denied employment in violation of her civil rights, the matter would still not be trivial.

It is also possible to argue that "nepotism" regulations discriminate by sex, not only in fact, and not only in civil rights law, but also in traditional family law. It is a well-settled principle, broken recently in only a few jurisdictions, that a married woman's domicile follows that of her husband.[29] If a husband moves to better his carrer, a wife must either follow, no matter what the effect on her career, or give grounds for divorce for desertion. If a husband chooses to stay when a wife has career opportunities elsewhere, and she chooses to leave, she, again, is the deserter. This dependence of domicile does not apply to any other adult "relatives," all of whom, including husbands, are legally free to move anywhere they choose.[30] It is, therefore, married women who, with their legal lack of mobility, are uniquely disadvantaged by "nepotism" rules.

Therefore, given HEW's interpretation of the Executive order, the new statutory provisions, the constitutional developments, the studies documenting sex discrimination in higher education, and the sociological and legal commonplaces discussed above, it seems clear to me that antinepotism regulations not narrowly framed to accomplish only the legitimate purpose of avoiding likely conflicts of

26. Fahey, "Policies and Practices Relating to the Employment of Relatives in Land-Grant Universities," Paper presented at Western Psychological Association convention, April 1971.

27. *The Woman Doctorate in America* (New York: Russell Sage Foundation, 1969), p. 29.

28. "Report of the Subcommittee on the Status of Academic Women on the Berkeley Campus," p. 11.

29. Restatement (Second) Conflict of Laws § 21 (1971).

30. Indeed, it is a constitutionally protected right. Shapiro v. Thompson, 394 U.S. 618 (1969); Aptheker v. Rusk, 378 U.S. 500 (1964).

interest are illegal. Unfortunately, this conclusion does not solve many of the problems facing married female academics and the administrators who want, or do not want, to hire them. The legal weapons will help those women who have been kept out of, or only temporarily and penuriously in, available positions for which they are exceptionally qualified. However, precisely suitable positions may simply not be open at their resident university, and the suitable position that is open at some other institution may not come with a job for the husband, or the position may be suitable, but not precisely so. Or the woman may have qualifications just as good or nearly as good as those of another applicant, but the other applicant from another institution will probably bring with him extrainstitutional contacts and reputation and be able to bargain with other offers. Those supporting the cause of academic women say that the obligation of affirmative action requires the institution to "bend" a little bit in these situations, and offer the woman the position if she is competent to fill it. If it does not, the academic couple's relative lack of mobility will disadvantage both of them but, social realities being what they are, chiefly the wife. Such a situation perpetuates the discrimination against qualified women that the Executive order and legislation are intended to correct. The administrator will answer that it is none of his business to cure social ills and promote the cause of female equality; his business is to get the very best (and best known) faculty available to upgrade the university's teaching and research staff and to promote the institution's national reputation. Giving preference to resident and incoming wives will not promote this goal. This latter point is, of course, legitimate and serious and requires a serious answer from advocates of academic women's rights.

At one academic conference I attended where the legality of sex discrimination was being discussed, an administrator on the panel protested, "I don't care if it is illegal; you've got to convince me that what you want is good for us." This attitude is the crux of the whole problem. The value system called "us" judges faculty merit (at least for purposes of status and remuneration) by mobility, and judges the merit of a university by the national reputation of its faculty. Is this value system the only possible system? We can ask further, isn't it also a positive value to extend the traditional purpose of the university, the education of free men, to include the education of free women? And if we do wish to educate free women, do we wish to do so in a way that will actively work to break up marriages, or in a way that will encourage marriages that reflect and foster more-or-less accepted social values? These are not rhetorical questions. It is perfectly possible that female equality and monogamous marriage are incompatible and that the values promoted by lifetime monogamous marriage are obsolete.[31] It is also perfectly possible that we have been headed for social disaster all these years in educating women in approximately the same way as men, encouraging independence of mind and individuality of ambition. However, "us" now has a stake in continuing such education, especially now that the end of the baby boom and the present disenchantment with higher education threaten to deplete the supply of undergraduate and, particularly, graduate students on which our livelihood depends. And it is difficult to answer the arguments that marriage offers values for child rearing and mutually helpful companionship that are not provided by other institutions. This discussion does not purport to resolve this "issue in 'nepotism' rules," but only state what it is.

If educational administrators do choose to further the values of female education and fairly settled monogamous marriages, they must balance this choice against the incompatible values represented by policies of faculty "merit" based on mobility and of institutional merit based on faculty reputation. One cannot educate women for academic careers, adopt a policy that prevents a substantial portion of those women who marry from pursuing the career, and purport to favor both the education and the marriage. With affirmative action "bending" the traditional merit rules a little, the purported espousal of social values is credible. The issue is whether administrators prefer to be comfortable and traditional or credible and legal.

31. See the extended argument to this effect in Mitchell, *Woman's Estate* (New York: Pantheon Books, 1971), pp. 99–158.

JACQUELYN A. MATTFELD

Many Are Called, But Few Are Chosen

IN COLLEGE AND UNIVERSITY organization, "the administration" denotes persons serving a broad spectrum of functions. Although the qualifications expected of administrators and the manner in which administrators are selected and advanced vary widely from one area of administration to another, among similar institutions the qualifications and manner of selection and advancement are strikingly similar.

Three general categories of administrators can be identified in the Ivy League schools and in most others. A first category includes persons who are employed to maintain and develop the physical plant and to manage the business operations, alumni and other public relations, and development. A second category is composed of those who work in admissions, financial aid, student affairs, the academic and personal counseling of students, placement, and the registrar's office. The final group comprises the academic leaders of the university—the president, chancellors, provosts, and the deans of faculties, of colleges, graduate and professional schools, and special programs. Almost everyone would, I hope, agree that the intelligence, abilities, and personal qualities that make for successful service in *any* of these areas of administration are to be found in women as well as in men. What, then, accounts for the persistent paucity of women in administration today? How and where can their numbers be increased?

The data I have collected on the administrators in the Ivy League universities and the Massachusetts Institute of Technology show that the categories delineated above derive not only from the types of jobs and the responsibilities entailed, but also from the qualifications traditionally set for admission to each of these categories. The data indicate that the problem of the paucity of women in the first two categories of administration is readily soluble *if* the habits of discrimination and chauvinism can be broken or weakened. Traditionally, the *men* hired for most of the openings in the first two areas—business and student services—have recently received a bachelor's or master's degree, are personable, and hold good academic records—men who want to remain in the university environment. Many are alumni, especially in the Ivies, which share a happy certainty that alums make the best administrators by ensuring the perpetuation and dissemination of a belief in the virtue of homogeneity of backgrounds and the unique character and excellence of the institution.

Category two (student services) includes a subset, some of whose members stand apart from the rest of the group and carry such titles as assistant or associate dean of students or student affairs, assistant or associate dean of "the college" or of "studies" or of "instruction," and tutors, house deans, and counselors. Their vitae are often indistinguishable from those of the assistants or associates in other administrative offices, as described above; but a number of them will have moved from the ranks of lecturers, instructors, or assistant professors into administration. If they have come from a faculty, they are rarely prolific writers or scholars before or after the move, although they are likely to have distinguished themselves as teachers, tutors, or departmental advisers of some sort before having been refused tenure and offered a substitute post. Some choose to become administrators of this kind directly after receiving the Ph.D. or during work on a dissertation that may never be finished. A very few volunteer for part-time counseling work or a stint of deaning while continuing as highly regarded members of their departments simply because they "like students" or wish to challenge themselves in this kind of work. They are trained on the job by the superiors who chose them, and their salary increases are paced to their growing general usefulness in the office and competency in a relatively narrow specialization.

There are plenty of qualified men for jobs in categories one and two and for the subgroup in two. However, no college or university community boasts a shortage of intelligent *women* with college degrees and other qualifications in every way comparable to those of the men being employed (except for the ties of the fraternity). Therefore, it seems probable that the good of economic sanction will hasten both the consciousness and correction of practices prejudicial to women. When it does, the representation of women in all but the top segment of the administration can increase immediately. Qualified women are available.

The rapidity with which even the courteously resistant Ivy League institutions have, under sustained pressure, found and employed women for such jobs in undergraduate and graduate administration bears out this assertion. Currently there are 41 women identified as administrators in category two as defined here. There are more than 120 men. A large proportion of these women work directly with students. This suggests either that work directly involving students may be less prestigious and therefore considered more appropriate for women than other areas of administration, or that women are more drawn to it. Whatever the reason, three of the nine Ivy League schools recently appointed women to serve as dean of students or dean of student affairs. Only these three among the 41 women identified as administrators in this study both head major offices in the Ivy League and have titles without prefixes. Nineteen women are labeled "assistant" or "associate" deans and do counseling and advising for undergraduates primarily or exclusively; four have similar responsibilities for graduate students; and four work in residence. The majority are instructed by the terms of their employment to have special concern for women students, and a few have their responsibilities limited to that cause. In other words, three-quarters of the women working as administrators in the Ivy League during academic year 1972–73 are unambiguously working in student services. Like their male alumni counterparts, many are alumnae. Like the men, they have attained academic degrees, ranging from bachelor through doctorate, in a wide range of subjects and have had employment in a variety of jobs before coming to this work. Like their male counterparts, too, only a few of these women will be promoted to positions of greater authority in their offices, and fewer still could meet the criteria that tradition has established for transfer and promotion into the top arena of administration.

TOP ADMINISTRATORS

The situation for women in top administration is quite different from that for women in student services. The primary officers of universities and colleges have customarily come from the school's own faculty or the faculty of a comparably prestigious institution and, notably, after many years of teaching and research. They have for the most part been drawn from those disciplines to which the nation was turning for leadership or salvation in the year of their appointment.

Both of these prerequisites for office militate against the employment of women in high academic posts. Although women have been admitted to the undergraduate, graduate, and professional schools of this country for more than a century, only a small fraction have entered the professions and even fewer have remained active in them. Moreover, women are least well represented in the very fields which society has elevated in the recent past—the sciences, economics, and now law. Whatever the explanations that social, economic, and political historians or behaviorists may give for the situation, the statistics are incontrovertible. Five years ago there were very few women in the regular faculty ranks of public or private coeducational or all-male universities and colleges, and even the numbers in women's colleges had dropped sharply. Today the situation is only slightly improved.

It is not surprising, therefore, to find that as recently as 1970–71 virtually no women were serving as officers in any coeducational or men's schools. Furthermore, in the women's colleges, as the proportion of women faculty plummeted, there was a parallel drop in the number and percentage of women at all levels of their administration, and most noticeably in the highest levels of academic administration. (The exceptions to this rule were the coordinate colleges of the Ivy League—Barnard, Pembroke, Radcliffe, and the College of Liberal Arts for Women in the University of Pennsylvania, which had autonomous administrative offices staffed entirely by women although instruction in all but one was provided by the faculty of the male college in joint classes. All but two of these have, of course, now been merged into the father institutions, with various patterns of resignation, retirement, and transfer of the original women administrators resulting.)

The popular view that the academic excellence and prestige of an institution are directly proportional to the number of men in it and to the prevalence of their values, interests, and concerns in all areas of its endeavors is pervasive in American higher education. But nowhere is it more obvious than in the Ivy League. Indeed, one notes regretfully that only the threat of economic retaliation by federal government funding agencies was a force strong enough in many cases to initiate even *apparent* compliance with calls for a change in the status quo.

However, where presidents and governing boards are sincerely committed to including qualified women within all areas of their institutions, they are hampered by the small size of the pool from which to select women candidates for top academic administration. This situation contrasts to the ready availability of qualified women in other areas of administration—in student services and in plant and business operation. In view of the traditions the Ivy League universities follow in selecting top administrators, there is truth in their contention that as of now few, if any, women in our country can both move and meet the time-honored criteria for presidencies, academic vice-presidencies, chancellorships, provostships, and even top deanships. In these nine institutions, of the two ranking academic officers (presidents and provosts), eleven of the eighteen received their doctorates from an Ivy League institution, and all but one have taught for many years in the university of which they have become provost or president. (Only two of the eighteen have taught for fewer than ten years full time.) Nine have their doctorates in the sciences (including psychology, mathematics, and engineering); seven, in economics and law; and one each, in Sinology, history, and urban studies.

In hard facts, none of the Ivy League graduate schools except Brown has even 30 percent of its women students preparing to enter the academic professions, and, as of 1971–72, eight of the nine institutions had a combined total of only 151 women in a tenured faculty (professors and associate professors) of 4,470 and only three women as department chairmen or cochairmen. Given these realities, the odds are overwhelmingly against finding senior women faculty with both the bent and the desire to enter academic administration after having arrived in the promised land of scholarly recognition in any of these institutions.

Under these circumstances, most of the Ivy institutions, pressed to appoint women to "high level" positions, have temporized. To be sure, one has appointed a woman to be dean of the undergraduate college and associate provost. But this exception proves the rule. The others have used familiar titles to designate positions dealing with matters that directly affect women (such as coeducation, affirmative action, recruitment of women faculty, and the well-being of women students) or dealing with new areas of university activity (such as continuing education, off-campus study, interinstitutional arrangements, and training programs in the health professions). In 1972–73 these twelve women account for: one part-time president of the remnant of a coordinate college, four special assistants to presidents, one vice-president, two assistant vice-presidents, one associate provost, one assistant dean of the faculty, one assistant dean of a college of liberal arts and sciences. They average nine months in their positions, and six of the eleven have been appointed only this current fiscal year. None of their jobs threatens the established hierarchies or territories, and more than half have the ultimate in protection—impending retirement of the new incumbent or provision for "self-destruct" of the position itself. Four have positions that even skillfully written publicity releases reveal as being temporary. Not only are the responsibilities of this group of administrators substantially different from those of the men with identical titles, but so also is their background except in education.

Eight of the twelve hold undergraduate degrees from the Seven Sister schools, and nine have doctorates from Ivy League universities. They do *not* have teaching or research experience comparable to that of the men who become presidents and provosts of the country's private elite colleges and universities. However, more than half *have* had the lower echelon administrative experience their male counterparts *lacked* at the time of their appointment.

Enlarging the Pool

It is interesting to speculate on the probable professional future of these women who, because of new political forces, have been elevated to positions of visibility and responsibility in schools that two years ago scarcely acknowledged the existence of women in the academic world. It appears that we may all be part of a grand accidental experiment testing the questions, first, whether the top administrative posts in American colleges and universities are to remain the final reward of the faculty member who has succeeded in the publish-or-perish system, and, second, whether the faculty of the elite schools will continue to accept academic leaders only from among their own ranks. Certainly there is no evidence that keen intelligence, sensitivity in relationship, financial acumen, organizational ability, or even insight into the nature of education and society are limited to, or even most likely to occur among, teaching scholars. But it remains to be seen whether tradition-bound prestige institutions can be brought to test or judge objectively the performance of members of alternative populations for their highest position. Positions of genuine authority in high-level academic administration will have to be filled by those who have served apprenticeships in the lower echelons of administration and in other professions before we will know whether such women (and men who come by this route) can bring a new and different perspective and skills that will aid institutions in important ways.

Whether or not this enlarged pool is accepted, many administrators will continue to come from the faculty. We must therefore increase *not only* the number of internship programs and affirmative action plans that will remove barriers to the employment of women in lower echelon administration, but also the number of women in the tenured faculty of the Ivy League schools and *all* our other schools. We must belatedly make it realistic for the most able women students of all ages, no less than their male peers, to aspire to and achieve normal progression on the academic ladder, including that last leap up to high academic administration for at least a few. To achieve this end, there must be a fundamental change in institutional attitudes and practices, not merely the appointment of officers of Equal Employment Opportunity and Committees on the Status of Women. Unless we who are the women already in higher administration can help bring *this change* about, there will be neither substance nor permanence to the small gains in opportunities for women in administration that we have seen in the past twenty-four months.

Rearrangements in Faculty Schedules

Full-status Part-time Faculty

SHEILA TOBIAS AND MARGARET L. RUMBARGER

IN ANY ATTEMPT to assess the status of women in the academic community, a summary of their numbers on the faculty can be misleading. For although women have been accepted in teaching and research positions—as blacks, Puerto Ricans, and Chicanos have not been—they have often been marginally placed so that they function as paraprofessionals, regardless of their training and aspirations. Their concentration in the lower ranks, particularly as lecturers and instructors, has important implications for their academic careers as well as for their salaries. In most institutions, faculty members in these ranks are not privileged to vote in faculty meetings, nor are they eligible for the full range of faculty benefits, such as leave, support for scholarship, tenure, and opportunity to participate in decision making. Marginal appointments, even if full time, carry one-year contracts, little possibility for promotion, little security, and almost no research stability. Women in science disciplines who were eligible to apply for grants have often had to forgo the opportunity because they could not guarantee a long-term university affiliation.

How and why are women concentrated in marginal positions, and what can be done about it? To start, the first appointment after the Ph.D. often determines the future pattern. A study of women historians undertaken by the American Historical Association showed that "while only 5% of the men employed have been engaged at the rank of Visiting Lecturer, Lecturer, and Instructor, these lower categories embrace the ranks at which 32% of the women were engaged."[1] In this survey, 77 percent of all men Ph.D.'s had been initially hired as assistant professors, as opposed to only

1. *Final Report of the Ad Hoc Committee on the Status of Women in the Historical Profession* (Washington: American Historical Association, May 25, 1971), p. 19.

47 percent of the women Ph.D.'s. The AHA report suggests that women do not have the same range of choices in employment that men have; 74 percent of the women surveyed had only one offer for that first job, whereas 54 percent of the employed men had received more than one offer. One explanation lies in the high incidence of dual academic careers among married couples. Generally the wife's opportunities have lower priority than the husband's; and, too often, geographical location (as the AHA questionnaire results document) is the most urgent consideration in a married woman's job hunt.

Of course, other factors also account for the concentration of women in the lower ranks. Women have been inclined to accept marginal employment because the probationary period for an assistant professor exactly overlaps the childbearing years. Requirements for tenure, often rigidly defined and inflexibly administered, assume that the years prior to tenure require a full-time commitment so rigorous that the married woman professional cannot hope to compete while rearing children.[2] Because she hesitates to face a tenure decision after seven years, she accepts a marginal position. Another source of marginally placed women faculty members is the late-bloomer who returns for graduate education after her children are grown. By the time she completes the doctorate, she is considered "too old" to be placed on the traditional career route.

Perhaps the most frequent reason women professionals have historically accepted marginal nonladder appointments has been their preference for part-time work during all or part of their careers. Although a part-time commitment to teaching has long been acceptable when it has been accompanied by a professorial title, by tenure, and in some cases grant funds, part-time service in the early professional years has been frowned on and discouraged. Nowhere else is the evidence clearer that women have had to adjust to career patterns that are convenient to and established by men. As Jo Freeman has noted, "The life styles of the population of intelligent, highly educated women are more heterogeneous than those of men. Yet the University is geared to serving the needs of men or of those who most closely resemble them. Only women

2. See Alice H. Cook, "Sex Discrimination at Universities: An Ombudsman's View," *AAUP Bulletin* 58:281.

who can organize their own lives, however uncomfortably, into the environment created for men, can succeed there."[3]

AAUP PRINCIPLES AND PRACTICES

The "1940 Statement of Principles on Academic Freedom and Tenure," jointly formulated by the American Association of University Professors and the Association of American Colleges, and endorsed by more than eighty educational associations and learned societies, is the basic document on tenure and the probationary period. The 1940 Statement explicitly provides that tenure should be awarded after seven years of "full-time service." It should be noted, however, that the 1940 Statement extends its protection of faculty members to include many of those who serve in marginal ranks; though one must teach a full-time load, title does not matter. In this respect the 1940 Statement extends its protections beyond the more exclusive tenure track found at some institutions.

According to AAUP policy, then, any person who enjoys faculty status should be regarded as having tenure after seven years of full-time service, regardless of whether the institution regards the rank involved as being "on the tenure track." Many institutions employ an "up or out" policy for instructors and others in nontenure-bearing positions, with the result that those in the marginal ranks may not have the same opportunities for tenure which accrue to those in the professorial ranks.

Under the standards set forth in the 1940 Statement and later standards which amplify those principles, the situation of part-timers is quite another matter. Although the principles do not *preclude* an individual's being given credit for part-time service, the AAUP has taken the position that such service does not *necessarily* accumulate credit toward tenure (provided, of course, the service is actually part time and not a full-time load masquerading in a technical part-time affiliation). To date, AAUP has not extended the protections of notification of nonrenewal of appointment to part-time faculty members. Thus an individual may in fact teach for many years on a part-time basis but have less security of employment than a first-year full-time appointee, who must be afforded notice at least by March 1 or three months prior to the

3. "Women in the University of Chicago" (Chicago: The University, 1970), p. 113.

expiration of the appointment. Not infrequently the part-timer is assured a position only when the enrollment figures permit and, consequently, may be informed as late as the beginning of the academic year that no appointment will be forthcoming.

REGULARIZING PART-TIME FACULTY

Part-time faculty no longer constitutes the monolithic (and usually expendable) work force that it has in the past. True, many persons take on part-time positions in addition to other professional affiliations, often at more than one institution in a given area; others, and particularly women, wish or need to teach part time because the exigencies of family situations preclude their devoting full time to professional responsibilities. For some women, a temporary part-time affiliation of short duration may be most convenient and agreeable to permit them to fulfill parental obligations and then return to the full-time professional duties for which their training has prepared them. Others may wish to remain in a part-time affiliation for a longer period, but feel that appropriate recognition of professional ability should accompany what is for them a full-time intellectual commitment. In both cases the women are usually out of luck, and are thrust against their will to the fringes of the profession, if not out of it altogether. And for men who may wish to devote time to raising a family, the practical possibility of so doing is simply ruled out, if not by economic or professional exigency, then by cultural mores.

Over the past several years several constructive responses have been developed to the problems of the "regular" part-time faculty member or the person who wishes temporarily to assume a reduced load, usually in the context of affording greater opportunity to academic women. One response permits a regular faculty member to assume a reduced teaching load for a short time in order to accommodate family responsibilities and to have the probationary period extended accordingly; another response has been the creation of a special but limited category of part-timers who may enjoy full faculty tenure in their part-time positions after the expiration of a stipulated probationary period. Still other institutions have moved to permit regular, but less than full-time, faculty members to enjoy professorial titles in accordance with their abilities as teachers and scholars, and to establish for them equitable standards for notification, pay scales, fringe benefits, and opportunities for community service.[4]

TOWARD MORE FLEXIBLE CAREER PATTERNS

The critical question appears to be, not how can a full and fair opportunity be provided to persons in positions considered marginal and expendable, but rather how can the concept of the academic career itself be changed so that they will be able without extraordinary means to develop and maintain themselves as professionals if, of necessity, they must assume a part-time teaching load. A few suggestions may stimulate others:

1. A first rule for all institutions: It should not be assumed that women want or need part-time positions as opposed to full-time positions. Nor should women be encouraged or compelled to accept a part-time affiliation if they are capable and willing to teach full time. Conveniently selective application of socialist principles to the contrary, not all women have husbands to support them, and even some of those who do might like to give their partner a chance to be relieved from full-time professional obligations for a while.

2. Professional persons who have heavy family responsibilities for a short period should have the opportunity to assume a reduced load temporarily, and to return to full-time status when their schedules permit. Maximum flexibility should be accorded particularly in the probationary period, during which tradition has decreed that thou shalt pursue mightily and with all thy strength until thou hast achieved Tenure. Men as well as women should be eligible for reduced load appointments.

3. Provision should be made for those who wish to teach regularly on a part-time basis to enjoy many of the rewards and benefits which accrue to regular faculty status. Regular part-timers should be willing to undergo the same critical professional evaluation accorded their full-time colleagues, and should be prepared to contribute time and energy in such areas as counseling, faculty committee work, and the maintaining of office hours. If they wish to gain acceptance in the mainstream, the regular part-timers must be

4. Institutions that have recently developed policies regularizing part-time faculty appointments include Columbia, Princeton, Yale, Cornell, Colgate, and Wesleyan Universities, and the University of Wisconsin. See appendix to the present paper for memorandum statement by Yale University Provost Charles H. Taylor, Jr., on "Part-Time Appointments in the Tenure System."

prepared to accept numerous obligations which may not have been required of them in the past. In return, an institution may gain tremendously from having a specialist teach on a regular part-time basis what could not be afforded in a full-time appointment.

Of course, some institutions will find it considerably easier than others to implement these policies. Especially those with a stable faculty and student body (not to mention endowment) will be in a better position to regularize their policies for part-time faculty than, say, a large urban multiversity with a floating student population and literally hundreds of part-timers moonlighting from other jobs. For example, Princeton University can say quite readily that it will inaugurate a "limited" policy of part-time tenure appointments; it is not so easy to ask New York University to distinguish among its regular and "irregular" part-time faculty members or to provide them the same expectation of continuity and benefits accorded the full-time faculty. Things must start somewhere, however, and a good start has been made in a number of colleges and universities in the East.

Faculties and administrators should be concerned about the exploitation of part-time faculty and about inflexibility which compels talented professional women to drop out of a system that demands too much from some at the wrong time. They should be equally willing to devise in the coming years workable programs to remedy the inequities created by the present system. The task may not be easy, but what worthwhile challenge is?

APPENDIX

Office of the Provost
Yale University

June 26, 1972

To: Department Chairmen in the Faculty of Arts and Sciences
Deans of the Professional Schools

From: Charles H. Taylor, Jr.

Concerning: Part-Time Appointments in the Tenure System

1. *Part-Time Appointments: General*

Yale, in common with other universities, has for many years made part-time appointments to its various faculties. These appointments usually, although not always, have been as Lecturer or at one of the professorial ranks but with the qualifying status of visiting or adjunct. In several of the professional schools, there have been occasional exceptions, with a full-time title being conferred upon persons with part-time appointments. In all schools, persons holding part-time appointments were not considered eligible for a number of the fringe benefits which Yale offers to its full-time employees; conversely, persons on part-time appointments have not been subject to the restrictions on outside employment which, in general, is prohibited to full-time employees.

The conditions and procedures set forth below are intended to make it possible for some individuals to serve part-time in the regular academic ranks and to become eligible for tenure in one of the University faculties. (Conditions of employment and fringe benefit eligibility for persons holding part-time appointments other than as Instructor, Assistant Professor, Associate Professor, and Professor are set forth in the *Faculty Handbook* of the University and in policies developed in the ten University faculties.)

2. *Part-Time Appointments: Definition and Purpose*

Part-time appointments may be made at the ranks of Instructor and Assistant, Associate, and full Professor in accord with the normal procedures for these ranks. Part-time appointments are intended to allow those faculty members with family commitments or health circumstances which make it difficult for them to work full-time to request an appointment, *or a reduction in appointment*, to part-time but not less than one-half time.

"Part-time" shall be interpreted to mean part-time not only with respect to teaching, but also with respect to research and to other faculty responsibilities, including committee work and other administrative obligations. A full-time faculty appointment includes the expectation that the individual will meet normal teaching and other obligations as a member of the department and of the University, and still have approximately one-half time available for research. The individual who holds a part-time appointment will be expected to devote half of the usual amount of time not only to teaching, but also to research and the obligations of faculty citizenship.

3. *Part-Time Appointments: Terms and Conditions of Appointments*

Part-time appointments at the professorial ranks will be made as a percentage of full-time (not less than 50%) continuing throughout the academic year. Appointments will not ordinarily be made on a one term on full-time, one term off basis. Persons holding part-time appointments within the tenure system may not accept employment outside the University except as specified in the *Faculty Handbook* for full-time employees.

Appointments to part-time status will be made only when such an arrangement is mutually advantageous to the department and to the faculty member. In any given year, no more than a small proportion of the faculty in any department or school should hold part-time appointments.

The recommendation to use a position on a part-time basis shall require the vote of the appropriate governing body in a department or school. In the Faculty of Arts and Sciences, a chairman should forward the recommendation to the Provost who may seek the advice of the Executive Committee. In the Professional Schools, the Dean should forward the recommendation to the Provost.

4. *Part-Time Appointments: Expectations Concerning Subsequent Adjustment of the Proportion of Time*

Since part-time status within the tenure system normally will be temporary, tentative agreement should be sought concerning the anticipated date of return to full-time status; this will facilitate departmental and budgetary planning. The funds which become available in the department budget by converting a full-time position to part-time shall remain available to the department for other purposes. These funds normally shall be used only for short-term appointments, including for example, teaching fellows or part-time Acting Instructors. Limiting the use of funds released by part-time appointments to short-term appointments will insure the feasibility of the conversion of part-time to full-time positions.

Occasionally, a person who is a candidate for a part-time appointment may not be able to specify when he or she will become available for full-time employment. In that case, the proportion of time specified at the outset of the appointment will apply to that appointment until continuing resources become available to increase the proportion of time.

In recommending a candidate for a part-time appointment, the standards and process of evaluation shall be independent of the proportion of time proposed. Should a change subsequently occur in the proportion of time, a second review will not take place.

5. *Part-Time Appointments Within the Tenure System: Extension of Term in Rank*

Faculty members who hold, or have held, part-time faculty appointments at the ranks of Instructor, Assistant or Associate Professor on term, will be allowed an extension in their existing term in rank if they request it. The total of such extensions shall not exceed the difference between the faculty member's part-time accumulated service at Yale and a normal full-time term of appointment. Normally, however, the total of such extensions shall not exceed three years. Any requests for extension of the term of appointments must be submitted to the Chairman of the Department and the Dean of the School before January 1 of the year preceding the final academic year of appointment. Extensions beyond the limit of three years will require the written approval of the appropriate Dean and the Provost, who may seek the advice of the appropriate appointments committee.

6. *Part-Time Appointments Within the Tenure System: Leaves and Benefits*

a. *Leaves without salary:* Faculty members holding part-time appointments shall be eligible for leaves of absence without salary on the same basis as persons holding full-time appointments in those ranks.

b. *Leaves with salary:* Faculty members holding part-time appointments shall be eligible for leaves of absence with salary on the same basis as persons holding full-time appointments in those ranks. The salary paid during leave shall be in proportion to the average fraction of full-time spent in the individual's appointment during the period creating eligibility for the leave. Thus, for example, an Associate Professor on half-time shall become eligible for a Triennial Leave of Absence with half-time salary in the third year following the initial appointment as Associate Professor. Junior faculty in the Arts and Sciences who hold a part-time appointment will be eligible to compete for Morse and Junior Faculty Fellowship leaves. The amount of the fellowship award will be in proportion to the time taught in the previous year.

c. *Summer compensation:* Faculty members holding part-time appointments shall be eligible for the summer stipend under the conditions specified in the *Faculty Handbook* for persons holding full-time appointments in those ranks. The amount of the stipend will be in proportion to the fraction of full-time to be taught in the next academic year.

d. *Travel grant:* Faculty members holding part-time appointments shall be eligible for the $300 travel grant under the same terms as faculty holding full-time appointments in those ranks.

e. *Retirement Plan:* Faculty members holding part-time appointments of not less than half-time in the ranks of Assistant, Associate, or full Professor shall be eligible for the Faculty Retirement Plan as outlined in the *By-Laws of the Yale Corporation.* Faculty members with tenure are required to participate in the plan.

f. *Health Plan:* Faculty members holding part-time appointments at not less than one-half time shall be eligible for enrollment in the Yale Health Plan and other medical and insurance plans on the same basis as faculty holding full-time appointments in those ranks. However, persons with part-time appointments cannot be enrolled in the University's Disability Plan, which is limited by contract to full-time employees.

g. *Mortgage Loan:* Faculty members holding part-time appointments in the ranks of Assistant, Associate, or full Professor shall be eligible for the Mortgage Loan Plan providing they can meet all other criteria expected of a person holding a full-time position.

h. *Group Life Insurance:* Faculty members holding part-time appointments of not less than half-time in the ranks of Instructor, and Assistant, Associate or full Professor and whose appointment is for a minimum of twelve months are eligible for the Group Life Insurance Plan.

Maternity Leave Policies

ANNE THORSEN TRUAX

MATERNITY LEAVE POLICIES in this country are regulated and influenced, as are many other issues in the women's rights movement, by outmoded moralistic beliefs, laws, and, in the private sector, contractual agreements. The moralistic beliefs, including the still common attitude that a woman's place is in the home, especially if she is pregnant, have resulted in clauses in group health insurance policies that deny maternity benefits to married couples unless they have been married a full nine months and in policies that unjustly deny any form of maternity coverage to single women. In most European countries, equitable maternity leave policies are secured through a single national health insurance program. In the United States, such policies are made by a great many agencies and are embodied in federal laws and regulations, state laws and guidelines, group health insurance contracts, institutional rules and policies, union bargaining agreements, and policy statements of professional organizations. The plethora of influences guarantees no uniformity of policy. Although maternity leave is sometimes included as a part of health insurance and sick leave policies, often it is specifically excluded.

Women teaching in elementary and secondary schools are going through a period of contradictory court decisions regarding the right of school boards to deny work to pregnant women. Although the majority of decisions appear to favor the woman who wishes to remain on the job, the fight for a just and equitable policy will be a long one. Nor is it assured that the passage of the Equal Rights Amendment (ERA) will make a difference in these decisions, inasmuch as an exactly analogous case to sick leave for men cannot be made.

Maternity Leave in Colleges and Universities

In the discussion that follows, the term "maternity leave policies" is to be interpreted as including both short-term leave to be taken at the time of giving birth and longer furloughs for the purpose of child rearing. Both kinds of leave are meant to apply to both mothers and fathers and to both adoptive and natural parents.

It is of primary importance that in both long-term and short-term cases, decision about when to begin leave and when to terminate it should be based on the individual case and not on any specific or mandatory length of time. Both kinds of leave should be granted equally to single and married women. In no case should the request for leave be used as an excuse to terminate the individual's appointment. After either kind of leave, the individual should have the right to return to a job of the same or similar responsibilities and equal pay. The granting of leave of any length should not interfere with consideration of the individual for an appointment with tenure. (Time off in this sense may be considered analogous to leave for military service.) For graduate students, time taken for any kind of parent-related leave should not be included in the time allocated for completion of a degree.

Childbirth leave. Some special considerations apply to childbirth leave, which can be considered to cover periods of a few weeks to no more than a semester. This leave should be treated as short-term leave and should not be considered a special case, either in terms of benefits or denial of rights. To give women special benefits would give employers an excuse not to hire them, and, if the ERA is adopted, such special benefits would come under attack. The parent who wants short-term childbirth leave should be able to utilize sick leave, vacation leave, or leave without pay. If sick leave is offered with pay, childbirth leave should also be paid. During childbirth leave, health insurance and retirement programs and the consideration of promotion and salary increases should be handled as they are during other short-term leaves.

Child-rearing furloughs. Such leave should be granted at the time the parent thinks the child most needs the parental presence and will not necessarily coincide with the early years of childhood. An individual desiring a long-term furlough should take into consideration the needs of the department and the institution, as well as personal needs. The child-rearing furlough should be arranged for a period of not more than a year, and should be extended beyond this only in extreme circumstances. The parent should arrive at an agreement, preferably in writing, with the departmental chairman, about returning to work and the effect of the furlough on tenure, salary, and fringe benefits. Departments and institutions, in turn, ought not to consider such furloughs as detrimental to the probationary process. During the furlough, if the individual wishes, he or she ought to be given priority consideration for part-time appointments in the department.

CONSIDERATIONS FOR THE FUTURE

Each educational institution should have a written policy on maternity leaves that conforms to existing state guidelines, federal requirements, and the policy statements of professional associations. Individual faculty members, women's organizations on campuses, and professional associations have a responsibility to press for such policies. These policies should include clear statements of their applicability to graduate students and nontenured faculty—the groups most likely to be affected. Information about current maternity leave policies and their effects is lacking and should be compiled. This step is important if uniformity of treatment is to be achieved. Consideration needs to be given to coverage of the costs of abortion as part of the policy. With the increase in collective bargaining agreements, faculty women must ensure that good maternity leave policies are made part of such agreements.

Day Care Services for Children
of Campus Employees

BEVERLY SCHMALZRIED

THE NEED for child day care services by selected groups in our population has been brought to national attention by welfare recipients, by the 1972 Democratic and Republican platform committees, by members of both houses of Congress, by factory workers, by the U.S. Department of Labor, and by members of the women's movement. In a quieter way this need for quality care for children is being voiced on campuses by students, faculty, staff, and administrators as they confront the problem. Unfortunately, day care services are often seen as a problem only for the women of the institution and not for the male parents of the children in need of care. In some cases the needs of the children themselves have been ignored when institutions rushed into poorly planned, poorly staffed, and poorly administered programs that serve no one well except those who want to "get rid of" children.

From the institution's standpoint, the availability of comprehensive child care services would reduce the complexities of arranging the faculty schedules by allowing faculty members who are also parents to teach early morning, late afternoon, or evening classes. Parents even of small children, including infants, could provide uninterrupted service to the institution. Staff absences now necessitated by minor illnesses of children could be reduced. However, until such time as family goals are seen to be as important as employment requirements, it seems preferable to allow parents to function as nearly as possible like nonparents in the work force.

NEEDS OF THE CAMPUS COMMUNITY

The various segments of the campus community each have unique needs for day care services. Student parents need inexpensive, part-day care located in or near the married student housing. They want and can afford child care for only those times when both are in class or studying, but not on holidays and during vacation periods. Ideally one or both parents might work in the center to help defray the expense, but in actuality the demands of course schedules and of housekeeping would in many instances prevent their doing so. Many times children of students need the same comprehensive services as children of the disadvantaged: tight budgets may prevent well-meaning young parents from providing the nutritional, medical, and dental care they know the child should have but feel must be delayed until after graduation and the first pay checks come in. Although members of this segment of the campus community are concerned about their children, they may not recognize the need for good day care, and often only the more vocal will work for the establishment of day care services through the married student housing association or the student government.

Staff members, the majority of whom are women employed as secretaries, have need for day care from 15–30 minutes before their work day begins to 15–30 minutes after its close. As classified employees, their work schedules do not follow the academic calendar, and they need the services during vacation periods but not on holidays. Because of the time span involved, day care for preschool children of staff members must provide for at least two meals (breakfast and lunch), two or more snacks, and a rest period (cots or mats are needed). In addition, an after-school program is needed for children age six through twelve. In small communities this service can be provided on campus; in larger communities school-age children should be cared for after school in their public school or neighborhood community until one parent returns home. Staff members may be willing to participate actively in the campaign for day care service if they anticipate several years of employment at the institution. Often, a student's wife who plans to work only one or two years, until her husband graduates, settles for care by an otherwise unemployed neighbor. Staff members may fear that their employer will discriminate against them if they work actively to convince the institution of its responsibility to provide quality care for children of employees. On the other hand, a quality campus day care center represents an employee benefit that would promote attracting and retaining competent employees for secretarial, maintenance, food service, and other positions.

For faculty members, both men and women, the needs in child care services differ somewhat from those of staff and students. Usually they are able to afford quality care and are more willing to pay for it and they are also more demanding in their purchase of care. Their hours are frequently more flexible, and husband and wife can arrange their schedules so that the child spends a shorter day at the center. Furthermore, the child is usually not at the center during holidays or vacation periods. The faculty family uses its own funds to provide adequate nutrition and medical and health care and to purchase any therapy or other services the child needs. Both fathers and mothers may be interested in telling the children about their academic specialty and may wish to participate in the policy making and administration of the program. Faculty members often need after-school care for older children. A unique need in this group is for around-the-clock care when parents are away at professional meetings, supervising off-campus students, or attending evening meetings or classes. Unlike the classified employees, their day does not usually end at four-thirty or five o'clock.

MEETING THE NEEDS

All three campus groups—staff, students, and faculty—need day care for children aged two weeks to twelve years. Few centers, public or private, can accommodate the entire age span. In fact, infant care centers are relatively new in this country, and after-school programs are difficult for most parents to find. For many years state licensing regulations prevented group care of infants and toddlers, and most early childhood educators still have reservations about this type of care. The studies of the University of North Carolina at Greensboro have helped to define the environment necessary to good infant and toddler care. Although a program of day care for children between three and six years of age has priority, the job is not finished until quality care for both younger and older children is provided.

There are several alternatives available to the institution that accepts the responsibility of providing child care services for children of faculty, staff, and students. One is to use existing child development laboratories or university laboratory schools designed for teacher-training purposes. These programs have traditionally been designed to provide part-day programs for the children of faculty or middle-income families. Such programs, with some modification of facilities, staff, and budget, could be used for day care. In fact, any early childhood education teacher-training program that does not provide its students with experience in a day care setting is not being realistic about the 1972 job situation.

Another alternative is to establish a day care center from institutional funds or funds collected as part of student fees. Student fees are used to support coffee house entertainers, bowling alleys, and a variety of student services and often represent a large pool of money controlled by the student government association. Sliding fee schedules may, of course, be used to supplement funds available through any university source. Campus ministries, service organizations, and fraternal and social organizations should be seen as potential sources of funds and volunteer services. Universities with declining enrollment may see an expenditure for day care centers as a way of increasing the enrollment of women and as a means of demonstrating an affirmative position toward equal employment of women. Now is the time to plan such an effort.

Although government support of day care was included in the platforms of both the 1972 Republican and Democratic parties, costs and conservative opposition will probably limit its availability for the next few years. Such funds as are available will probably be restricted in use to children of families in work training programs designed to reduce welfare costs. Some states are beginning to incorporate perschool programs into their educational budget. In higher education, the institution should assume the costs for child care until federal or state support is available.

Institutions that are unable to provide direct child care service might act as coordinator in helping employees locate and use services available in the community. Employees and students with limited income may be able to enroll their children in a Head Start center; those in work training programs may receive funds for purchase-of-care in public or private centers. The college or university center for women could bring students or women seeking employment in child care together with faculty, students, and staff who need child care. A network of faculty families might be established to care for children while one parent or both are away on an overnight trip. In most situations a university will be unable to secure quality child care provided by other agencies and individuals.

In assuming responsibility for child care in the campus community, the following should be considered:

1. The costs of quality child care should not be underestimated. Estimates of $15–$35 per week per child may be reduced somewhat

by the institutional donation of space, utilities, food service, transportation, and janitorial services. Sample budgets are available to help estimate the cost in representative local communities.

2. A program should not rely heavily on volunteer help from students and the community. Children need the presence of adults who provide continuity of care. Volunteers are often irregular attenders and disappear on vacations and during exam periods. Certainly they can help enrich the daily program, but a regular, paid staff of professionals and paraprofessionals should be on hand at all times.

3. The university child care program should exemplify quality child care. The program must, of course, comply with state licensing regulations for group care. However, these are usually minimal and in most cases less demanding than an institution's own standards of excellence. A certified early childhood teacher or day care worker and a competent paraprofessional staff are the first step toward quality.

4. Provision should be made to care for children with minor illnesses. Many public and private centers send children home at the first sign of illness; this practice does not help any parent employee in maintaining job status. Isolation rooms, extra staff, medical services, and other precautions are necessary to provide for the sick child in the center.

5. When possible, the parent should be permitted to join the child in the center during coffee periods and the lunch hour. The day care center staff may find visits disruptive, but occasional visits and luncheons together should be seen as helping the child and parent strengthen their relationship. The day care center should be viewed as a service to the whole family, not the child alone. Parent education, marriage and family counseling, food service, and other programs may further give the employee the help she needs to function most effectively in the institutional work force.

Universities traditionally provide parking lots, recreational facilities, food service, emergency medical care, group health and life insurance, and many other benefits for their employees. Quality care for the children of employees should be a first, not the last, service provided by an institution concerned about the development of individuals.

ANN L. FULLER

Liberating the Administrator's Wife

IT IS TACITLY ASSUMED in colleges and universities that when a man is hired as a senior administrator, his wife also will perform services for the institution. No similar assumption applies to the husband of the woman administrator, for a man's work role takes precedence over his other roles. His job precludes service to his wife's employer, just as it excuses him from a major role in house-keeping and child rearing. A woman, even if she is employed, is expected to take charge of the housekeeping and the children and is also expected to help her husband in his career. If he is a college administrator, this last responsibility means that she must render service to the college.

Now that women are reassessing their roles in society, the role of the administrator's wife takes on special significance. Women traditionally aspire to become the wives of successful men, and the role of administrator's wife is a particularly seductive one. A more varied, demanding, and glamorous version of the familiar role of housewife, the role of administrator's wife also involves the exercise of more power—power to direct and influence other people—than women usually enjoy in our society. The work has many of the characteristics of a job; it requires a variety of skills and, often, long hours. However, because society has labeled it as "volunteer work," it lacks the pay and status of regular employment. The role embodies the painful, frustrating ambivalence of women's customary position in this society: it represents the epitome of success for many women, but it is also a powerful symbol of the subordinate status of women to men in society generally. From this perspective I shall describe the job of the administrator's wife, analyze the compensation she receives for her work, and suggest a new way of viewing and treating the job.

JOB DESCRIPTION

To some extent, all faculty wives and wives of administrators are encouraged to perform services for the institution for which their husbands work. They are expected to entertain students, colleagues, visiting speakers, and candidates for jobs, bake cookies for faculty wives teas, and attend numerous events. However, these duties are more time-consuming and obligatory for the wives of a few senior administrators whose roles go beyond participation in college entertaining. The roles that an administrator's wife plays may vary with the type of institution, its size and location, and her capabilities and interests. The point is that in every college someone plays these roles and that someone is rarely in a paid position.

The minimum requirement of the job of administrator's wife is to plan and conduct social gatherings for all the constituencies with which her husband must deal—students, faculty, administration, trustees, alumni, parents, townspeople, and visitors to the college. Her attendance at these and other events (which may include parties given by faculty members, lectures, concerts, and student functions) has long been virtually compulsory. She directs the efforts of people who facilitate college entertaining (food service, buildings and grounds, maids, printers), manages a college building (the president's house), and keeps the entertainment accounts. She is expected to work with the faculty wives' organization, primarily to plan further social events, and she provides encouragement to, and appreciation of, other administrators' wives in their similar work for the college.

She is also expected to involve herself in community volunteer work in the spirit of noblesse oblige. Her participation may range in degree from figurehead to full-time work. Common choices of community activities include church or hospital work, tutoring, service on college-related committees, or work in some not-too-controversial form of political activity such as the League of Women Voters or environmental protection. She may also serve as an advocate, working for certain causes she is interested in such as day care, the arts, or a town recreation program for youth. It is viewed as inappropriate that she work openly in partisan politics or for controversial causes.

The administrator's wife is used as an ombudswoman, receiving information and complaints from many sources for transmission to her husband. She is also called upon to interpret, explain, and defend administration policies.

COMPENSATION

How is the administrator's wife compensated for her work? The assumption is that she is rewarded by: (1) the high standard of living her husband's salary provides her; (2) her share of his fringe benefits, which may include free house, car, and household help; (3) a certain amount of "free" travel to such things as alumni events; and (4) reflected prestige and elevated social standing, that is, emotional rewards.

How valid is the assumption that these *are* rewards for her work? Is any part of the administrator's salary and fringe benefits intended as compensation for the wife's work? Put another way, Would a bachelor college president with similar qualifications receive a lower salary and fewer fringe benefits than a married man? The answer is that the single man might have a harder time getting the job since the employment structure is geared to married men, but once given the job, he would receive a similar salary and the usual presidential fringe benefits. He would also be provided with a paid social secretary to take care of planning and conducting official entertainment. As for "free" travel, the amount is small, and the traveling wife must work for it by participating in alumni events. Thus the administrator's compensation is not increased because of his wife's work nor is she paid directly.

Now let us look at the emotional rewards of the job. These include the inner sense of accomplishment derived from doing socially useful work, giving good parties, and supporting other people's efforts. Since she enjoys the status of a socially prominent person because of her husband's position, her activities are noticed by the community and may result in its approbation. However, because her status is derivative, support for her is influenced strongly by attitudes toward her husband. When college administrators come under attack, the feelings toward her are bound to be ambivalent, if not hostile.

Certain problems, inherent in the nature of high-level administrative work, affect her perception of the emotional rewards of her position. Her husband carries a heavy work load and has constant demands made on him by others so that he has little uninterrupted time to spend with his family. Consequently she must deal with both her personal adjustment problems and those of her children, who also have pressures caused by their father's job. These problems are especially acute in the first year of a job, when she is defining her role in the college, meeting new people, and making decisions about house decor, entertaining, and other matters, mostly without the help of her busy husband. Complicating her adjustment is the difficulty in forming satisfying friendships. Ambivalent feelings toward her husband affect all relations between his wife and people who have some connection with the college. The foreknowledge that local gossip will feed on what various members of her family say and do also interferes with making friends. She becomes aware that some people try to use relationships with administrators and their families to gain political favors. For the administrator's wife and children, a lack of friends, added to the other strains of the position, may in some cases lead to feelings of isolation and depression.

An administrator's wife has her problems compounded if she has independent career aspirations, and especially if she is young and her career is not yet fully developed. Her husband's acceptance of the job will very likely upset her own career plans. If she lives in a geographically isolated area, certain career options may be unavailable or require more commuting time than is feasible, given the institutional and family demands on her. To work at a paid job, she must counter preconceptions of what her proper role is. To others, it seems suitable for her to work only if she is engaged in a high-prestige occupation, such as college teaching, law, or medicine. Even in these professions, if she is to achieve any professional status in her own right, she must be in a regular career ladder position, rather than in the marginal ones usually occupied by women. To the community, her status as wife is more important than her status as worker. Lack of any recognition for her work and the disparity between her worldly success and that of her husband may undermine her self-respect and determination to pursue a career.

The administrator's wife, then, is expected to be a gracious hostess, social secretary, house manager, bookkeeper, ombudswoman, and volunteer in both the college and community. These duties are an extension of the housewife role to a grander stage than the individual family. Though she can use her personality and position to do social good, she is essentially limited to roles with no decision-making power. Her activities in the community are an extension of her nurturing role in the family: she helps others in polite, feminine, loving ways and stays out of the controversial men's arena of college and partisan politics. So long as she helps to maintain the status quo by exemplifying traditional women's roles, she receives public, though essentially ambivalent, reinforcement.

The job of administrator's wife requires much time-consuming work for which the rewards are inadequate. Not only is she not paid for her work, but also the emotional rewards are mixed. If she attempts to break out of the stereotyped concept of her proper role by taking a paid job, she may be accused of shirking her wifely duty and putting personal gain ahead of community betterment. If instead of taking a paid job, she involves herself deeply, in a professional way, in some aspect of the college's operations (say, in planning a conference), her work is quite unlikely to be taken seriously, even though it is performed competently, because she is not working as a paid administrator. On the other hand, if—in spite of the difficulties that result—she deviates from her stereotyped role, the rejection of the role can have positive effects. If she has the self-confidence to administer her own life in an independent and personally fulfilling way, her actions may give sanction to other women in the community to search for more enriching roles.

Liberating the Administrator's Wife

How can the responsibilities of the administrator's wife be redefined to remedy any unfair treatment she now receives? First of all, more acceptable options for these women should be established. For a diminishing number of them, the present system may remain satisfactory. Others may want to combine career and family roles with a part-time job as administrator's wife. Still others may choose to do no work for the college, in which case the college should hire someone else to do the work. Second, the administrator's wife who chooses to work for the college should be paid. Pay would help curb the exploitation, eliminate some of the antiquated make-work in the job, and give her the self-respect that unpaid workers in the society now lack. Salary should be determined on the usual basis of qualifications, experience, and fraction of full time worked. The person who fills the job, whether administrator's wife or not, should be interviewed for it, and, when hired, provided with title, office space, secretarial help, and budget. (In the present system, the administrator's wife is "looked over" to see whether she is socially acceptable; this is a covert hiring process, because the job is treated as a nonjob.)

Why should a college concern itself with redefining the role of the administrator's wife? Academic institutions are in the process of examining their policies concerning women employees and students. In academe, as elsewhere in the labor market, women work mainly as secretaries and service workers. Women are underrepresented, relative to their educational attainments, in faculty and administrative positions. As faculty members, they are concentrated in "women's fields" (for example, nursing, education, home economics, and social work). In order to achieve economic equality for women in colleges and society at large, efforts must be made to upgrade jobs and widen employment opportunities beyond careers and occupations now accepted as appropriate for women. One barrier to their success in the professions is the assumption that women must perform most of the unpaid labor in the society. If, along with increased recruitment of women for faculty and administrative jobs and other efforts to improve the status of women in higher education, colleges abolish expectations that faculty and administrators' wives will serve them in volunteer jobs, another step will have been taken in improving women's position in society. Inasmuch as the practices of college communities stand as models for many of society's other institutions, it is important that colleges discontinue this kind of exploitation.

What is the current feasibility of a plan to liberate or pay the administrator's wife? Most older faculty members and faculty wives oppose it. Many younger faculty members, male and female, and faculty wives would feel that the faculty wife should not be expected to do unpaid work for the institution but would be uncertain about extending that policy to the administrator's wife. Both the traditional view of the administrator's wife as a quasi-aristocrat and the disparity between salaries of junior faculty members and senior administrators make it difficult for junior faculty and their wives to feel that the administrator's wife should be freed of institutional responsibilities or paid for her work. At this point, little support comes from other administrators' wives either; most would feel—perhaps rightly—that they can do more interesting work and have more power as an administrator's wife than in a paid job or as a full-time housewife. Although some might not object to being paid for their work, it is doubtful they would fight for monetary recognition.

The impetus for change is most likely to come from the young administrator's wife who sees a more interesting alternative career for herself or who objects to being expected to perform work not of her own choosing. One potential ally is the woman administrator who is handicapped in comparison to a married man by her lack of "wife." Since she must work both as administrator and as hostess, she will be likely to welcome professionalization of the "wife" functions.

Once an administrative post has been accepted, it is difficult to modify the traditional role. Thus, a couple should be aware from the beginning of the hiring process of the need to negotiate their separate positions. As dual careers in a family become more common in the society, colleges will have to become more sensitive to the needs of spouses of potential employees if they are to recruit people of high caliber.

Changing expectations for the administrator's wife will affect the job of the administrator also. If the administrator's wife refuses to perform ceremonial, insubstantial roles at social functions, many social functions may be recognized for what they are: business meetings held for political purposes. The administrator may become more professional about the performance of his job, and the social side of his life will become private. Accordingly, he will no longer live in a rent-free college building. Some of the strain administrators and their families now feel will be relieved and some of the dehumanizing aspects of their jobs removed.

The role of the administrator's wife must be redefined to become consistent with the changing concepts of sex roles in the society. The contributions made by the administrator's wife who chooses to work for the college must be recognized by payment.

The woman who chooses to follow other interests must be given that option. Whichever option is chosen, the administrator's wife serves, to some degree, as a role model for all women in the community because her position is prestigious and highly visible. The role has usually been used to support traditional "wifely" behavior in women. It can, however, exemplify new directions for women and help bring about changes in the society that will improve the lives of both women and men.

Part Four

ACADEMIC PROGRAMS

BARBARA SICHERMAN

The Invisible Woman:
The Case for Women's Studies

THE MOST EXCITING CURRICULAR INNOVATION of the past two years has been the dramatic appearance of studies for and about women. In October 1971, over six hundred courses in a variety of fields had been registered by the Commission on the Status of Women of the Modern Language Association, an estimated half or third of the actual number. Courses included freshman writing seminars, multidisciplinary offerings such as Female and Male, courses on Patriarchal Politics and The Many Faces of Eve, and specialized offerings on The Psychology of Women, Sociology of the Female Labor Force, and Roman Women. Women's studies courses have also been offered in high schools and in professional schools of social work, education, and law.

Today the emphasis is on establishing programs. At the start of the 1971–72 academic year, plans for at least seventeen programs had been announced, but that figure was hopelessly out of date by June 1972.[1] At Richmond College of City University of New York, seven students have already graduated with majors in women's studies, and beginning in 1972 Sarah Lawrence College is offering a master's degree in women's history. Appropriate professional conferences and journals are keeping pace.

Many individuals have shared ideas and materials about women's studies with me. I am especially indebted to Phyllis Ackman, Barbara Debs, Marlene Fisher, Dolores Kreisman, and Dorothy G. Singer for reading a draft of this paper. Special thanks are also owed to the students at Manhattanville College who took the course Women in America in spring 1972 for their ideas on women's studies and for the experience of the course itself.

1. Course outlines and bibliographies are reprinted in *Female Studies:* I, II, and III, and in Betty E. Chmaj, ed., *American Women and American Studies.* For descriptions of programs, see *Female Studies:* III, pp. 140–81. See also the Bibliography, "References on Women's Studies." (The Bibliography also cites in full other references on women's studies and related subjects, published and unpublished, including those for which only abbreviated citations appear in the footnotes of this paper.)

The rising demand for women's courses and programs—they have been extremely popular—can be charted by the progress of the women's liberation movement. Carl Degler, who taught about women long before it became fashionable, found that students at Vassar initially considered feminism and women's roles in contemporary society dead issues "or what was worse: only of historical interest," an attitude that began to change following publication of *The Feminine Mystique*. Now at Stanford, he has found a tremendous surge of interest in women's history in the past two years.[2]

The women's studies movement, though still in its infancy, has already had a striking impact on women faculty members. Many younger professors undoubtedly came to women's studies from their involvement in the women's liberation movement. Those educated in the postwar years, however, had long played down their feminine roles in order to be fully accepted as professionals. Until recently, most academic women avoided "women's subjects" like the plague; to do otherwise was to diminish their chances of being considered serious intellectual contenders in traditionally male fields. The remark of a radical young woman to a distinguished woman sociologist says it all: "How did you manage to get stuck in a low status field like marriage and the family?"[3] Many women had idealistically believed they could succeed on the basis of personal competence, but in practice encountered severe discrimination, even humiliation. Some painfully recalled medical school interviews probing into their sex lives or the requirement of asking "permission" to appear at work during the last stages of pregnancy.

The recent formation of women's caucuses in professional associations, the closer collaboration among women colleagues, and the enthusiastic embracing of "women's topics" all reflect the changed perceptions and raised consciousness of many women.

Deterrents to Women's Achievement

The gap between the achievement of schoolgirls and the vocational attainments of adult women is one of the most disturbing educational realities of our time. Girls consistently receive higher

2. Letter from Carl Degler, May 10, 1972.
3. Quoted in Pauline B. Bart, "Sexism and Social Science," p. 736.

grades than boys, and often seem to make school their careers. Along the way, many have developed skills and entertained ambitions that might lead them to strive for professional achievement in the adult world.

Yet a girl is caught in a double bind. While encouraged to do well in school, she has also been brought up to believe that her primary goal in life is to be a wife and mother. Socialization into adult sex roles begins extremely early. One has only to examine children's books to discover the extent to which men's and women's adult roles are depicted as totally separate, almost mutually exclusive: men are frequently portrayed as doers, and work at a variety of occupations, while women, who are primarily mothers, look out windows and doors at the interesting action outside. Fathers are often called upon to resolve family crises, so helpless apparently are mothers. Even Madame Curie has been made to appear primarily as her husband's helper.[4] In nursery school, children may be ridiculed for engaging in activities considered appropriate to the other sex. At this stage, boys probably suffer more acutely, for sissies are more deplored than tomboys. In later grades, segregation of boys in shop and girls in home economics has often been mandatory. Although this pattern is changing in some schools, many fathers flinch when confronted with cookie-baking sons.

Psychologists maintain that all humans possess an innate drive for competence and intrinsic motives for learning which depend not on any external reward, but on successful completion of a given task.[5] Children's development of cognitive skills seems to depend in part on opportunities to explore the external environment freely. It may be that men and women, if given complete freedom of choice, would value different kinds of achievement. But by rewarding girls primarily for activities appropriate to their traditional roles, and by limiting their activities, we have artificially stunted their cognitive as well as their emotional development. In a careful review of the literature on sex differences in intellectual development, Eleanor Maccoby concludes that in both sexes the more passive, dependent children tend to perform poorly on a variety of intellectual tasks, whereas more independent children

4. Marjorie B. U'Ren, "The Image of Woman in Textbooks," pp. 218–25. See also Florence Howe, "Sexual Stereotypes Start Early," pp. 76–82, 92–94.

5. Robert White, "Motivation Reconsidered: The Concept of Competence," pp. 297–333; Jerome S. Bruner, "The Will to Learn," pp. 41–46.

excel. One study found that children whose IQ's had increased from preschool years to age ten were "competitive, self-assertive, independent, and dominant in interaction with other children," a veritable inventory of "male" traits. A number of studies also suggest that analytic thinking, creativity, and high general intelligence are more likely to be achieved by boys and girls who are high in traits characteristically ascribed to the other sex.[6]

Moreover, the traditional "female virtues"—passivity, dependency, and conformity—do not meet current criteria for healthy adult behavior. Recently, clinical psychologists have ascribed the same characteristics to the "healthy male" and the "healthy adult," but not to the "healthy female." If the "healthy female" is not a "healthy adult," there must be something wrong with the definitions of health, or with society's expectations of women, or both.[7]

Nor does emphasis on women's dependency square with the real ways in which women behave, or even with all men's expectations of them. Women frequently act autonomously, and men sometimes encourage them to do so. The point is, however, that many women have internalized the presumed norms, and believe that assertions of independence or competitiveness are incompatible with their femininity. As a result, women may fear success or experience intense anxiety on achieving it. Matina Horner suggests that, typically, college women develop a "motive to avoid success" because they believe achievement will diminish their popularity. She found they did less well on competitive tests than when working alone. Only when they were threatened with loss of popularity for not succeeding did their need to achieve increase. Men improved their performances simply on being told they had done poorly on the tests.[8]

In college, the conflict between the desire to achieve—which, in a highly competitive society like ours, probably affects almost everyone—and traditional definitions of femininity become particularly acute. Unless highly motivated to begin with and consistently supported by her environment, it is easy for the young woman to choose the path that minimizes or eliminates the conflict. Not surprisingly, women, but not men, report their college years to be

6. "Sex Differences in Intellectual Functioning," especially pp. 29–31, 35–36, 45. Quotation is from Maccoby, "Woman's Intellect," p. 33.

7. See Bart, "Sexism and Social Science," pp. 740–41.

8. Matina Horner, "Fail: Bright Women," pp. 36–38, 62.

progressively less happy, and until recently many also noted diminishing interest in careers.

Formerly the women's colleges educated girls in a "protected" and inspirational environment that allowed them to postpone assuming adult female roles. M. Carey Thomas, for twenty-eight years feminist president of Bryn Mawr, believed that college must "make it possible for the few women of creative and constructive genius in any generation to join the few men of genius in their generation in the service of their common race."[9] Other feminist administrators and professors at women's colleges also exhorted students to strive for the highest attainments and themselves exemplified what women could achieve. Even in the early 1950s these colleges provided a climate in which students were expected to achieve; those who succumbed to "the feminine mystique" found themselves on the defensive.

In the recent past, colleges offered little encouragement to succeed or assistance in coping with ambivalence. Mary Bunting has noted the "climate of unexpectation" in which girls are educated.[10] Although the process begins in childhood, college women even today receive numerous cues from professors, administrators, and peers—not to mention parents—that they are not expected to achieve great things, and that they are not very interesting students or persons. Although relatively little is known about the kinds of educational environments from which successful women emerge, the effects of indifference, discouragement, and hostility are only too apparent.

The facts about declining proportions of women attending college, obtaining Ph.D.'s, and teaching in universities in 1960, as compared to the 1920s and 1930s, are well known. Clearly, despite the expectations of Carey Thomas, education alone did not drastically alter women's roles or inevitably increase their realistic options. Nor did the increased reliability of birth control: college women in the 1950s married earlier and oftener and had more children at younger ages than their nineteenth-century predecessors.

The conventional portrayal of women as wives and mothers is, however, no longer an adequate reflection of present-day reality.

9. Quoted in Barbara M. Cross, ed., *The Educated Woman in America*, p. 169.
10. Bunting, "Educational Determinants in Individual Life Experiences," Speech delivered at Conference on Successful Women in the Sciences, in *Annals of the New York Academy of Sciences* (New York: The Academy, forthcoming).

A woman who has two children spaced two years apart spends only seven years, approximately 13 percent, of her adult life caring for preschool children. What of her other estimated forty-nine adult years?[11] In 1966, the average mother was twenty-six at the birth of her last child; by the time her last child attended school full time, she was thirty-two.[12] Not surprisingly, women, especially those between the ages of thirty-five and fifty-four, have entered the labor force in ever-increasing numbers. In 1970, 43 percent of all adult women worked, as compared to 23 percent in 1920.[13] Women today constitute 37 percent of all those employed; over half of them are married. In fact, one-third of all married women work.[14] These trends have not significantly altered cultural patterns, and will not until many women occupy high-status positions. Even professional work does not necessarily alter traditional family roles, for in most two-career families, the husband is considered the primary breadwinner, and his career invariably comes first.

In view of the changes in the shape of the family life cycle and women's employment, there is much truth to the assertion that if women's liberation did not already exist, it would necessarily have been invented. New cultural goals, reflected in declining birth rates, only increase the urgency of finding new life styles for women and men. If colleges are to encourage individuals of all ages to plan constructively for the future, they must examine not only curricular offerings and hiring practices, but the entire range of relationships among faculty, students, and administrators. Only then will it be possible to provide a genuinely humane and challenging environment for all individuals.

WOMEN'S STUDIES: A SOLUTION

A major goal of a liberal education, particularly in the humanities, has been to learn to place oneself in the perspective of an honored cultural tradition. Presumably this objective inspired the original survey courses on Western civilization, with their emphasis on the Judeo-Christian and Greek intellectual traditions. That women occupied a degraded position in Greek society or blacks in the Western hemisphere was, of course, considered beside the point. Educators assumed that all groups attending college partook

11. Alice S. Rossi, "Family Development in a Changing World," pp. 1058–59.
12. Bernice L. Neugarten, "Education and the Life-Cycle," pp. 210–11.
13. *New York Times*, April 9, 1971.
14. Cynthia Fuchs Epstein, *Woman's Place*, pp. 15, 95.

equally of this tradition or, if they did not, it was nevertheless the only one worth aspiring to. Recently blacks have made explicit their view that this has not been their exclusive heritage, and that it is not one in which they can take unmitigated pleasure. Thus, by assuming that a highly selected set of facts constituted *the* Western tradition, the curriculum fostered notions of racial inferiority and hindered blacks from acquiring a positive self-image.

The relationship of women to this heritage is probably even more complex. In contrast to other low-status groups, women— however deprived as a group of economic, social, and political rights—as individuals have always reaped rewards from the status and power of their fathers or husbands. In aristocratic societies, queens sometimes wielded considerable power as their birthright. The occasional precedents, however, do not alter the fact that women were rarely mentioned; nor do they provide much comfort for young women in democratic societies. The traditional curriculum, while assumed to be blind to sex, only confirmed the woman student's conscious or unconscious conviction that women were inferior to men, that their achievements were virtually nonexistent, or, if noted at all, distinctly second rate. It told her in addition that only as a wife and mother could she be completely fulfilled.

Women and the disciplines

Because the study of history has traditionally been concerned with politics, war, and diplomacy, it is fairly obvious why women have been largely invisible. David M. Potter a decade ago noted the distortions caused by this exclusion:

> What we say about the character of the American people should be said not in terms of half of the American population—even if it is the male half—but in terms of the character of the totality of the people. In this sense, also, attention to the historic character of American women is important not only as a specialty for female scholars or for men who happen to take an interest in feminism, but as a coordinate major part of the overall, comprehensive study of the American character as a whole. For the character of any nation is the composite of the character of its men and of its women and though these may be deeply similar in many ways, they are almost never entirely the same.[15]

15. Potter, "National Character," p. 445.

Despite Potter's challenge, historians have continued to make generalizations about frontier life and what "Americans" in any given period thought, without considering half the population.

Before women can be fully integrated into the national past, however, more must be learned about the realities of their lives. The experiences of women as women and as members of specific reference groups must be explored. Scholars are now examining the work and family patterns of women of different classes and nationalities, women's organizations, women who defied the system, and the relationships of women of different classes to each other—social workers and clients, slave women and their owners, ladies and mill girls. Only after the objectives and behavior of women in a wide variety of situations have been studied will we know whether in fact there have been common "feminine" cultural styles that cut across women's participation in charitable and religious organizations, temperance and abolition movements, labor and farm organizations, as well as feminist groups.

Special attention must be given to the experiences central to the lives of most women, particularly marriage and the family. Recent demographic studies have yielded considerable information about family life cycles in different periods, such as age at marriage, number and spacing of children, longevity and stability, but the implications of these findings for women's lives have been too little explored. Historians must use nonquantitative as well as census data if they are to reconstruct women's roles as wives and mothers. Medical records, for example, although biased in some respects, are often extremely revealing about women's health, family life, and, sometimes overcoming Victorian reticence, even about female and male sexuality.

Historians are now searching out quantities of archival and manuscript materials relating to many aspects of women's lives. These should prove particularly revealing about women's roles in local communities. As Gerda Lerner has suggested, when this material has been fully analyzed, women may well emerge as the real community builders, not only as teachers and social workers, but also through their voluntary efforts as conservationists and as patrons of the arts and religion.[16]

16. Lerner, "New Approaches to the Study of Women in American History," p. 60.

Despite the undeniable contributions women have made to literature, women writers have frequently been judged by a double standard. Charlotte Brontë's and George Eliot's novels received more negative critical appraisals after the feminine identities of their authors were revealed.[17] The designation "woman's novel" is still derogatory, and is generally equated with "a narrow focus." Even the accepted views of women's sexual experiences have been those proposed by male novelists. In view of the personal attacks on writers like Brontë and Eliot for suggesting that women have sexual feelings, it is little wonder that only recently have women begun to overcome self-imposed censorship in writing about their unique experiences.

In psychology and sociology the conventional wisdom about women's roles has often been purveyed as scientific law or cultural imperative. How many courses in personality, for example, have portrayed women exclusively in terms of classic Freudian assumptions about women's unusual superego and sexual developments, formulations based ultimately on the belief that women were essentially deficient men? Even childbearing, in this view, became a compensatory experience for not being male. Masters and Johnson have recently demonstrated that many of Freud's ideas about female sexuality were dead wrong. Traditional studies of "masculine" and "feminine" traits have assumed one scale ranging from most "masculine" to most "feminine." It has recently been observed, however, that girls who are designated "masculine" by certain tests do not necessarily lack "feminine" traits, and that the most creative people may be high in traits attributed to both sexes. How many current beliefs about women would be destroyed if examined impartially?

Some psychologists have recently found that the failure to study sex differences and their possible significance is a major shortcoming of personality research. Most studies are carried out on male students and, in order to control variables, subsequent research generally follows suit. Some researchers, assuming male behavior as the norm, consider women inconsistent or incomprehensible when scales and findings don't hold up. Rae Carlson has severely criticized the experimental approach that has dominated academic personality research and that has been particularly unfortunate for

17. Elaine Showalter, "Women Writers and the Double Standard."

the study of women. She questions whether most experimental studies, which are mainly carried out on white, middle-class, college males at a single session and then analyzed statistically, actually reveal much about individual personality, surely a complex entity. Carlson argues persuasively for putting the person back into personality research by studying individual behavior over longer periods of time and investigating the personal meanings of the individual experiences of men and women.[18]

Sociologists have long offered courses on marriage and the family which focused on women's roles as wives and mothers and emphasized the necessity of "adjustment" to these roles. Accepting the view that men fulfilled "instrumental" or more active roles, and women more "expressive" or emotional ones, courses and research failed to look at alternative behavior or else considered it "deviant." What followed were separate studies of men's "instrumental" roles and women's "expressive" ones. There are few studies of men as husbands and fathers, despite the tremendous importance of both roles. Although studies of working women are more numerous, scholars frequently fail to consider women in nonfamily settings or compare the work experiences of men and women. Women suffer from depression three times more frequently than men, but were excluded from a recent study of social structure and depression on the grounds that, for them, occupation was not an appropriate variable—this despite the fact that 43 percent of all American women worked in 1970.[19]

How functional are such distinctions in today's world—at any level? Recent research suggests that corporation managers are less exclusively concerned with substantive expertise than in the past, and are increasingly called on to demonstrate such "expressive" skills as cooperation and adaptability.[20] On the personal level, Alice Rossi has eloquently stated the advantages of men and women sharing in personality traits traditionally associated with the other sex.[21] To encourage women to become exactly like men supposedly have been is surely just as dysfunctional as insisting on complete

18. Carlson, "Where Is the Person in Personality Research?"
19. Good critiques of research on marriage, the family, and sex roles may be found in Bart, "Sexism and Social Science," and Marcia Millman, "Observations on Sex Role Research."
20. Millman, pp. 775–76.
21. Rossi, "Equality Between the Sexes."

segregation of traits. For this reason, a recent disparagement of Jane Addams for falling into "the compassion trap" is doubly unfortunate. The real Jane Addams was not simply a compassionate woman who brought maternal feelings to the larger family of the social settlement; she was an effective community organizer who also withstood obscene letters from ward heelers and bitter personal attack for refusing to support America's entry into World War I. Moreover, might not more, rather than less, compassion be appropriate in male as well as female leaders?

Those now working in women's studies have the unique opportunity, and responsibility, of extending basic knowledge about women in many fields. They will also have to conduct "men's studies" if the old cultural myths are not to be perpetuated. As women's pasts are re-created and their present honestly explored, it is to be hoped that the knowledge gained may be utilized to create educational and social forms capable of bringing out the full potential of women and men. For women's studies not only augurs well for scholarship, but has more immediately pragmatic aims.

The goals of women's studies

The major goal of women's studies courses and programs today is the fostering of intellectual and personal autonomy in women. To attain this objective, the negative self-image that many women have internalized, the burdens of socialization, ambivalence, and anxiety in the face of success must all be eliminated. Courses that reveal the actual experiences of women make women visible for the first time as important subjects and even as role models. Students learn how socialization and cultural myths have restricted their own lives. By analyzing institutional restrictions on women's roles, they may be started on a search for alternative personal and social strategies that will provide them and their children with greater options. By confronting the historical and social realities of women's lives in supportive classroom settings, students are able to place their own lives in perspective. For many, this strengthens motivation and improves self-confidence, intellectual élan, and emotional realism. Some will be freed to make choices about careers and marriage based on what really seems best for them. Obviously, one course, or even several, cannot entirely counteract the effects of early socialization and later cultural pressures. In one notable experiment, however, college women (but not men) considerably improved their performances at problem solving after group discussions had emphasized that it was socially acceptable to excel at the required tasks.[22]

To those who charge that this is "consciousness raising" and has no place in the classroom, I would argue that raising consciousness is a primary goal of liberal education. An education that does not encourage the student to raise difficult questions about her society, about her relationship to that society and to significant persons in her life, that does not encourage her to relate her own experiences to larger intellectual and social concerns will not equip her to grapple realistically with the world around her.

The participation of older women in women's studies courses is vital in many ways. For younger classmates, their ideas and experiences, their very presence, are likely to be more instructive than any lecture. For the student who returns to college at age thirty-five or forty, courses about women may provide a significant point of reentry into academic life. Some older women consider themselves casualties of "the feminine mystique." Faced with redefining their goals as their children approach college, growing older in a society obsessed with youth, many find the return to college traumatic. If they still have young children, they often feel guilty about "leaving home." They not only lack confidence in their own intellectual ability, but sometimes encounter hostility in the classroom where they compete with students who are the age of their own children. By starting with material that is close to their own experience, some continuing students may more readily regain the tools and confidence needed to fulfill their new goals.

Finally, what of the male student taking women's studies? The motivation of those who have ventured into courses has reportedly varied from fraternity brothers who enrolled "as a joke," to the young man whose girlfriend wanted him to be more "masculine" and who sought group support for moving out of stereotyped roles. Although some proponents of women's studies would exclude men or place them in separate discussion sections, it seems particularly important that men take the courses if any real changes in role definitions in our society are to occur. Exposure to

22. Maccoby, *Development of Sex Differences*, p. 51.

the issues may force the young man to reevaluate his own behavior, attitudes, and expectations; he may also understand better what's troubling his sister or girlfriend and, increasingly, his mother. He will certainly be better prepared for his future as employer, colleague, husband, father, and even subordinate of women.[23]

IMPLICATIONS OF WOMEN'S STUDIES

The questions raised by women's studies about the relationships between subject matter, teaching, and motivation are central issues in education today, and they apply to the majority of students of both sexes. Indeed, current complaints about student apathy and withdrawal are precisely those leveled in the past against women students. If "marking time" for four years, intellectual disengagement, and passivity toward learning have become norms for many students, women's studies courses can provide clues to circumstances eliciting genuine enthusiasm for learning. Obviously, recent curricular innovations did not begin (nor will they end) in women's courses. But proponents of women's studies are among those who have most seriously considered ways to integrate subject matter and teaching strategies to foster genuine intellectual commitment.

Changes in teaching

It is striking that almost all writers on women's studies—a highly diverse group—have emphasized the importance of the teaching experience, a concern frequently missing in curriculum discussions.[24] To greater or lesser degree, teachers of women's studies reject the traditional pattern of authority where the teacher (possibly supplemented by a textbook) is the primary source of wisdom, the lecture is regarded as the most effective teaching medium, and the student is expected to digest facts to be reproduced on final examinations. Instead, those teaching about women have adopted the model of the professor as a resource, the classroom as a shared learning experience, and the student as an active participant in her own education as well as in that of her peers and her professor.

23. On teaching male students, see Sheila Tobias, "Teaching Female Studies," pp. 6–8, and *Female Studies*, IV.
24. The emphasis on teaching may be found in *Female Studies*, IV; and *Female Studies*, V: *Women and Education: A Feminist Perspective*.

One reason for the flexibility in teaching is the novelty of the subject matter. Because there is no "official" body of knowledge to be covered, professors have been willing to admit that they too were learners rather than "experts." Students have participated enthusiastically in experimental classes and have benefited from the opportunity—sometimes a necessity—of doing basic research. In a field like history, which some students initially perceived as "irrelevant," exposure to primary sources vividly conveyed how people lived, felt, and thought in other eras, and provided a concrete context for historical study and comparison. Students became their own historians, immersed themselves in the material, and learned to draw their own conclusions, however tentatively. Intellectual excitement and an uncommon appreciation of the value of historical research often followed. After reading the five hundred pages of volume one of Emma Goldman's autobiography, students not always noted for their diligence asked where they could find volume two, and indicated they wanted to pursue the topic further.

Teachers of women's studies have employed a variety of techniques to encourage maximum participation. Chief among them has been the small group discussion. In large lecture classes, extra discussion sections have often been requested by students, if not previously initiated by faculty. In some instances, every student has been asked to comment on a particular question, an attempt to counteract passivity and timidity. If students come away from such discussions with a greater respect for themselves and each other, it is a major triumph. Another innovation has been the journal, a private record of the student's reactions to readings, discussions, lectures, and personal experiences during the course, a device that sometimes helps overcome previous writing blocks. Some professors have eliminated grades and encouraged collective research projects, in part to redefine the classroom as a cooperative rather than a competitive endeavor. Growing rapport in the classroom sometimes led to increased interaction among students and faculty after hours. Some classes met for meals; a few living or working collectives were organized.

It is unlikely that many of those adopting these teaching styles had studied the literature of achievement motivation. It is striking, however, that in providing an atmosphere in which self-expression and critical thought are not only socially valued and supported by peers, but also expected by those in authority, professors are in fact re-creating the kind of situation in which women presumably learn best. Furthermore, the teacher, however unwittingly, provides a role model for students previously convinced that women must conform exclusively to conventional social norms or be considered deviant. It is difficult as yet to measure the results of these courses by objective criteria, but the subjective perceptions of students are often quite moving. One of my students described the changes she experienced:

> Before coming into this course, I was aware that women have held an inferior position but not for how long or far this extended. Before this course, Women's Lib meant a bunch of crazy ladies who got tired of being housewives and decided to be truckdrivers and construction workers. I was so totally anti-Women's Lib that I never would have even thought of having anything to do with it. Now, I see the inferior position society has, is, and will foster upon us and I really believe that something should be done about it. I'm still not into the Women's Lib movement but I am trying to find my place. I cannot deny that motherhood is a beautiful thing—but only for those who desire it. We should not be typed into that one role while men can pick and choose.

The experiences of women's studies with multidisciplinary offerings may be useful to others seeking to break down overspecialization of knowledge. Almost everyone who has taught a course about women, in almost any field, has soon concluded that the subject transcends disciplinary boundaries. Published course outlines reveal not only how often nontraditional source materials are utilized, but also the variety of approaches to multidisciplinary teaching that are feasible and desirable. Not all courses need be jointly taught; qualified faculty members can introduce material from other fields into literature and history courses. Those who have taught multidisciplinary courses acknowledge that, for them, much of the excitement comes from putting subject matter together in new ways. Programs which insist that faculty members routinely offer reruns of material they or others have already developed would therefore be self-defeating. Indeed, if women's studies programs can find ways to ensure flexibility while building on a growing body of knowledge, they will make a major contribution to academic life.

Participants in multidisciplinary ventures report many benefits of learning from colleagues. Joint teaching not only proved the quickest way to expand each person's store of knowledge, but the experience also generated new approaches to specialized courses in their own disciplines. Academic women who previously felt isolated from intellectual life because of personal demands on their time or exclusion from informal male social networks found the experience of learning from peers both intellectually stimulating and, when it led to collaborative research, professionally fruitful as well.[25]

Women's studies and the community

Perhaps the most controversial aspect of women's studies today is its relationship to "the community," which often consists of registered students, nonacademic staff, and individuals with no official institutional connection. Some have charged that women's studies is a political movement rather than an academic endeavor because, in some instances, it was community pressure that initiated women's courses in "liberation" schools and later in regular academic settings. For some radical feminists, moreover, the avowed goal of these programs is revolutionary change—change in existing relationships between women and men, and in the capitalist system.[26] Proposals to link the academy through the women's movement to a variety of revolutionary groups gave professors the discomforting sense that free inquiry might be sacrificed to politics. In some cases, conflicts developed when groups sought to bypass traditional institutional criteria for establishing courses and hiring faculty.

Although each college or university will develop responses to its own community, few are likely to succumb to pressures for "community control" of women's studies programs. In fact, many radical feminists, fearful of co-optation, are themselves dubious about the connection between their programs and academic institutions.[27] A university may, however, find new ways to represent its diverse constituency. At Cornell, for example, a recent proposal for women's studies provides for an advisory body of graduate and

25. See Tobias, "Teaching Female Studies," pp. 4–6, 8–9.
26. Roberta Salper, "Women's Studies."
27. Ibid.; Marilyn Salzman-Webb, "Feminist Studies: Frill or Necessity?" in *Female Studies*, V.

undergraduate students, adjunct faculty, staff, and community members to work with a faculty board.[28] It will be interesting to see whether these groups can together develop an effective and challenging program.

Women's studies programs may, in fact, prove advantageous to institutions seeking to create new links with the community—an act of survival for some. A number have encouraged "open classrooms" that welcome participants not officially enrolled. Among them are likely to be women who, after an exploratory course or two, may decide to register. Some professors have invited secretaries and other staff members to attend the courses, thus attempting to break down the rigid hierarchies that academic life often fosters. In many places women's centers have been established to house information about all issues affecting women within and outside the institution. The centers might also serve as informal meeting places for older women who, particularly in their first year as students, have an almost desperate need to meet and talk over common problems with other women.

Organization of women's studies

How women's courses are to be transformed into programs will depend on institutional traditions, resources, and the goals of faculty members.[29] Small colleges that have encouraged faculty experimentation, self-designed majors, independent study, and field work may need no special arrangements. At institutions which discourage multidisciplinary majors, a coordinating committee drawn from several departments may establish requirements for concentrations and generate new courses. Some existing programs, such as American Studies, may provide acceptable working models.

At large universities, or wherever there are rigid departmental controls, separate programs may prove necessary. Where powerful department chairmen exercise tight control over faculty time, and oppose women's studies, it is unlikely that faculty members will be able to develop courses. Moreover, for women's studies to survive in such a setting, a person with prestige and know-how may

28. "Proposed Women's Studies Program at Cornell."
29. For two quite different approaches to women's studies programs, see those of Barnard College and Richmond College, in *Female Studies*, III, pp. 140–41, 168–70.

be needed to secure funds. Establishment of a separate major, staffed by faculty unattached to regular departments, carries serious dangers, however. Such appointments offer highly uncertain protection to professors when the inevitable budgetary crises arise. Faculty in isolated women's studies programs could quickly become the university's newest second-class citizens. To what extent is it already true that individuals are hired for "women's positions" with less care and respect than professors customarily bestow on potential colleagues? Even if the women's studies program survived financially, would it suffer the fate of home economics?

To protect teachers and programs, therefore, it seems important that faculty members in women's studies programs receive joint appointments. Regular departmental appointments offer protection in the face of economic crisis or declining interest. Scholars care about other aspects of their disciplines besides women, and will favor—even insist on—keeping formal ties with other colleagues. Besides, if women's studies is to have a major impact on academic life, its findings must be shared and integrated into the rest of the curriculum. The current trend of appointing an official troubleshooter or "conscience" on all matters relating to women is encouraging because it ensures a highly placed spokeswoman for women's studies.

Whatever the organizational format, a good program must emphasize research. Women's studies might encourage the university to become an educational laboratory to test the validity of its fundamental assumptions about learning, as well as the specific situations which foster creativity in female and male students. Faculty members should be freed to engage advanced students in primary research on some of the hypotheses advanced in this paper. Are there significant differences in the subsequent motivation, academic careers, and professional choices of those who take women's courses and those who do not? If so, what accounts for them? Do students respond differently to male and female professors? What happens when men and women are paired as teachers? Research, not limited to women's courses, might enable students and faculty together to discover a more genuine basis for ordering educational offerings. Others might study the effects of socialization on young children—research made feasible by the growth of day care centers on campus—or the influence of early childhood and peer groups on the motivation and intellectual styles of college students. An institution that systematically sought constant feedback about the effects of particular courses and teaching styles, of advising and living arrangements, would be an exciting place. With students impatiently seeking answers to a host of pressing social problems, emphasis on practical research might both improve morale and research techniques and enhance the long-range possibility of securing significant educational and social changes.

What of the future of women's studies? Is it simply a passing trend, as some have charged? Or will it help to alter colleges and universities in important respects, as its supporters maintain? The real question is not the precise form women's studies will take in the future, but how well it fulfills its goals. Will the programs lead women to fuller participation in intellectual and professional life? If women really cease to experience conflict between their professional and affiliative goals, no special programs will be needed, but there is no reason to believe that resolution will be readily achieved. Today's trends toward earlier involvement between the sexes and general cultural pessimism may make the development of personal autonomy more, rather than less, difficult. There may actually be a growing need for special programs for women, particularly in coeducational settings, for some time. Women's studies is our own solution to the "educated woman problem," as the women's colleges were in the nineteenth century. If these programs are to retain the inspirational, even "protective," quality which women's colleges ultimately lost, they must continue to encourage genuine innovation and commitment on the part of both faculty and students.

And finally, how are the findings of women's studies to be integrated into the curriculum? In the immediate future, interested individuals must be encouraged to devote attention and energy to developing research and new courses. Until basic knowledge is extended in many disciplines, materials about women can receive only token integration into the curriculum. Ultimately, however, women's studies cannot be separated from men's studies, for its lasting impact will come only when all students—not just those already concerned—are exposed to the full range of human experience. Then it will be possible at last to teach genuinely human studies.

BIBLIOGRAPHY

References on Women's Studies

Baxter, Annette, and Wemple, Suzanne F. "Thoughts on 'Women's Studies' at Barnard." Mimeographed. New York: Barnard College, n.d.

*Chmaj, Betty E. *American Women and American Studies*. American Studies Association, Commission on the Status of Women. Women's Free Press, 1971.

Female Studies, I: *A Collection of College Syllabi and Reading Lists*. Edited by Sheila Tobias. Pittsburgh, Pa.: KNOW, Inc., n.d.

Female Studies, II. Edited by Florence Howe for the Commission on the Status of Women, Modern Language Association. Pittsburgh, Pa.: KNOW, Inc., n.d.

Female Studies, III. Edited by Florence Howe and Carol Ahlum for the Commission on the Status of Women, Modern Language Association. Pittsburgh, Pa.: KNOW, Inc., 1971.

Female Studies, IV: *Teaching about Women*. Edited by Elaine Showalter and Carol Ohmann for the Commission on the Status of Women, Modern Language Association. Pittsburgh, Pa.: KNOW, Inc., 1971.

Female Studies, V: *Women and Education: A Feminist Perspective*. (Conference sponsored by the University of Pittsburgh and the Commission on the Status of Women, Modern Language Association, Nov. 5–7, 1971.) Pittsburgh, Pa.: KNOW, Inc., forthcoming.

The New Guide to Current Female Studies. Edited by Carol Ahlum and Florence Howe for the Commission on the Status of Women, Modern Language Association. Pittsburgh, Pa.: KNOW, Inc., 1971.

"Proposed Women's Studies Program at Cornell: Rationale." Mimeographed. Ithaca, N.Y.: Cornell University, n.d.

Salper, Roberta. "Women's Studies," *Ramparts*, December 1971, pp. 56–60.

*Showalter, Elaine. "Introduction: Teaching about Women." In *Female Studies*, IV: i–xii. Pittsburgh, Pa.: KNOW, Inc., 1971.

Tobias, Sheila. "Female Studies: Its Origins, Its Organization and Its Prospects." Mimeographed.

———. "Teaching Female Studies: Looking Back Over Three Years." (Talk before the Association of American Colleges, Jan. 11, 1972.) Mimeographed. Washington: The Association, 1972.

* May be ordered from KNOW, Inc., P.O. Box 86031, Pittsburgh, Pa., 15221.

————. "Women's Liberation, Phase II." *Middletown* (Conn.) *Press,* March 17, 1972.

Trecker, Janice Law. "Woman's Place Is in the Curriculum." *Saturday Review,* Oct. 16, 1971, pp. 83–86, 92.

Other References

Bardwick, Judith M. *Psychology of Women: A Study of Bio-Cultural Conflicts.* New York: Harper & Row, 1971.

Bart, Pauline B. "Sexism and Social Science: From the Gilded Cage to the Iron Cage, or, the Perils of Pauline." *Journal of Marriage and the Family* 33 (1971): 734–45.

Baruch, Grace. "Research in Psychology Relevant to the Situation of Women." In *Female Studies,* V. Pittsburgh, Pa.: KNOW, Inc., forthcoming.

Bernard, Jessie. "Sexism and Discrimination." *American Sociologist* 5 (1970): 374–75.

Bruner, Jerome S. "The Will to Learn." *Commentary* 41 (1966): 41–46.

Carlson, Rae. "Where Is the Person in Personality Research?" *Psychological Bulletin* 75 (1971): 203–19.

Cross, Barbara M., ed. *The Educated Woman in America.* New York: Teachers College Press, 1965.

Degler, Carl N. "Revolution without Ideology: The Changing Place of Women in America." In *The Woman in America,* edited by Robert J. Lifton. Boston: Beacon Press, 1964. Pp. 193–210.

Epstein, Cynthia Fuchs. *Woman's Place: Options and Limits in Professional Careers.* Berkeley & Los Angeles: University of California Press, 1971.

Freeman, Jo. "Women's Liberation and Its Impact on the Campus." *Liberal Education* 57 (1971): 468–78.

Gordon, Ann D.; Buhle, Mari Jo; and Schrom, Nancy E. "Women in American Society: An Historical Contribution." *Radical America* 5 (1971): 3–66.

Hareven, Tamara K. "The History of the Family as an Interdisciplinary Field." *Journal of Interdisciplinary History* 2 (1971): 399–414.

Horner, Matina. "Fail: Bright Women." *Psychology Today* 3 (1969): 36–38, 62.

Howe, Florence. "Sexual Stereotypes Start Early." *Saturday Review,* Oct. 16, 1971, pp. 76–82, 92–94.

Husbands, Sandra Acker. "Women's Place in Higher Education?" *School Review* 80 (1972): 261–74.

Lerner, Gerda. "The Feminists: A Second Look." *Columbia Forum* 13 (1970): 24–30.

———. "The Lady and the Mill Girl: Changes in the Status of Women in the Age of Jackson." *Midcontinent American Studies Journal* 10 (1969): 5–15.

———. "New Approaches to the Study of Women in American History." *Journal of Social History* 3 (1969): 53–62.

Lynn, David B. "Determinants of Intellectual Growth in Women." *School Review* 80 (1972): 241–60.

Maccoby, Eleanor E. "Sex Differences in Intellectual Functioning." In *The Development of Sex Differences*, edited by Eleanor E. Maccoby. Stanford, Calif.: Stanford University Press, 1966. Pp. 25–55.

———. "Woman's Intellect." In *The Potential of Woman*, edited by Seymour M. Farber and Roger H. L. Wilson. New York: McGraw-Hill, 1963. Pp. 24–39.

Millman, Marcia. "Observations on Sex Role Research." *Journal of Marriage and the Family* 33 (1971): 772–76.

Neugarten, Bernice L. "Education and the Life-Cycle." *School Review* 80 (1972): 209–16.

Newcomer, Mabel. *A Century of Higher Education for Women.* New York: Harper & Bros., 1959.

Nochlin, Linda. "Why Are There No Great Women Artists?" In *Woman in Sexist Society*, edited by Vivian Gornick and Barbara K. Moran. New York: Basic Books, 1971. Pp. 344–66.

Potter, David M. "National Character." In *American History and the Social Sciences*, edited by Edward N. Saveth. New York: Free Press, 1964. Pp. 427–45.

Rosen, Norma. "Mount Holyoke Forever Will Be For Women Only." *New York Times Magazine*, April 9, 1972, pp. 36–37, 56–72.

Rossi, Alice S. "Equality Between the Sexes: An Immodest Proposal." In *The Woman in America*, edited by Robert J. Lifton. Boston: Beacon Press, 1964. Pp. 98–143.

———. "Family Development in a Changing World." *American Journal of Psychiatry* 128 (1972): 1057–66.

"Sexism in Family Studies." (Special issues.) *Journal of Marriage and the Family* 33 (August, November 1971).

Showalter, Elaine. "Women Writers and the Double Standard." In *Woman in Sexist Society*, edited by Vivian Gornick and Barbara K. Moran. New York: Basic Books, 1971. Pp. 323–43.

U'Ren, Marjorie B. "The Image of Woman in Textbooks." In *Woman in*

Sexist Society, edited by Vivian Gornick and Barbara K. Moran. New York: Basic Books, 1971. Pp. 218–25.

Weisstein, Naomi. " 'Kinde, Kuche, Kirche' as Scientific Law: Psychology Constructs the Female." In *Sisterhood Is Powerful*, edited by Robin Morgan. New York: Random House, 1970. Pp. 205–22.

White, Robert. "Motivation Reconsidered: The Concept of Competence." *Psychological Review* 66 (1959): 297–333.

"Women and Education." (Special issue.) *School Review* 80 (February 1972).

Woody, Thomas. *A History of Women's Education in the United States*. New York: Science Press, 1929. 2 vols.

UNPUBLISHED MATERIALS

"A College Education for Women." (Report of the Ad Hoc Committee on the Education of Women.) Mimeographed. New Brunswick, N.J.: Douglass College, 1970.

"Conference on Successful Women in the Sciences: An Analysis of Determinants." (Sponsored by the New York Academy of Sciences, May 11–13, 1972.) *Annals of the New York Academy of Sciences*. New York: The Academy, forthcoming.

Currier, Barbara. "Special Approaches to Women's Education: A Model Coeducational Plan." (A Report for Hampshire College, June 23, 1969.) MS.

Morgan, Sherry Ward, and Mausner, Bernard. "Behavioral and Fantasied Indicators of Success in Men and Women." Mimeographed.

"A New Plan for Manhattanville College." Mimeographed. Purchase, N.Y.: The College, August 1971.

MINA REES

The Graduate Education of Women

AT A 1970 MEETING called to discuss problems in graduate education at which I was the only woman present, a professor of history from a leading Eastern university turned to me, without any preliminaries, and said, "Why don't those girls write their dissertations?" It developed that he was the one member of his department who insisted on giving fellowships to women, and department members were up in arms because women have been receiving fellowships for several years and not one had completed her dissertation. I was a bit dismayed by the sudden attack, and riposted with, "Why don't you appoint a woman graduate dean?" This suggestion seemed a little radical to my questioner; but it may be that Representative Martha Griffiths of Michigan was right when she suggested, in 1970, that what we need is heroines. Nonetheless, the complaint is common on many campuses, and I want to focus on this point and other myths and realities in the graduate education of women.

The problems of graduate school women differ for unmarried women recently out of college and for married women with children (both those who return while their children are young and those who postpone graduate work until their children are in school). The most striking difference seems to stem from the attitudes of faculties toward granting financial assistance, and it is closely related to the ability of a woman to study full time (though often the attitude of the usually male faculty toward the appropriateness of graduate work for a married woman plays an important role). A married woman has additional problems, even if the university will permit her to study part time. Are courses available at times and places that fit her schedule (different women have different needs)? Is there a day care center where she can leave her young children? Is there any possibility of getting some financial assistance even though she is a part-time student?

For those young women who enter graduate school without

substantial family obligations, there are other sex-related problems. Though claims are made that all women are discriminated against when financial aid for graduate study is distributed, there is substantial evidence that this generality does not hold for full-time students. Helen Astin reports that, in her study of all women who received their degrees in 1957 and 1958, the percentage of women doctorates who had had financial assistance was about the same as the percentage of the 1955 men doctorates studied by Harmon.[1] This finding is confirmed in a Yale study initiated in 1966[2] and by National Science Foundation studies. Most recent studies indicate no discrimination in admissions. Yet there are real problems.

Virgil K. Whitaker, former dean of the Stanford Graduate School, has said,

> A much thornier problem, especially in the humanities, is provided by the young ladies. They mostly profess an undying devotion to learning, at least on their applications. But for many of them the need to find a place in the world that plagues both sexes is complicated, to speak bluntly, by the need to find a man. A fellowship provides support while they continue the hunt.... There is ... ample statistical support for the proposition that the hard-pressed American taxpayer or even the generous donor is not getting his money's worth out of women graduate students if Ph.D.'s practicing their profession is the goal.[3]

The ambivalence of women about combining career and family has been commented on by many writers. The problem is most acute in precisely those years when men are preparing for a career. As Graham has said:

> Some young women are able to do graduate work and to do it well in these years, but few pass through this period without severe qualms about the desirability of planning for a demanding professional life. Men, too, are beset by a variety of doubts during these years, but for the majority of them, at least, academic success does not bring substantial psychic problems as it does for women.... To expect young women to buck the cultural standards for females is to demand of

1. Astin, The Woman Doctorate in America (New York: Russell Sage Foundation, 1969), p. 103.

2. Summarized in E. Wight Bakke, "Graduate Education for Women at Yale," *Ventures, Magazine of the Yale Graduate School* 9 (1969): 11–25.

3. "Graduate Study in the Humanities—Substance and Support," in *Graduate Education Today and Tomorrow*, ed. Leonard J. Kent and George P. Springer (Albuquerque: University of New Mexico Press, 1972), p. 201.

them much more than is expected of any man attempting to succeed in his field, since men are supposed to be successful.[4]

This problem is real and will not be solved easily. The recent changes brought about, at least partially, by various aspects of the women's lib movement, have encouraged the development and increasing approval of a greater variety of life styles for women than has previously characterized our society, and we may be making progress. But in this, as in other facets of professional achievement, women simply have a harder time than men because of the expectations of our society. For a married professional woman like me, a trivial but recurring frustration is the necessity that all invitations and all thank-you notes come from the distaff side of the family.

I am giving little special attention here to the problems of unmarried women because most of the information and opinion seem to concern either the married woman or all women. Further, most of the reported studies are based on data collected at least five years ago, and substantial changes are occurring partly as a result of changes in laws and related regulations and partly as a result of a new climate of opinion among women and among men.

Yale and CUNY

I referred earlier to a complaint that women do not finish their work for the Ph.D. This is just one in a set of familiar complaints I shall address. They are summarized in the report of the Yale study, mentioned earlier, concerning the policies and practices of the Graduate School with respect to the admission, financial aid, and to a certain extent the graduate educational programs of women. Most of the present and past directors of graduate studies in the forty-six graduate degree-granting departments reported, in response to a questionnaire, that there were several conclusions about differences between men and women students which most felt it necessary to take into account if they were to discharge responsibly their obligations to all students, to the Graduate School, to their colleagues, to the profession, and to society. I should emphasize that Yale has a policy of nondiscrimination, and there was very little reported opinion, among students and alumni responding

4. Patricia A. Graham, "Women in Academe," *Science* 169 (1970): 1284–90.

to questionnaires, that discrimination existed in administrative or faculty practices.

I shall now turn to some of the Yale conclusions on which objective evidence exists both at Yale and at my own institution, the Graduate School of the City University of New York, where we have recently completed a study (as yet unpublished) of the records of all students admitted from its establishment in 1962 through 1970. Our study included 3,204 students, of whom 36 percent were women.

The Yale directors of graduate studies reported that academic achievement and promise of women applicants as measured by college records and Graduate Record Examination scores were less than those of male applicants, that women take longer to get their degrees, and that their dropout rate is higher. On the first point, at Yale the men's GRE scores on the average surpassed the women's by substantial margins in the quantitative and advanced tests, whereas the women had a somewhat smaller margin of superiority on the verbal test. Moreover, with the exception of the performance of the English Department applicants on the advanced test, the best male score was considerably higher than the best female score.

At the City University, on the other hand, although the men's score on the quantitative test is, indeed, higher, and the women's score on the verbal is higher, the differences are about the same. Moreover, although the mean of the advanced test is five points higher for women than for men and more women than men had a score over 710, the variations by disciplines were considerable. This finding accords with the expectations of the staff of the Educational Testing Service, though they have no nationwide study that verifies it. One finding that seems to be uniform at the City University, on the basis of a study of eight separate disciplines, is that the undergraduate grade point average of the women is higher than that of the men. I recognize that a graduate school in a large urban center may attract many particularly able women who are bound by family obligations to study where they live. But there are many such graduate schools, so that I would argue that the evidence for high promise among women is at least as good as among men.

The finding that women take longer to get their degrees and

that their dropout rate is higher has considerable evidence to support it. A 1967 study of Woodrow Wilson fellows found that a greater proportion of women fellows than men fellows interrupt or discontinue their graduate training and that only 17 percent of the women fellows had received their Ph.D. six to eight years after they entered graduate training as compared with 42 percent of the men fellows. Rossi, in her special study of graduate sociology departments, found that although 39 percent of the students at the University of Chicago were women, over a nine-year period only 18 percent of the Ph.D. graduates were women. And at Wisconsin, although 28 percent of the graduate students were women, only 4 percent of the degrees awarded went to women. Rossi reports, however, that the practice of registering all students as candidates for the Ph.D. tends to confuse the picture, inasmuch as a number of women in sociology aspire to find a career in social work or education and have the master's in sociology as a goal.[5]

Whether the City University study reports a unique situation, or whether it reports phenomena more recent than those considered in the literature I cannot be sure; but it contains some findings on the subject of attrition and completion rates that are at variance with published studies. Since the only degree now granted by the CUNY Graduate School is the Ph.D., one source of confusion is eliminated; but we still have the problem of defining "success." Three so-called bench-marks were used in our study: the completion of the first or qualifying examination, the completion of all requirements for the degree except the dissertation, and the completion of the degree. At the time of the study, a smaller percentage of women than men had dropped out before completing the qualifying examination, and in the humanities and the social sciences a larger percentage of women had passed the examination; in the sciences 53.4 percent of the men and 51.9 percent of the women had passed the examination. At the all-but-dissertation stage, fewer women than men had dropped out in the humanities and social sciences, but more in the sciences; more women had completed the oral examination in the humanities, but fewer in the social sciences and the sciences. As to the completion of the degree, 35.7 percent of the students admitted between 1962 and 1970 were women; and of the 477 Ph.D.'s conferred by 1973, 31.7 percent

5. Alice S. Rossi, "Women in Science: Why So Few?" *Science* 148 (1965): 1196–1202.

went to women. Our records seem to present strong evidence that, at least at the City University, attrition rates are about the same for men as for women and women do complete the degree though it takes them almost a half-year longer than men. It will be interesting to see whether current studies in other schools replicate our findings. The fact that the CUNY Graduate School is in an urban center is probably significant. The fact that the head of the institution has been a woman has probably had an effect. But I suspect that, among women, the general expectation has changed enough recently to bring about changed attrition and completion rates on a national basis.

In any consideration of attrition, attention must be given to the variety of reasons having nothing to do with ability or motivation that may lead women to drop out or postpone their graduate work. Husbands' mobility and other problems connected with marriage and the family hit women in a distinctively different way from men. And, in today's educational world, the fields that women find particularly attractive are often the ones in which getting a job is particularly difficult. Graduate schools should act to accommodate the special problems of women. Day care centers are an obvious need. For those women who wish to pursue graduate work before their children are grown or in school, part-time work for the Ph.D. (a rare commodity at many of the most prestigious schools) and part-time financial aid must be considered, particularly in the urban universities. When women's problems are seriously discussed, one discovers that making changes to accommodate women would introduce innovations that would be responsive to the needs of many men; provision for part-time work is one example. Another striking instance is the obligation, not yet met by many graduate schools, to provide solid postdegree work on the graduate level for men and for women. If the universities respond to this demand, as they should, women who need to update their competence before returning to the university for a graduate degree could be greatly aided; for many women, the length of time to a degree could be reduced. But I believe we are moving, as the recent Carnegie Commission report *Less Time, More Options*[6] suggests, to an increasing recognition that individual styles will vary, and that, although some students should move ahead

6. New York: McGraw-Hill Book Co., 1971.

quickly to the completion of the degree, there will be able students who should move out of the university to participate in other experiences before completing their work. When this point of view becomes widely accepted, many women will find the graduate experience more attractive, and there will be less reason to believe (with the Yale findings) that the professional objectives of women students are fuzzier than those of men and that marriage and motherhood will dominate the career patterns of most of them. Women are beginning to recognize that, even if they marry and have a family, there will be twenty to thirty years in which they will work; and they are beginning to plan their lives to prepare for this expectation. They are beginning to face up to the problem of choosing a life pattern which will enable them to seek a career that will combine with marriage and a family, if that is what they want. But there must be greater concern for providing models that encourage girls and women to choose the life style that suits them. It seems to me that when there are more women on college and university faculties who can serve as models and counselors for students, the women who enter graduate school will do so with a better understanding of the kind of commitment they are undertaking.

After Graduate School

The discussion thus far has addressed three major attitudes of graduate faculties that often make life at graduate schools difficult for women: concern that they are more interested in finding a husband than in getting an education; the conviction that they show less promise of intellectual distinction than men; and the expectation that their attrition rates will be higher and that they will not complete the degree. Two other attitudes need brief attention: first, the conviction that the scholarly and scientific contributions of women, on the whole, are not equal to those of men; second, the concern that women Ph.D.'s do not use their education.

On the first, there is some important evidence. The Yale study reported:

> The record of professional utilization of their education is ... not as good as that of men. Just over half the women reported present full-time employment, ... Close to the same proportion of both men and women employed were serving in educational institutions, about two-thirds in each case. Junior colleges or secondary schools, however, provided an operational field for women to a much greater extent than

for men, and in the four-year colleges and universities the proportion of men in full professorships and top administrative posts was over three times as great as the proportion of women. The proportion of women who reported publishing nothing (25%) was twice the proportion of men.[7]

Further comments on this question have been provided by both Helen Astin and Alice Rossi. After observing that a particularly difficult problem for women is the interruption of their careers for marriage during precisely those years which have been found to be the most creative, Rossi says:

> Women (however) will not be strongly motivated to remain active professionally during the early years of child rearing simply out of concern for the effect of withdrawal upon their intellectual creativity. The development of their children is a concern equal to if not greater than their own work.[8]

And Astin concludes:

> All the evidence indicates that women, however highly talented and well educated, tend not to be as successful (if success is measured by large salary and high position) in their professional lives as men.... It is ... possible that women are less competitive ... by choice. The woman may consciously decline to compete for salary and status because she knows that if she becomes more involved in the world of work, she cannot devote as much time and energy to her family. Even the most capable, ambitious, and well-educated woman will usually choose husband and children over career if conflicts arise between these two areas of her life. She will, for instance, leave a job to move to another area if her husband decides to move. Or she will give up work entirely if one of her children is sick and needs her attention.[9]

Dr. Astin then remarks that this preference for the role of wife and mother is not peculiar to American women, that it is equally prevalent in the Soviet Union, and that, even in the fields in which Soviet women dominate (for example, medicine), they hold few of the top administrative positions.

The evidence here adduced and the comments of two such astute observers as Rossi and Astin can certainly not be ignored. But we may see here a self-fulfilling prophecy if women are denied the opportunity to qualify for leadership positions in academia because, in the past, they have not been appointed to them. I

7. Bakke, "Graduate Education for Women at Yale," p. 19.
8. "Women in Science," p. 1199.
9. *The Woman Doctorate*, pp. 91–92.

suspect that, as usual, the truth will be found between the two extreme positions: there are substantial numbers of women whose achievements would have been outstanding had they not been victims of discrimination; but many women would prefer to accept lesser roles in order to meet what they perceive to be the needs and best interests of their families. But, as Rossi concludes, "No society can consider that the disadvantages of women have been overcome so long as the pursuit of a career exacts a personal deprivation of marriage and parenthood, or the pursuit of happiness in marriage and family life robs a woman of fulfillment in meaningful work."

The last point to which I wish to address myself is the claim so often made, and implied in Dean Whitaker's remarks, that women fail to use their education after they have received it. Recent studies bear on this point. Astin's survey of women who received their Ph.D.'s in 1957 and 1958 found that 91 percent of the more than fifteen hundred women who responded to her questionnaires were employed. To quote from Joseph Katz's foreword to her book, *The Woman Doctorate in America,*

> These women are also very stable in their employment patterns. Almost half have stayed with the same employer, and an additional 30 percent have changed jobs only once since they received their degrees.... The women doctorates are found in a great variety of important and productive jobs. Ten years after receiving their degrees, over half of them have achieved the status or full or associate professorships. For a large number of them, a full-time occupational life has been combined with marriage and raising children. It is indeed a remarkable record of achievement, particularly because the path to professional productivity has been made difficult for many by discrimination against women, geographical dislocation due to their husband's job mobility, and the ever-present scarcity of competent domestic help.[10]

Another study of 1,764 women Ph.D.'s who received their degrees between 1958 and 1963 also found the rate of employment of women Ph.D.'s to be high: 96.4 percent of the unmarried women, 90.7 percent of the married women without children, and 83.8 percent of the married women with children. Moreover, the scholarly productivity of the women Ph.D.'s was comparable to that of men. Of the men, 57.5 percent had published at least one article; in comparison, 57.9 percent of the unmarried women, 66.2

10. Ibid., p. vii.

percent of the married women, and 63.9 percent of the women with children had also published at least one article.[11]

It is clear that the claim that women Ph.D.'s do not use their education is a myth. As Astin says, "Once a woman decides to invest herself, her time, and her energy in pursuit of specialized training, the likelihood of her maintaining a strong career interest and commitment is very high."[12] Thus, I do not agree with Virgil Whitaker that it is a waste of time and money to encourage women to seek advanced degrees.

In view of the job market in the humanities and the social sciences, where most of the academic women are found, I am cheered that the head of our placement office, a woman, reports that the colleges and universities are now playing the hiring game for real, that they are really seeking to employ able women, and that, even in this tight job market, women are faring well. Women, like men, will still have occasion to change their jobs and sometimes their career goals. Such changes won't be easy, but it is worth quoting a remark made by one of the women professors whom Helen Astin asked for an extensive report in connection with her study: "If there is any moral to be drawn from my experience, I suppose it is this. When somebody opens a door, don't just stand there. Walk through it!"[13]

The Motive to Achieve Limited Success: The New Woman Law School Applicant

THELMA Z. LAVINE

DR. REES has admirably defended the woman graduate student against a variety of stereotypical criticisms, and she strikes a note of optimism with her suggestions for meeting the problems of women by the introduction of day care centers, part-time work toward the Ph.D., financial aid for part-time students, and post-degree updating courses.

I shall turn my consideration to another area of postbaccalaureate studies for women, the law school, and to the astonishing and

11. R. Simon, S. Clark, and K. Galway, "The Woman Ph.D.: A Recent Profile," *Social Problems* 15 (1967).

12. *The Woman Doctorate*, p. 149

13. Ibid., p. 126.

unexplained increase in number of women applying to law schools over the past five to six years. The Educational Testing Service has provided comparative data on the registration of women for the Law School Admissions Test (LSAT), as shown in Table 1. I shall hazard some explanations.

TABLE 1: *Registration of Women for Law School Admissions Test, 1966–67—1970–71*

Year	Women Registrants	
	Number	Percentage of Registrants
1966–67..............	3,040	6.5
1967–68..............	3,802	7.6
1968–69..............	5,081	8.5
1969–70..............	8,273	10.8
1970–71..............	13,891	13.3

First, the vast increase in number of women applying to law schools, from 3,000 to nearly 14,000 registrants for the LSAT in a five-year period, reflects a significant upsurge in women's pursuit of professional careers and in what may be characterized as their "motive to achieve" in the professions.

Second, along with the growing tendency for women to seek entrance to the professions, there persists, although perhaps in diminished strength, the cultural ideals of feminine personality and behavior which are incompatible with the drive to success in a professional career. A conflict thus emerges between the motive to achieve and the fear that achieving will be perceived as a deviance from the cultural feminine norms and as a threat to social acceptance, marriageability, popularity, and so on. That career-oriented achievement is anxiety-producing for women college students has been vividly demonstrated by social psychologist Horner, now president of Radcliffe College, through the use of a story-completion test based on the following clue: "*After first-term finals, Anne [John* was substituted for the boys taking the test] *finds herself at the top of her medical-school class.*"[1] Over 65 percent of the girls, as against less than 10 percent of the boys, told stories that express anxiety with regard to this success, ranging from (*a*) fear of social rejection ("Anne is pretty damn proud of herself, but everyone hates and envies her"; "Anne doesn't want to be number one in her class. . . . She drops down to ninth in the

1. Matina Horner, "Woman's Will to Fail," *Psychology Today* 3 (1969): 36 ff.

class and then marries the boy who graduates number one."[2]) to
(*b*) doubts about the compatibility of femininity and success
("Unfortunately Anne no longer feels so certain that she wants
to be a doctor. She is worried about herself and wonders if perhaps
she isn't normal. . . . She will finally have a nervous breakdown and
quit medical school, and marry a successful, young doctor.") to
(*c*) the extreme anxiety-response of denying the reality of Anne's
success ("Anne is a code name for a non-existent person created
by a group of medical students. They take turns writing exams
for Anne."). Horner concludes that "for women, then, the desire
to achieve is often contaminated by what I call the *motive to avoid
success.*" The bright woman is caught in the double-bind of
anxiety about failure in her career, and anxiety about success.

Third, what is the relationship of the two antithetical elements
—(*a*) the increase in the numbers of women pursuing professional
careers and exhibiting *the motive to achieve professional success*
and (*b*) *the motive on the part of women to avoid success*, flowing
from fears of social disapproval, guilt, and the like—to the unprecedented upswing of women's aspirations for law school? I
suggest that women's choice of law as a profession represents an
effort to overcome the conflict between the two—the motive for
professional success and the motive to fulfill or at least not to
flout social ideals of the female. As a result, the motive to achieve
is modified or "contaminated" by the motive to avoid success. The
outlook for the new woman in the law school is therefore problematic.

The current competition to gain admission to law school applies,
of course, to men as well as to women and is partially triggered
by the utility of legal knowledge and skills in the liberal-activist
spectrum of reform-revolution within the student culture, as well
as by the decline in academic job opportunities. For women, however, law may be perceived as undercutting social disapproval of
careerist drive and ambition in women, inasmuch as the practice
of law entails a *fusion* of aggressive and helping-humanitarian
traits, thus mitigating the social disapproval of feminine aggressive
behavior. But do not all the professions characteristically represent
the same fusion of drive and humanitarianism, medicine perhaps

2. Compare with: "Anne starts proclaiming her surprise and joy. Her fellow
classmates are so disgusted with her behavior that they jump on her in a body
and beat her. She is maimed for life."

most conspicuously? By contrast with medicine, however, undergraduate preparation for a legal career is seen by women to be relatively undemanding and does not require the regimen of undergraduate mathematics-science courses which are forbidding to many women. The law school curriculum itself is seen to be less rigorous and to require a lesser investment of time, effort, and money than medicine. The practice of law appears to offer a greater variety of jobs, more flexibility of hours, more opportunities for part-time practice, and more job mobility than does medicine. Moreover, as compared with medicine or most of the sciences and humanities, training in law is seen to be akin to learning a skill that can, without significant loss, be practiced intermittently or fallen back upon later in life, as against mastering a constantly changing and growing body of knowledge. Finally, the completion of the LL.B. appears to require less career single-mindedness and less complete mobilization of the total self than the M.D. or Ph.D.

These determinants for choosing law school among postbaccalaureate career studies (which are based on interviews with George Washington University women undergraduates) are negative (less demanding, no undergraduate requirements, shorter time for completion, etc.) and extrinsic (part-time work options, mobility, etc.). The reasons suggest, then, that the choice of the legal career is currently not determined by strong, specific motivation toward the profession (such as often characterizes highly motivated women in medicine and the woman law-aspirant of the past).[3] Instead, for a cross section of undergraduate women, the legal career is viewed as subserving the career of wife and mother, with its requirements of part-time work, postponed work, mobility according to the husband's job, and intermittent use of skills, rather than planned development of a career within a supportive social frame.

College women of the late 1960s and early 1970s may feel they *should* want a professional career, just as, according to sociologist Jessie Bernard, in the 1940s and 1950s, whether women wanted babies or not, they felt they *should* want them.[4] In any event, the

3. See James J. White, "Women in the Law," *Michigan Law Reveiw* 65 (1967): 1051–122.
4. Bernard, *Academic Women* (University Park: Pennsylvania State University Press, 1964), p. 62.

current rush of women to law school indeed reflects the motive to achieve success in a legal career. But their motive to achieve success is visibly contaminated by the motive to avoid success, on two counts. They are handling their fear of social disapproval of their career aggression, not by independence or defiance, but by disavowing career single-mindedness and seeking to accommodate law school and law practice to the vicissitudes of the superordinate career of wifehood and motherhood. The predictable story completion is that of innumerable law school Annes, destined to find happiness outside career achievement, but without even the initial brief success of medical school Anne in Horner's Thematic Apperception Test.

Even more important evidence of the motive to avoid success is entailed in their misperceiving the structure of the legal profession. Rather than providing a haven for part-timers, migrants, and intermittent or late entrants, the legal profession reserves its rewards, as Epstein points out, for aggressive and ambitious male lawyers who work unusually long hours and are sponsored for jobs and partnerships by a male protégé system within an informal, exclusively male network of communication. Epstein finds "arbitrary and illogical sex typing" in the legal specializations, the conventional women's fields being the low-ranking, low-paying ones of the semiwelfare work of legal aid societies, domestic relations, and trust and estate law.[5] Much of the work within these areas is regarded by the male-dominated profession as merely paralegal, involving primarily social work and routine legal operations.

The appeal of law school is drawing unprecedented numbers of women into a professional career. Perhaps a majority will become paralegal Annes, forming a new subgroup of migrant workers who are poorly paid, uncertain of their locus or status, without the benefits of established workers in their field, and a potential source of private if not social discontent. A note of cautious optimism may nevertheless be sounded: Is not the aspiration of so many women, however ambivalent, to a professional career a potent and dynamic sign that the motive to avoid success is waning?

---

5. Cynthia Fuchs Epstein, *Woman's Place: Options and Limits in Professional Careers* (Berkeley and Los Angeles: University of California Press, 1970), pp. 163–64. The new and growing field of public interest law appears to cut across both male/female and high-motivation/motive-to-avoid-success categories.

Alternative Patterns
for Recurrent Education

The Nontraditional Student in Academe

JEAN W. CAMPBELL

THE AMERICAN COUNCIL on Education in 1957 held a landmark conference on the education of women. There it was often noted that talented young women did not go on to higher education in nearly the same numbers as their male counterparts and that the discrepancy increased successively at higher degree levels. Even then, when economic and cultural pressures combined to encourage women to concentrate on home and children, the waste was called appalling. Inefficiency in women's education was attributed by some leaders to the inflexible character of the educational establishment. Why must education be consecutive and full time? Could not women combine study and homemaking until the children were in school and be prepared then to move into jobs worthy of their talents? Should they not be able to leave school to marry and care for their small children and then return? Institutions were exhorted to develop programs that would be responsive to the discontinuities in women's lives and to women's educational purposes and at the same time suit institutional structures and characteristics. Some of them did.[1]

In 1962 the American Council again focused national attention on women's education through a conference largely devoted to exploring the new programs for women who were continuing their education. These programs demonstrated that women with families could return to school or combine their family responsibilities and their educational programs without interruption if the colleges and universities would make some adjustments.[2] The continuing educa-

1. See Opal D. David, ed., *The Education of Women: Signs for the Future* (Washington: American Council on Education, 1959).
2. See Lawrence E. Dennis, ed., *Education and a Woman's Life* (Washington: American Council on Education, 1963).

tion programs of 1962, astonishingly varied in design, were the patterns for several hundred others that have come to life since, with variations of their own.

After ten years that have been long on experience and anecdote and short on hard data, what understanding do we have of the effort to accommodate "recurrent education" in the traditional structures? What has been gleaned in the efforts to provide continuing education for the woman whose education has been interrupted, who often must be a part-time student while she works or takes care of her family or both, and who may live almost beyond reach of the campus?

First, we now understand that she was a bellwether. Adjustments that were or might have been made for her have become important for other populations. She has been joined on the campus by blacks and other minority group members, whose disadvantaged status often requires unusual institutional adjustments; by youth, whose testing of social values and the achievement ethic has challenged every tradition and requirement; by men in mid-career who seek further education or, in growing numbers, want to try for a more compatible second career; and by intermittent students, characterized by their mobility. It is commonplace these days for university presidents and for governance reports to foretell a more flexible traditional institution that will welcome the motivated, qualified adult student. The fact that educational leaders are now widely advocating institutional flexibilities, some of which have long been sought for the returning woman, is a fair comment that they are not yet commonly accepted. The demand for a more flexible campus may now be assuming critical proportions; unfortunately declining budgets seem, at least temporarily, to be creating increased resistance within the traditional structures to the necessary adjustments.

Some model programs of continuing education for women have circumvented institutional rigidities by their administrative structures: a separate identity has been created for the program. Women have then been recruited and carefully selected under special admissions criteria. In some of these cases the women have been segregated from the regular students for a transitional period of course work; in others there is no separation. These programs are essentially degree-oriented. Other model programs neither select nor admit students but offer a variety of supportive services and seek to lower institutional barriers through institutionwide adjustments. These programs usually provide entrée to degree programs. The model I represent (and the bias from which I speak) falls in the latter category.

UNIVERSITY OF MICHIGAN CENTER

The Center for Continuing Education of Women at the University of Michigan, although open to any woman who wishes to counsel about her educational and vocational choices and plans, essentially helps women return to formal education as mainstream degree-seeking students. Women whose educational purposes are more limited may become special students.

The women may go to other institutions or directly to employment or postpone action. The majority of them intend to work. However, according to a recent study, their motivations are complicated and the more general goals and values of education are at least as important to them as their preparation for work. We have counseled more than four thousand women and served several thousand more through discussion groups, conferences, workshops, a working library, a merit scholarship program, and emergency financial assistance. We have sought to reach a larger community of women indirectly through a newsletter and a series of publications as well as through staff professional activities and consultations with other programs. These services have evolved gradually and in recent years have been expanded to include both an evening program of regular credit courses for student wives and working women who cannot attend daytime classes and a varied program for undergraduate women in cooperation with the residence halls. We have shared campus concerns for affirmative action through membership on the Commission for Women and for the development of a program for women's studies as part of the Committee for Women's Studies, to which we contribute the services of a staff member. The center was initially supported by alumnae fund raising, but is now part of the university budget and reports administratively to the Office of Academic Affairs. The UM Center was specifically charged to recommend policy and procedural improvements to the university on behalf of the women it proposed to help.

The center has made some progress in developing more flexible arrangements, and our experiences may be sufficiently prototypical to provide a base for discussion. University policy approves part-time options for qualified returning women students, but not all units of the university welcome those who must be part-time for part of their education. Understanding sought by the center and cooperative efforts with other parts of the university often make it possible to place women in programs on an individual basis. Returning women need not take the required examination for admission (though they are asked to take it as a matter of record). Admissions officers are sensitive to the special motivation of adult students and recognize that it may not be reflected in undergraduate grade records. There are various admission categories that provide some flexibilities at both the graduate and undergraduate levels. Women may establish their own residency (apart from their husbands) for in-state fees. Part-time students may receive financial assistance through the center or in cooperation with the financial aids offices. But the routine assumption that serious, qualified part-time students have as justifiable a claim on financial aid as full-time students remains elusive. Federal government policies limiting aid to full-time students are a major barrier to reform efforts on the campus.

Credit by examination is not yet widely used. Credit for past experience is unheard of, even though the university is accustomed to evaluating clinical courses, internships, and undergraduate "outreach" experiences. The university does not yet believe that credits from institutions of comparable quality should be completely transferable for those who cannot avoid moving from institution to institution. Again, individual relief can sometimes be obtained. Adults are taking advantage of other changes: the elimination of mandatory physical education and language requirements, the development of a general studies degree, and a greatly relaxed attitude toward self-designed education and curricular innovations at all levels. The Graduate School has initiated a study of women students which will include an assessment of the deterring effect of current practices on the returning woman student.

This cursory review of one university's experience in lowering the institutional barriers experienced by the woman who is combining her education with other responsibilities suggests that progress is slow and fragile even when the circumstances are favorable. Women are resuming their education in sizable numbers but still without the full acceptance that their qualifications and purposes should command. This situation, of course, is related to the status of all women in academe and to faculty and staff attitudes toward women generally.

The effort to lower institutional barriers is quite clearly only a part of the picture. How shall the supportive impact of these programs be assessed? Thus far, the answer is partial and impressionistic, but new bibliographies and surveys of the literature, reports from pioneer programs, and some new research are providing the tools for a better evaluation in the near future. The following observations may offer additional illumination.

SOME POINTERS FOR EVALUATIONS

1. Knowledgeable counseling is perhaps the single most important service to nontraditional students. Most Center for Continuing Education of Women programs either provide it or hope to. Many programs revolve around it. New interest in adult development and counseling has paralleled the continuing education movement. One important evaluation study determined that counseling at the New York State Guidance Center for Women had an impact on the decisions of 83 percent of its clients and recommended that every community college in New York develop an adult guidance center. A sample survey of our UM Center's population indicates that 87 percent felt they had received some help. As demonstrated through a questionnaire administered to 400 women in the Grand Rapids, Michigan, area in 1971, overwhelming numbers of women still do not know what their options are or how to take a first step.

2. As this study in mid-America Grand Rapids suggests, the demand by women not now in school for programs and services is growing, even as budgets for higher education are shrinking. The UM Center has experienced a steady, gradual increase in use, but in 1971, 43 percent more women were counseled than in 1970— a sharper increase than we anticipated. It is difficult to escape the inference that a more militant feminism has directed the attention of more women to their growth and development. Another bit of evidence can be read in the mail of established centers, which

have always been inundated with requests for information about their programs and for "how to" advice. In July and August 1972, the UM Center responded to 20 percent more such requests than in the preceding six months. They were mainly from Midwestern universities, large and small, but requests from, for example, New York, California, Georgia, and Montreal suggest that the heightened demand is not a regional phenomenon.

3. This picture of demand tells us that the situation of the out-of-school and underemployed educated woman is little different in character from a decade ago. Today, however, the data are better.

For example, an outstanding 1970 UM thesis in clinical psychology, comparing honors graduates (1945–55) who are single and have always worked, married always worked, and married never worked, concludes that married women now in their middle years who have never worked have significantly lower self-esteem than married, career-committed professional women with children, or even than single professional women. The homemakers more often tended to rate their general mental and emotional health as only poor to average, feel more lonely, and are more likely to miss a sense of challenge and of creative involvement in their lives, feel less attractive to men, and feel less certain of who they are and what to do with themselves.

Similarly, a 1972 unpublished national survey from the UM Institute for Social Research on satisfactions with life experiences shows that white housewives and white employed wives bear a high degree of similarity to each other in their general sense of well-being and in their assessment of the major areas of their lives until they are divided on the dimension of education. Although the number of cases is small (and the conclusions must be provisional), the data show that, except among college graduates, positive attitudes increase as education increases. The scores of housewives who have graduated from college reverse the upward trend of women with lower levels of education, and they are clearly less positive than employed wives who have graduated from college. Further, college women who are employed are considerably more likely to see their lives as very interesting and very challenging than are those who do not work outside the home. Married college women who have accepted employment outside the home do not describe their marriages in more unfavorable terms than college women who have remained housewives. On the contrary, it is the highly educated housewife who does not have an outside job whose marriage seems most likely to be beset by disagreements, lack of understanding and companionship, doubts, and dissatisfactions.

Middle-class educated women are obviously not the only population of concern to continuing education programs. However, their needs were the original impetus for redesigning traditional institutions for greater flexibility, and they are still valid. Longer lives, fewer children, and a generally minimized domestic role are the facts of life.

4. Returning women do well academically and, when they have clear goals, stay in school. Women's academic capacity is unquestioned. In recent years, the functional intelligence of adults and their ability to learn have not been in doubt. It is not surprising then that 91 percent of the women answering the UM Center questionnaire report grades as good as, or better than, they had previously earned. The ten-year report from the Sarah Lawrence College Center for Continuing Education of Women is, in its entirety, a comment on the effectiveness of the women as students.

5. Returning to school has a profound effect on women. As reported in the sample survey of the four thousand women who have used the UM Center, 85 percent of those who returned to school enjoyed it very much and another 12 percent, somewhat. This affirmation was virtually unanimous in spite of changes in their home and family life: 76 percent noted at least some change; 33 percent said there was not enough time for home and family life; 74 percent, not enough time for housework, entertaining, and related activities; 10 percent felt pressured. When asked if they experienced changes in their own lives, 75 percent said they did; 61 percent indicated they felt new confidence and self-respect; 65 percent noted their increased knowledge and understanding; 17 percent gained respect from family; 10 percent valued new friends; 2.5 percent said returning to school resulted in an unhappy and divided family.

6. The profile of women coming to the UM Center—and no doubt to other centers—has changed since 1964. They are very much younger (37.5, 29.5) and they represent a wider range of backgrounds. More are single, widowed, or divorced (10 percent,

33 percent). Those who are married (81 percent, 65 percent) have fewer children (2.8, 2.1). There is growing interest in new occupational fields. There is a lively interest in sharing roles in two-career families, in which the children also share responsibilities (shades of Rossi, 1964[3]). More women than in the past are interrupting their educations to test their values and to try to find themselves. More are returning to school with an apparent willingness to postpone marriage and children until their education is complete.

7. Programs facilitating women's efficient use of higher education will be needed into the indefinite future. We may hope these programs will influence the direction of change in higher education. They will continue to be as varied in design as in the past, but they will be more comprehensive. They are already helping women at all stages of their educational and life planning; they are advocates of wider options and equality of opportunity. Many of them had a primary interest in programming, for example, in renewal education and stretched-out graduate professional degrees.

Responding intelligently as institutions to women students on the campus and, in this electronic age, beyond the campus, remains a challenge.

Expanding Opportunities
Through Continuing Education

ROSALIND LORING

IN THE MIDST of today's assessing, critiquing, and mental-spanking of much of higher education for not serving society as it could and should, one part of the structure has offered and continues to offer viable alternatives to women. Called "continuing education" or "university extension," this division of the traditional system has provided the means for a diversity of people to select those topics, educational experiences, or curricula which best meet their needs. Indeed, the extension students' demands have required ad-

3. Alice S. Rossi, "Equality Between the Sexes: An Immodest Proposal," in *The Woman in America*, ed. Robert J. Lifton (Boston: Beacon Press, 1964), pp. 98–143.

ministrators and teachers to be relevant, experimental, available, and creative problem solvers.

Extension personnel, aware of trends in the society and in close communication with their students, were early on the scene with program developments conducive to learning in untraditional ways, using variants in location, timing, scheduling, and methodology. Moreover, credit toward undergraduate degrees and for professional upgrading has been available for over fifty years through correspondence courses, and for seven years by means of television.

Extension divisions in most public universities and many private ones have offered a range of programs sized and shaped by their enrollees. Educational activities especially designed for women, who constitute 55–60 percent of the students, have been growing over the past dozen years, at first slowly but accelerating rapidly in the last five years. In 1971, *Continuing Education Programs and Services for Women*, issued by the Women's Bureau, U.S. Department of Labor, listed more than 450 institutions with some type of programming for women.

What has this development meant in facilitating education opportunities for women? A major contribution of extension has been an energetic attack on the formidable barriers defined by the Task Force on Higher Education, particularly the assumptions of both men and women regarding the role of women in our society. Almost all extension programs for women include courses in the psychology and sociology of women; counseling to uncover and then encourage development of personal potential; and awareness-inducing educational experiences that deal with contemporary issues of work, family, marriage, education, and community relationships.

Women have utilized these opportunities to take lower- and upper-division courses, some of which carry credit transferable to the "regular" campus toward an undergraduate degree. For many, extension is a safe place to check on learning ability that has not recently been tested. Others are attracted by the convenience of schedule, time, off-campus location, and the absence of a required minimum number of units to be taken.

Many a Ms. X discovered some years ago that extension courses in History of Western Civilization or The Education of Emotionally Handicapped Children or Skills for Community Action not only satisfied her plan for college-level curriculum but also were available *without* a two-mile hike from the parking lot, an expensive day long babysitter, and a teacher who questioned the validity of her class participation. And, after several years of studying part time, Ms. X, refurbished with new knowledge and revitalized by a fresh self-concept, has frequently enrolled in a full-time college program.

There are, of course, problems. Even today few major institutions grant a bachelor's degree to an extension student (more are considering the possibility); graduate degrees remain elusive. Furthermore, the cost of providing convenience and accessibility is real. Few states subsidize education for adults; few banks provide loans for part-time students. And the values of our society are just beginning to commend the expenditure of family income on continuing the education of women. Small wonder, then, that women extension students, on the whole, are both mature and middle class. Yet it is they who have been seeking to change the traditional images of themselves as dull, uninteresting, plastic, not-quite-bright persons.

Thus the most recent thrust of continuing education is to extend the continuum of offerings from standard credit courses to new formulations that combine the acceptability and credibility of the College-Level Examination Program (CLEP), external degrees, and certified training, all of which may enable women to reach wider, clearer, and more accessible goals. Increasingly these are work-related.

For example, a recent creation of extension is the certificate denoting the achievement of a specified body of knowledge. In response to expressions of conviction by public officials, educational administrators, and women themselves, in a growing number of fields an acceptable alternative to a bachelor's or a master's degree may be a certificate for a concentrated, integrated curriculum which designates competence in a single field. Such a certificate gives the term "paraprofessional" another definition, denoting a new career at a level exceedingly close to the definition of "professional." For liberal arts graduates, for second careers, for the middle-aged, or for the young in a hurry, these programs are briefer in length than university professional education yet encompass content and process challenging to the minds, energies, and psyches of women.

Two examples from UCLA Extension will illustrate newly conceived certificate programs with women as the primary enrollees. I quote from the official program descriptions.

PROBATE ADMINISTRATOR

Provides paraprofessional training for adults who wish to develop knowledge and skills as specialists in the administration and transfer of property through estates and trusts and in the fundamentals of legal bibliography and research applicable to probate and related legal matters. Designed as a response to the need for trained paraprofessionals to function as middle-level members of the law office team, between the attorney and the general office staff. A concentrated training program combining theory and applied learning, provided 20 units of credit, and including a minimum of 200 hours of instruction supplemented by assignments, research, and tutorial assistance. Classes are scheduled five days per week for twelve weeks, at the rate of three to five hours of instruction per day.

Program content contains both the concepts and the procedures involved in all aspects of probate, including legal research, estate administration, fiduciary accounting, and income, estate and inheritance taxation. Emphasis on conceptual training as well as training in procedural matters can thus enable the paraprofessional to perform tasks at the discretion of the attorney which traditionally have been performed by the attorney.

Requirements for admission

Each applicant must have a bachelor's degree or its equivalent in education and/or experience, and perform satisfactorily on the entrance examination to be considered for admission to the program. The standardized entrance examination is designed to measure numerical reasoning, critical thinking, concept mastery, and verbal aptitude. The depth to which applicants meet these requirements is evaluated to determine the selection of participants.

Content and format

A comprehensive Curriculum Outline and a Model Estate were developed for student and instructor use by two attorneys who are members of the Advisory Committee and teaching staff. Assignments and examinations are scheduled frequently as learning tools. In addition, all lectures and discussions in each of the fourteen sections are tape recorded for use by students in review and clarification outside class. A two-day comprehensive final examination measures the student's performance, and combines with the student's total performance record of assignments, short examinations, and attendance to comprise certification criteria.

COUNSELING SPECIALIST FOR ADULTS

Provides an alternative to graduate programs for adults with bachelor's degrees who wish to study in an organized and comprehensive approach to the information, theories, and practice of counseling adults in the areas of marriage, family, education, career, retirement, and aging. Designed as a response to the need for an expression of counseling services to a larger and more diverse community population. Offers specialized education to the increasing number of adults interested in becoming instrumental in human services. A concentrated training program of six courses and a practicum combining theory and related practice in adult counseling, providing 24 units of University of California professional credit with a minimum of 240 hours of instruction and supervised practicum.

Student-participants are encouraged to attend special programs and courses outside the Counseling Specialist for Adults program which are related to the areas of adult growth, development, and counseling adults.

Program design

To provide opportunities for interrelated learning experiences throughout the entire program, six courses are organized in two parallel sequences. One sequence of three courses is in the area of "Growth and Crises of the Adult Personality," and the other sequence of three courses includes "Theories and Practice of Adult Counseling." Courses are scheduled in mutually complementary pairs, with one course from each sequence scheduled each quarter. Each course in the first sequence is scheduled with the related course in the second sequence.

The quarter in which the practicum is scheduled is determined by the individual student-participant's academic achievement, readiness for field work experience, and interests.

There are, of course, numerous other programs around the nation. On many campuses, temporary teams of faculty, facilitators, and students are engaged in grand designs for combining the scholarly stance with realities of practitioners.

Whatever the particular combination, I strongly support the idea of certificates or credentials as alternatives to a degree. We need a middle path that will facilitate educational experiences between high school diploma and a bachelor's degree or between a B.A. and a master's or a doctorate. Such validation should be defined as occupational in orientation, related either to a new career or to professional upgrading. In order for a credential or certificate to be valuable, it should be nationally recognized and accepted, as, for example, are CLEP and the more traditional degrees. Thus, a national board or committee would be needed to establish and promote its value. Included in the criteria necessary to foster acceptance are such items as the establishment of measurable performance, the evaluation of competence at the specialist level, and the use of teaching staff who combine academic and professional expertise.

The concept of credentialing was adopted long ago, a B.A. for a certain number of units, an M.A. for additional time, effort, and concentration, and so on. If we are serious about extending the range of alternatives, we may find other designations useful within the concept of recurrent or, to use a now-familiar term, lifelong education.

Part Five

AFFIRMATIVE ACTION

MARGARET L. RUMBARGER

The Great Quota Debate and Other Issues in Affirmative Action

THE PAST MONTHS have witnessed a continuing debate on campuses about the equal employment opportunity requirements for universities and colleges holding federal contracts. It has been argued, for example, that enforcement of the law against discrimination will somehow compromise what in conventional wisdom are the egalitarian principles of professional and scholarly excellence upon which institutions of higher education were founded and have flourished. It has been argued that the traditional prerogatives of departments and faculties will be compromised by affirmative action requirements in the hiring and promotion of faculty. It has been further argued, and I believe more seriously, that affirmative action hiring will discriminate against white men, inasmuch as most colleges and universities are under an obligation to increase the number of women and minority-group personnel on their staffs, both academic and nonacademic.

More specifically, the complaint has been raised that the federal government seems obliquely to be calling for the use of quotas, even if not by name, by making compliance otherwise so expensive and difficult, or the demonstration of good faith so arduous, that as a practical matter administrative instructions to departments would result in preferential hiring, even at the expense of diluting professional quality. Given the current academic job market (which already discriminates against those who have spent the better part of their adult lives in training for employment or in actual employment in the academy), the consternation of young white men turned away or even dismissed in the name of affirmative action poses a particular dilemma for the academic profession.

A case was made in the now-infamous letter quoted by John Bunzel in the *Wall Street Journal*, July 27, 1972, in which an aspiring candidate was informed that

although the Department of ——— saw you as our top candidate we
will not be able to make you an offer for our new position in ———.
——— University is an Affirmative Action Employer and the department must attempt to fill the new position with an individual from a
recognized oppressed minority group. Although the department
initially viewed your ——— ancestry as satisfying the requirements
of Affirmative Action, consultation with our institutional advisors in
the Affirmative Action Program indicated to us that your ancestry
does not qualify you as an oppressed minority.

This and other less stark, but no less overzealous and heavy-handed,
responses to affirmative action cast serious doubt that those in positions of authority understand what it really means. If they understand it, then one suspects that they are reluctant to accept its
implications for their own domination of the academy.

Nondiscrimination and Affirmative Action

It may be helpful to note here some points about the law that
has caused the stir and given rise to a new spectre of quotas and
exclusionary preference in the academic community.

Executive Order 11246, prohibiting discrimination on grounds
of race, sex, color, national origin, and religion by federal contractors, has been the focus of most of the debate within the
academic community. It embodies two concepts: nondiscrimination
and affirmative action. *Nondiscrimination* requires that all remnants
of discriminatory treatment, whether purposeful or inadvertent,
be eliminated. *Affirmative action* requires a contractor to go beyond
the passive stance of not discriminating: it requires him to seek to
employ members of groups which have traditionally been excluded,
thereby mitigating the effect of discrimination in the society at
large. The premise behind affirmative action in the Executive order
is that there is both deliberate and inadvertent discrimination in
employment, and unless positive action is taken to overcome its
effects, a benign neutrality today will only preserve yesterday's
conditions and project them into the future.

The affirmative action concept requires a contractor to determine whether women and minorities are "underutilized" in its work
force and, if so, to develop as a part of his affirmative action program specific goals and timetables designed to "overcome" that
underutilization. Regulations promulgated by the Department of
Labor pursuant to the Executive order define *underutilization* as

"having fewer women or minorities in a particular job than would *reasonably* be expected by their availability." Underutilization is distinguished from a lack of representation resulting from discriminatory employment decisions by the contractor himself. In other words, a contractor must not only remedy identified discrimination against a particular person or group, but must also, if women and minorities are not fairly represented in his work force, make good faith efforts to increase their number.

This concept does not mean that the U.S. Department of Health, Education, and Welfare (the agency designated to monitor compliance in colleges and universities holding federal contracts) is seeking racial, ethnic, or sexual balance in faculties. It does mean that the relative absence of women and minorities on faculties indicates a suspect condition that will require systematic, effective efforts to locate persons from the underrepresented segments and encourage their candidacy. Statistical evidence can serve as an important indicator of whether recruitment and hiring practices (as well as promotion and tenure policies) should be carefully examined for their possible exclusionary effect.

Unfortunately, what affirmative action has meant in practice is often far from its intentions. In order to avoid establishing expensive and time-consuming recruiting programs, for example, an institution or department may simply decide to impose its own kind of quota system: "If HEW wants women, by God they'll get them." The spectre of compensatory hiring (not long ago encouraged in the construction industry by the very same academics who now recoil in horror as it appears in their own backyards) is raised in hushed and not so hushed tones at faculty meetings, the arguments both pro and con assuming that women and minority candidates must be judged by lower standards lest they not make the grade. These quasi-quota systems tend to reinforce stereotypes about women and minorities which we can ill afford to perpetuate. We can compete on our own terms, thank you, and if the rules of the game change to permit a broader and intellectually more defensible definition of what has traditionally been accepted as "quality" and "potential," so much the better.

The arguments of the critics of affirmative action seem to rest on two assumptions. According to the first assumption, we are in a zero-sum game, where efforts to right historical injury to one or more groups will inevitably and necessarily inflict corresponding injury on others. The second assumption maintains that traditional modes of faculty selection have resulted in—if not the best of all possible worlds—at least as good a world as we might aspire to, and thus any change in these modes must be for the worse. The reaction has been, I am sorry to say, an assertion of a proprietary instinct to which we can no longer defer.

Response to affirmative action demands has been curiously contradictory. On the one hand, there has been a sudden reassertion of those standards of excellence which had earlier been under attack from within the academy itself, but which now apparently are to be defended as the last barricade of the white male majority. On the other hand, there have been hasty and ill-conceived efforts to hire women and minorities at any price, in the belief that they cannot hope to compete on equal terms with white men. Thus, "compensatory" measures, conceived as such, are taken to see that women and minorities are included at the banquet table, in accordance with one's conscience and federal directives. The irony of liberal opposition to quotas has been noted by John Rumbarger in a letter to the editor in the May 1972 *Commentary*, for in the not-too-distant future quotas may be the only way for white male chauvinists to remain in academe's grove.

There are, of course, some real and difficult questions confronting the academy as it moves to remedy past injustices in the context of self-imposed or government-directed affirmative action requirements. Are patterns of discrimination against women and minorities in academic employment so deeply imbedded that some more drastic remedy than simple nondiscrimination is called for? To what extent are statistics useful in determining whether discrimination exists, and to what extent are they useful in devising remedies? Under what circumstances, if any, may it be appropriate to take into consideration such factors as race, sex, or ethnic origin in the selection, promotion, and retention process? Should the effectiveness of affirmative action be measured in terms of goals and time-tables or in terms of the institution's record of "good faith efforts"? Should faculties and institutions be required to make explicit their standards and criteria for appointment and promotion, or would open formalization constitute an unwarranted intrusion into the delicate fabric of peer judgments?

The dilemma seemingly reflected in these and related problems confronting the academic profession is illustrated in a simple example I encountered as a staff member of the American Association of University Professors. The Council Committee on Discrimination, having concluded that the association's position on discrimination must be made crystal clear in its operating policy documents, made a very specific recommendation to Committee A on Academic Freedom and Tenure that it incorporate into its Recommended Institutional Regulations a statement to the effect that faculty appointments be made on the basis of prospective fitness as teacher and scholar, without regard to considerations involving prejudice on grounds of race, sex, religion, or national origin. Committee A, considering this seemingly innocuous addition to its policy, was concerned to know what the Committee on Discrimination had in mind by "prejudice" or "discrimination." One member asked whether this statement would prohibit an institution —because of its desire to attract women to fulfill its affirmative action goals—from offering an appointment to A, a woman, over B, a man. Given the context of the debate noted above, adoption of the recommendation in the absence of precise association policy on this and related apparent ambiguities might appear to be reactionary. Should the AAUP state that race and sex are factors which should not be considered *at all*, or only *benignly*? *If* we are in a zero-sum game, does not benign consideration in one case imply *malign* consideration in another? If AAUP were to take the position that race and sex are not to be considered *at all*, could it also continue its active support of efforts among faculties and administrations to rectify decades of injustice by seeking out and appointing qualified women and minorities to now-scarce faculty positions? Above all, are these *real* problems, or are they simply self-generated by an academy that has lost the ability and perhaps even the will to seek out new modes of expression and operation?

The dilemma of Committee A is a real one for the profession, and one which demands hard thinking and reevaluation of past practices and assumptions, including assumptions about such things as "standards" and "quality."

The Committee on Discrimination has recently focused on these and related problems, and hopes to have a statement in draft form to present to Committee A's Council at the end of October.[1] The

1. See "Affirmative Action in Higher Education: A Report by the Council Commission on Discrimination," *AAUP Bulletin* 59 (1973): 178–83.

premise of the AAUP committee's work is that the eradication of all remnants of invidious discrimination *and* the protection of institutional autonomy and academic excellence are two highly desirable and not incompatible goals. But I suspect that its deliberation will produce no simple yardstick or system of measurement for faculties and institutions wishing guidance in this matter. I may be accused of suggesting that the wheel be reinvented, but the problem of "what is discrimination" is not as simple as it appears at first glance. Certainly I have no easy answers. I can say that I do not personally believe that the solution sought by the Democratic party in its 1972 convention (that is, that all groups should be represented according to their presence in the population) can be easily implemented, or is necessarily desirable, in academic employment. Take the case of the predominantly black college which believes that its goals as an educational institution are best furthered by a predominantly black faculty. Can we in justice, and in consideration of valid educational goals, demand that it move toward a balance of all races, in proportion to their presence in the population, or even their availability in the work force? Similarly, those women's colleges that have chosen not to become coeducational and have made this choice for what are, in their view, valid educational reasons would take an analogous position with regard to women faculty.

In spite of our eagerness to move toward eliminating inequities, or perhaps because of it, there has still been some basis for individual concern that the affirmative action concept is in fact operating to deny opportunity to persons on the sole grounds of their race and sex. It is even possible that some university administrators cultivate this overreaction to create divisiveness and hence impotence in their faculties, while using their faculties' so-called intransigence to excuse their own failures to the government and to the groups which they continue to exclude.

Toward Valid Academic Goals

The important issue, it seems to me, is not so much whether an institution will move to include women and minority group persons in its faculty ranks and enhance the status of those who are already there, but, more critically, whether it can afford not to. Once the commitment is made, the issue becomes whether it will be implemented with the same patronizing attitude that virtually assures continuation of the second-class citizenship which has characterized the treatment of women and minorities in the past. I suggest to women and minority persons that we can ill afford to let white males impose quotas even upon themselves for our alleged benefit. We must insist that techniques be developed to afford all persons equal opportunity, based upon clearly understood standards of professional excellence, to serve their students, their colleagues, their institutions, and their community. We must insist that standards which have traditionally assigned women and minorities a priori to a lesser, weaker, and certainly *different* category, be thrown out and new ones be adopted that are based on individual potential as teacher and scholar. These may, in the short run at least, include a candidate's experience and sensitivity as a member of a heretofore excluded group. And we must insist that affirmative action be directed toward bettering the academic community itself and the experience of those within it, not simply toward redistributing pieces of the same old pie. After all, I would hate to think that if women were ever to control the academy, as men now control it, it would be the same as it is today.

The academy *must* change to accommodate this new intellectual capacity. It must do more than simply provide jobs for persons who have been excluded from opportunities to compete; it must also reorganize itself to fulfill its basic commitment to those who are concerned to maintain the academic institution as a vital force in our society. There are fresh ideas, new life perspectives and experiences, valuable intellectual contributions which we cannot afford to leave untapped. We should not talk of diluting standards or debasing criteria, but rather look forward to the transfusion these groups can give to our intellectual life. If our aim is to strengthen the academy in all of its aspects, then we cannot tolerate a continued neglect of these valuable intellectual resources.

The problems arising from affirmative action are real ones, for men and women, black and white, faculty, administrator, trustee, and student alike. One must hope they will be the subject of a more enlightened debate in the future than they have in the past. Nor should criticism of affirmative action be dismissed as pure liberal male chauvinist piggery; certainly the present glutted academic market gives it added force, and in a period of economic retrenchment and scarce jobs, sensitive and difficult issues are raised in the context of efforts to remedy discrimination and exclusion. But these concerns are and must remain technical problems, well within the power of the gathered intellect and ingenuity at any given institution to resolve—given the will to do so. I am convinced that the twin spectres of lost institutional autonomy and debased standards of excellence which have served as the points of attack and rebuttal have obscured the real objectives of the law against discrimination, of women and minority groups, and of the academic institution itself. In the institution, the objective in part is to discover, preserve, and transmit knowledge and experience, not selectively for one group, but for all people.

In the past two decades perhaps no sector has been more vocal than the academic community in its advocacy of equity in educational opportunity, employment, housing, and health care. When the issue of equity comes close to home, the academic community's response should be no less imaginative and intelligent than it has been in dealing with more purely academic problems. The academy should tolerate no sloppy, self-imposed quotas, no harbored attitudes of distaste for newcomers who lack the markings of the traditional academic, no refusal to undertake new and possibly time-consuming efforts to seek out the best teachers and administrators, no subtle (or not so subtle) discouragement of career patterns that do not conform to the "norm." The response must be to seize the opportunity to translate advocacy into results, to persuade slow learners that much can be won by expanding one's horizons, and to acknowledge that much can be lost by refusing to make way for those who demand entrance to the academy and to the profession as a need that confers a right.

LEO KANOWITZ

Some Legal Aspects
of Affirmative Action Programs

SOME OF THE LEGAL and constitutional issues that are raised by the concept of affirmative action programs are of especial interest to institutions of higher education. Stated briefly, these programs require employers subject to them to take positive steps to redress existing sex discrimination in their employment practices or to prevent such discrimination from occurring in the first place.

The circumstances under which a college or university can be required to formulate such an affirmative action program are varied. Recent impetus for their development has come, for example, from the requirements of Executive Order 11246, as amended by E.O. 11375, covering enterprises that contract with the federal government. Since few institutions of higher learning, whether private or public, do not hold substantial federal contracts supporting research or other activities, most have been subject to the affirmative action requirement of that Executive order, which prohibits employment discrimination on the basis of sex, among other grounds.

Where complaints alleging sex discrimination have been brought under title VII of the 1964 Civil Rights Act, the Equal Employment Opportunity Commission (EEOC), which administers that federal statute prohibiting employment discrimination on the basis of race, religion, national origin, or sex, has often, in its conciliation efforts, accepted an employer's agreement to institute an affirmative action program as part of the settlement reached between the complaining party and the employer. Until recently, teachers were exempted from coverage under title VII—as were employees of state and local governments. Congressional repeal of those exemptions early in 1972 now permits affirmative action programs designed to redress a sex imbalance in the work force of higher education institutions to become a common feature of EEOC-supervised settle-

215

ments in that realm, and also to become part of the remedies ordered by the courts in title VII suits affecting such institutions.

We should not overlook the possibility, realized in a number of instances, that a college or university may voluntarily institute an affirmative action program. Perhaps a more accurate description would say that such plans result from a "quasi-voluntary" decision, inasmuch as they are often stimulated by concerned campus groups, such as local Committee W's (on the Status of Women in the Academic Profession) of the American Association of University Professors or by special university committees that have investigated the situation of men and women employees on campus.

At this point I should emphasize that in using the term "employees," rather than "teachers," I chose the word deliberately. Although the most serious problems in this sphere require a substantial increase in the number of women faculty members (to serve as role models for women students, among other reasons) and improvements in their salary and rank, special efforts are also needed to desegregate by sex some of the nonteaching occupations commonly encountered in a campus environment. For example, students (about nine million right now) need exposure to the idea that secretarial or clerical work is an appropriate occupation for men as well as women. Meeting this idea at one of the most crucial stages of their personal development should influence them positively in the occupations they fill in their postcollege and postuniversity days. Of course, should large numbers of men be recruited for secretarial work on our nation's campuses, they would probably not tolerate for long the low wages generally paid to women clerical and secretarial workers. Their inevitable insistence on adequate compensation for their services, coupled with the requirements of title VII and the federal Equal Pay Act of 1963 that no wage discrimination be permitted on the basis of sex, would soon lead to an improvement—much needed—in the economic situation of many thousand women clerks, typists, and secretaries on campuses.

An important question about affirmative action programs is whether they permit "preferential" hiring of women for faculty positions or men for secretarial positions to implement the goals of the Executive order and title VII to end sex stereotyping in our nation's economic life. At first blush, there appear to be some constitutional impediments to this kind of program. A Washington State court, in the 1972 *De Funis* case, has held, for example, that a preferential admissions policy of the University of Washington Law School under which some black students were admitted though their paper credentials (undergraduate grade-point averages and test scores) were less impressive than those of some nonblack applicants who were denied admission, violated the prohibition against official race discrimination implicit in the Fourteenth Amendment's equal protection clause and enunciated in the famous school desegregation decision of 1954, *Brown* v. *Board of Education*. The *De Funis* case was appealed to the Supreme Court of Washington State.[1] Briefs on behalf of the University of Washington and "friends of the court" in that case argued that, for a variety of reasons, discriminatory practices *in favor* of a racial group that had historically been the victims of official discrimination, when those practices are designed to redress the balance, are compatible with both the Fourteenth Amendment's equal protection clause and the *Brown* decision.

A federal court has held the same with regard to the well-known Philadelphia Plan, requiring the hiring of a given percentage of black employees in that area's construction industry, as a specific application of the affirmative action requirements of Executive Order 11246.

One potentially troublesome possibility, surprisingly, may stem from ratification of the Twenty-seventh Amendment to the United States Constitution—Equal Rights Amendment (ERA). That amendment expressly prohibits official sex discrimination. It is generally recognized that the tests for determining whether a violation of the ERA has occurred would be even more stringent than those devised under the Fourteenth Amendment. Thus, even if a state could satisfy the most restrictive test under the Fourteenth Amendment, and thereby justify a sex discriminatory rule by proving that such discrimination is necessary to effectuate a "compelling" or "overwhelming" state interest, it may still be in violation of the ERA. Under the new amendment, official sex discrimination would be absolutely prohibited. A state could not sustain its right to discriminate on grounds of sex even if it established a need to do so in

---

1. The Washington Supreme Court's decision reversed that of the lower court.

order to effectuate a compelling state interest. Only in extremely limited circumstances, as where a person's sex was inextricably related to the area of a state's regulation—for example, permitting only males to be licensed as sperm donors or females as wet nurses —would sex distinctions in the law be permitted under the ERA.

If the standards under the ERA truly surpass those under the Fourteenth Amendment's equal protection clause, the question arises whether the new constitutional amendment might prohibit "benign quotas" or preferential hiring to redress historical discrimination, assuming that such quotas do not presently contravene the existing constitutional guarantees of equal protection and due process.

Given the legislative history of the Equal Rights Amendment, a strong case can be made for the proposition that, despite the amendments absolute prohibition of official sex discrimination, neither Congress nor the amendment's sponsors intended to preclude official action aimed at redressing past sex discrimination, even by according occasional and temporary "preferential" treatment to members of the historically discriminated-against sex group. Should the ERA be ratified, however, this matter would undoubtedly have to be decided by the courts.

MARTHA P. ROGERS

The Role of the Equal Employment Opportunity Commission

WHEN THE EQUAL EMPLOYMENT Opportunity Commission (EEOC) was first given its mandate by Congress in July 1965 to eliminate job discrimination based on race, color, religion, sex, or national origin, academic personnel were excluded from its coverage. Title VII of the Civil Rights Act of 1964, which created the EEOC, specifically exempted faculty and administrators. However, on March 24, 1972, President Nixon signed into law the Equal Employment Opportunity Act of 1972, which amended title VII to include an estimated four million employees of educational institutions.

The years since the passage of the Civil Rights Act have seen a revitalization of the women's rights movement and an increasing focus on the status of women in higher education. Numerous studies, including the 1970 hearings by Representative Edith Green's Special Subcommittee on Education, have examined this problem. Without exception, the studies documented a massive and invidious pattern of discrimination against women in American higher education. During the February 1972 Senate debate on including educational institutions under title VII, Senator Harrison Williams argued:

> Perhaps the most extensive discrimination in educational institutions is found in the treatment of women.... In institutions of higher education women are almost totally absent in the position of academic dean, and are grossly underrepresented in all other major faculty positions. Also, I would add, that this discrimination does not only exist as regards to the acquiring of jobs, but that it is similarly prevalent in the area of salaries and promotions, where studies have shown a well-established pattern of unlawful wage differentials and discriminatory promotion policies.

The Senate twice defeated attempts to continue the exclusion of employees of educational institutions. The Senate took the position that practices complained of in educational institutions paralleled illegal actions encountered in business. More important, it is essential that these employees be given the same opportunity to redress their grievances as were available to other employees in the other sectors of business. But, first, a few words about how the complaint process works.

A complaint of discrimination may be filed by (1) an individual, (2) one of the five EEOC commissioners, or (3) an individual or organization filing on behalf of another individual. After an investigation, if a finding of discrimination is made and the respondent fails to conciliate the charge, the individual may file suit or the commission, under the 1972 amendment, may elect to file suit. Although the EEOC may file suit against private institutions, suits against state universities will be handled slightly differently: only the U.S. Attorney General may bring suit against a state university. Up to October 1972, no such suit has been filed by either the EEOC or the Justice Department.

What has happened at EEOC vis-à-vis the academic community since March 24, 1972? To be brutally honest, the EEOC must profess ignorance about how institutions of higher learning operate, how faculty decisions are made, and what employment processes exist. The commission is currently developing procedures for handling charges of discrimination from the educational sector and attempting to develop a sensitivity to employment problems unique to academia, such as tenure and antinepotism policies. In order to ensure that informed judgments are made in developing commission policy, the commission has enlisted the services of George La Noue, professor of political science, formerly of Columbia University and now on leave from the University of Maryland. He will be meeting with professional groups and women and minority group members in the academic community.

Some persons view the commission's new jurisdiction as unwarranted interference with the right of the university to deal with its professional personnel according to traditional academic norms and standards. The point is: the EEOC *responds* to complaints. The commission does not initiate compliance reviews; it investigates charges. Because no uniform set of rules has yet been devised, complaints will be handled on a case-by-case basis. However, the Commission will attempt to apply what it has learned in seven years about combating job discrimination in the industrial sector.

Because the EEOC's practical knowledge in academic matters has been limited, I shall cite some analogies with the commission's experience in the industrial sector, recognizing that not all analogies are accurate. How could a pattern of sex discrimination develop and thrive in institutions whose members most pride themselves on objectivity and enlightened social policies? The answer seems to be: the same way as in industry.

Recruitment policies offer an example. Theodore Caplow and R. J. McGee, in *The Academic Marketplace*,[1] indicate that available positions are not advertised regularly. Rather, names of candidates and job openings are transmitted through informal channels consisting primarily of department heads and senior men in the discipline, usually at the annual or regional meetings of the discipline, and through personal contact and correspondence. Admittedly, *The Academic Marketplace* was published in 1958; some of these policies are changing; and advertising faculty positions has become widespread in some disciplines. However, a closed system of recruiting is still characteristic in many institutions and clearly works to the disadvantage of women and any other groups not already in "the system." Analogously, the EEOC found that a word-of-mouth recruitment policy conducted by a substantially all-white work force, without supplementary recruitment in the minority community, violated title VII. As the court said in *Parham v. Southwestern Bell* (CA-8, October 28, 1970): "With an almost entirely white workforce, it is hardly surprising that such a system of recruitment produced few, if any, black applicants. As might be expected, existing white employees tended to recommend their own relatives, friends, and neighbors, who would likely be of the same race." Likewise, it is probable than an overwhelmingly white male faculty would perpetuate itself by the same methods.

Employee selection techniques and promotion standards offer another means to discriminate unlawfully. In order to remedy inequities that exist, institutions of higher learning may have to reexamine their hiring standards in light of the new social sensitivity

1. Garden City, N.Y.: Doubleday & Co., 1958.

and new law. In the *Griggs v. Duke Power Company* decision, the U.S. Supreme Court ruled unanimously that title VII prohibits the use of such employment criteria as standardized tests and educational requirements in the hiring, transfer, or promotion of employees *where the employment criteria are not job-related and the use of such criteria has a disproportionately adverse effect on minority group members.* In the words of the Court: "Congress did not intend by title VII, however, to guarantee a job to every person regardless of qualifications. In short, the Act does not command that any person be hired simply because he was formerly a subject of discrimination or because he is a member of a minority group. . . . Congress has not commanded that the less qualified be preferred over the better qualified simply because of minority origins."

The commission, too, will be examining hiring standards in the academic community. It will be attempting to determine the "job-relatedness" of procedures, whether they are relevant to the ability to perform, and whether they are used to exclude minorities and women.

Another concern of the commission has been maternity leave policies. Policies that discriminate against women and severely hamper their careers are widespread in both industry and education. Many educational institutions maintain mandatory pregnancy leave policies which result in the loss of tenure and seniority. The EEOC issued revised Guidelines on Sex Discrimination in April 1972 which state that disabilities caused or contributed to by pregnancy are, for all job-related purposes, temporary disabilities. Although there are no court cases testing this guideline as such, a court decision on this topic was handed down on September 15, 1972, in the case of *Cohen v. Chesterfield County School Board.* This case was decided on constitutional, rather than title VII, grounds. The Fourth U.S. Circuit Court of Appeals ruled that the school board's policy of *requiring* teachers to take leaves of absence after the fifth month of pregnancy was discriminatory. The court said the policy violated the constitutional right to equal protection of the law in that it treated pregnancy differently from other medical situations.

In view of the legal responsibility of employers to provide equal employment opportunity to all individuals, institutions of higher education can no longer be allowed to stand aloof from the skirmishes of the secular world. There is no need here to cite statistics and past history to illustrate the extent of sex discrimination in the academic community for the staggering waste of education and talent among American women is well known. The commission is now empowered to obtain relief for those who have been victims of discrimination in academia. It will pursue that responsibility with seriousness but with some sensitivity to the autonomous role of the unversity in our society. I see no inherent conflict between proper institutional autonomy and the EEOC's goal of ensuring equal protection under the law.

ROBBEN W. FLEMING

The Implementation of
Affirmative Action Programs

THE EMPHASIS of the Council's 1972 meeting is on the role of
women in academia, and I shall, therefore, discuss affirmative action
programs only as they relate to women, though there are equally
important programs for minority groups. Since it is unlikely that
everyone agrees on all dimensions of the topic, I shall state the
point from which I start my analysis.

There has been discrimination against women in academic institutions. One need not concede the discrimination as deliberate to
recognize that it has existed. Indeed, from my point of view, most
of it has not been deliberate unless that term is defined as the product of long-held societal perceptions of the "proper" roles of men
and women. Those perceptions are now changing, as is the law.
Our task in higher education is to work together in eradicating the
discrimination that exists. The cause is little helped by male
prophets of doom who want no change in the status quo or by
female activists who adopt the simplistic view that the only problem is male chauvinism.

The basic elements in an affirmative action program are well
known and need not be repeated here. At the University of Michigan we know that discrimination has existed, and we are spending
substantial amounts of time and money in trying to end it. But I
cannot pretend that there are no problems. Some of them are practical; others have a philosophical overtone.

On the practical side, counterpressures are at work to make
implementation of affirmative action programs difficult. Practically
all colleges and universities are in financial trouble: inflationary
pressures, slackening enrollments, public disenchantment with
higher education, and demands for greater "productivity" from
academic personnel combine to tighten the academic personnel
market. Students of productivity know that in industrial terms a

university would be classified as a high "people" industry, that is, a very high proportion of its budget is in personnel. Significantly increased productivity and accompanying decreased costs can be achieved only by a diminution in personnel. Since both public and private institutions are in financial trouble, and since savings can be attained principally through a reduction in personnel, it follows that openings in the academic world will be fewer in number and the competition for them greater than in the past.

At the same time that pressure is being exerted for greater productivity, there is a general impression abroad—which may or may not turn out to be right—that too many graduate students are being trained to be absorbed by existing markets. Many of the leading graduate schools have deliberately reduced their enrollments, and all are suffering from a reduction in government support in the form of grants and fellowships. Thus, elimination of discrimination against women in graduate schools comes on the scene just when both financial support and opportunities are being reduced.

Finally, the essentially negative character of legislation against discrimination leads to many frustrations which could be alleviated by some positive help. It is easier and cheaper for a legislative body to say that there shall not be discrimination than it is to persuade itself that certain kinds of positive help might do a great deal more to resolve the situation. Two illustrations will make the point.

In recent years an enormous number of men have been enabled to attend graduate school through the support of government grants. Many of them could not have attended without that help. There is "equality" now, but, as noted above, there is insufficient funding for all graduate students. A government-financed program to encourage women and minority groups to attend graduate school would be a step in the right direction, and also give inestimable incentive to departments to enroll such students.

By way of further example, affirmative action employers are exhorted to move women into administrative and executive assignments. Equality with males in competing for these positions means that the normal channels of advancement must be opened up. This is where women have been at a disadvantage. Departmental chairmen are chosen from among senior faculty members; deans usually have the experience of departmental chairmanships; vice-presidents and presidents have invariably had some significant administrative experience. There have been few women on faculties, and they have normally not been considered for academic administrative posts. If this practice is to be altered and if institutions are to appoint top officials with experience, some way must be found to start women on the administrative ladder.

The experience of the past twenty years with respect to men reveals that both foundations and the government recognized a need for additional qualified administrators and therefore established internships whereby persons identified as having potential administrative talent were placed in supporting roles with established administrators in order to gain experience. This same practice for women and minority members would help immeasurably in getting them started in administrative fields, but I do not yet see such financial support emerging.

For some of us, the philosophical problems posed by affirmative action programs have been as difficult as the practical problems. Three examples will illustrate.

One of the first confrontations that usually takes place when the Department of Health, Education, and Welfare comes to a campus in connection with affirmative action concerns the confidentiality of records. In other contexts, university administrators have grown sensitive on this issue. Both students and faculty have felt strongly that information in their files is confidential and ought to be shielded from inquiring government agents. Human nature being what it is, this principle is readily sacrificed by female activists who charge that the university refuses to reveal its files only because it has something to hide. Some of us still think that records are confidential, and believe that one cannot say on one occasion to a government agency that it may not look into our files, and then say on another occasion that it may.

If a university with a poor record of shielding its files from inquiry suddenly stands on principle with respect to information about women employees, there may be valid ground for suspecting its motives. But if the policy of the university to protect files is clear and firmly administered, files are likely to remain confidential. As a practical matter, we at Michigan have found that we can work with HEW in supplying the information it wants without doing violence to our policy. We have been able to do so, I should add, because the HEW people with whom we have worked have shown sensitivity to the problem.

A second matter that has troubled us at Michigan may be identified as "due process." It has been easy for our critics to identify lack of due process when the university deals with a grievant, but much harder for them to agree that in its dealings with HEW the university is entitled to a fair opportunity to present its case. In one initial go-around, for instance, the university was threatened with withdrawal of federal funds, though the conclusion of the HEW investigative team rested on information obtained through unilateral interviews without an opportunity for the university to refute any of the charges. This error was remedied at a higher level of authority, but the matter remains troublesome not only to us but also to all university administrators. It is obvious that adequate hearings delay conclusions, but such is the price to be paid for fair proceedings. In the long run, our critics will stand to gain as much as the universities if fair procedures are applied.

Third, there is that most sensitive of all areas, the question of whether there should be something called "goals" or "quotas" in recruitment. The answer is not easy. If one concedes that there has been discrimination against women and minorities, and I do, then a simple argument in equity can be made for preferment in employment until such time as equity is achieved. Unfortunately, the problem is not that simple. America is a country of minorities, and preferment for one only leads to demands for preferment for another. This situation is documented by an affirmative action proposal published in the *Federal Register* as a possible addition to chapter 60 of title 41 of the Code of Federal Regulations, part 60-30. It is designed to promote equal employment opportunities for various religious and ethnic minorities, such as Jews, Catholics, Italians, Greeks, Poles, and Slovaks. Carried to its logical extreme, the principle of preference is unworkable. It is worth noting how many Jewish groups, themselves long-time targets of discrimination, register opposition to the principle of preference. Out of a bitter experience, they see how divisive it is and how unworkable it is when claimed by all groups that can show one form or another of discrimination. Regardless of views on goals and quotas, we are likely to have them unless we voluntarily do a first-class job of recruiting women and minorities and unless we display complete bona fides in considering and hiring them. Whether we will do so remains to be seen.

Finally, there is a factor that we view with mixed emotions. The University of Michigan has grown great partly because it is a decentralized university. We at the central administration level have known that deans and directors are likely to know more about their business than we do, and that their performance is likely to be better if they have considerable authority. One effect of the affirmative action programs (along with such other legislation as the application of unemployment compensation laws to universities) has been that we are having to run an increasingly centralized shop. We will find it difficult to permit disparate practices which expose us to the claim that we are inconsistent even though in the past we have thought these differences justified. The sheer volume of the enforcement problem makes it unlikely that any agency charged with monitoring affirmative action programs can spend the time necessary to differentiate between practices within a university. Therefore, when another set of critics belabors us for inflexibility and unwillingness to adjust to the individual problems that arise, we find ourselves pressed on the affirmative action front to make our practices conform to a single model.

Although I have dwelt on some of the problems connected with affirmative action programs, I do not wish to be understood to be opposed to the objectives they seek to accomplish, or to be listed in the ranks of those who propose to be dragged kicking and screaming into a new world. We will, in fact, do everything we can at the University of Michigan to eliminate discrimination, and to make our affirmative action programs effective.

KATHERINE M. KLOTZBURGER

Advisory Committee Role in Constructing Affirmative Action Programs

WHAT ROLE can an ad hoc advisory committee contribute to the construction of an affirmative action plan? The experiences of the Chancellor's Advisory Committee on the Status of Women at the City University of New York (CUNY) aptly illustrate some functions of such a committee.

In late 1971, Chancellor Robert J. Kibbee appointed the CACSW to recommend changes in policy to redress discrimination against women and to advance the status of women at CUNY. "Its mission is important," said Chancellor Kibbee, "not only for CUNY, but because it suggests a new mechanism for providing university administrators with women's perspective in matters relating to employment of women."

The committee was not assigned a direct role in developing a comprehensive affirmative action program for the university. However, because affirmative action guidelines were, at that time, the sole legal means of achieving equality of opportunity and treatment for women in academe, the committee decided to give particular attention to the university's formulation of an affirmative action program.

The committee early decided that, to carry out its mandate, it must necessarily undertake a comprehensive statistical investigation and assessment of the status of women at CUNY, encompassing an employment inventory in line with affirmative action considerations for federal contractors. As a first step in determining any patterns of job discrimination against women at CUNY, the committee consulted the basic data files only to discover that the computer roster listed employees by last name and first initial, without indication of sex. Clearly, then, a major committee responsibility was

I wish to acknowledge the assistance of Linn Shapiro and Amy Bridges, members of the research staff of the CACSW, in the preparation of this paper.

to devise a method of collecting data that would produce an information base sufficiently accurate to permit identifying problems of, or deficiencies for, women. Such a research function has contrasted with the functioning of other university-appointed advisory committees, which have tended to review policies and individual grievances, solicit views of women associated with the institution, and the like.

The committee study was designed to determine both the status of women at CUNY and the status of CUNY as a federal contractor subject to Executive Order 11246 and the implementing regulations of the U.S. Department of Labor. For example, individual job categories (or wage groupings) were examined for female presence and participation. Data on the CUNY work force were compared to the available labor force both locally and nationally, to ascertain whether women were being underutilized in job categories or wage groupings. For, without the two determinations—the current status of women at CUNY itself and in relation to availability data—the committee could not have developed many of the policies it recommended for removing employment inequities against women.

To carry out the study, the committee employed a research staff trained in data collection and analysis and sensitive to the manifestations of discrimination against women in academe. (Few affirmative action offices, let alone advisory groups on the status of women, within higher education institutions appear to have taken this step.) In carrying out data analyses from this dual perspective—awareness of affirmative action consideration *and* awareness of the needs of women in academe—an essential role that an ad hoc advisory committee serves in constructing an affirmative action program becomes clear: the statistics provide a knowledge base from which the problem areas most significant for women can be determined and the information transmitted to those responsible for writing and implementing affirmative action plans. Furthermore, once the original design has been executed, future researchers can update the materials periodically to reveal progress trends or new areas of need. A few examples of the committee's role in developing this inclusive data base illustrate the operation.

1. *Awareness of affirmative action guidelines.* From the inception of its research, the committee recognized it needed to deter-

mine whether women were underrepresented, on the basis of availability data, in selected job categories. The committee's data on current CUNY employees were compiled by job category, by rank, by department, by college, and by college grouping—senior college, community college. The results were then compared with national and New York City metropolitan area availability figures. Availability data—in academe, a measure of "presence" through the use of census data and earned degrees conferred—constituted the base from which obstacles to equal employment opportunity were analyzed and goals and timetables for remediation developed. This development follows the assumption (upon which affirmative action is based) that opportunities for distinct groups to gain employment (in society and in CUNY) should be at least in proportion to the rates of their presence in society. Within this framework, utilization patterns for women employees can be formulated at each of the functional and organizational levels mentioned—by rank, by department, by college, and so on. Without these basic data for comparison—the profile of current employees, and the availability data—the drafting of affirmative action plans could easily mock affirmative action requirements and the public interest.

Because affirmative action requirements would have profound significance in the status of women in higher education, the committee also surveyed the CUNY affirmative action plans for the twenty colleges in the CUNY system to see whether they conformed to implementing regulations. Overall, the survey showed that, to the extent that the plans presented goals and timetables, few specified how many women employees were to be hired by certain dates. Even the proposed universitywide affirmative action program considered women only as a percentage of total work force; it gave no breakdown of presence or absence of women in job categories.

2. *Sensitivity to sex discrimination in academe.* The committee also recognized the need to examine how certain sex-typed "women's fields" fared in terms of faculty ranks. Researchers unfamiliar with, or insensitive to, the subtle ways in which women face discrimination might not give priority to such an investigation. Our study revealed that rank distribution in the nine CUNY nursing departments differed considerably from rank distribution in the total faculty: in each college, the allocation of faculty lines was

such that nursing departments were allocated upper-rank faculty lines with less frequency than they appeared throughout the colleges. Thus, an overwhelmingly female department experiences de facto discrimination through restricted access to high faculty position (and concomitant higher salary).

Another example of data analyses further illustrates the necessity for a dual perspective in the research. One CUNY office recently investigated the employment of CUNY doctorates within the university and passed the results on to the committee. Data showed that of 440 persons who received their doctorates at City University since 1967, 127, or almost 29 percent, were employed by one of the CUNY colleges. The sex breakdown indicated that women were being employed at a slightly higher percentage rate than men. On the surface, then, these data do not seem to sustain the contention that CUNY hiring policies discriminate against women. But the definitive question has never been asked: Given the number of positions open and the relative proportion of CUNY graduates to other available graduates, are CUNY graduates hired in proportion to their availability? Since the data do not reveal how many positions were open, or the recruitment practice(s), or the availability profile, or the rank at which the persons were hired, it seems fair to suggest that we do not know whether CUNY was discriminating against all of its graduates, against only its women graduates, or not at all.

The absence of an inclusive data base and incisive information, illustrated by the above examples, could only result in less than complete affirmative action plans. From the committee's examination, it must be concluded that few of the CUNY plans seem to take seriously the need for affirmative action for women. One community college spoke of women as a "second priority," and stated efforts need be made only "to secure female representation where they are conspicuous by their absence." One senior college did not even give a sex breakdown for its hiring projections. The committee hopes that the deficiencies occurred because the colleges lacked the data necessary to prepare adequate plans to remedy their respective institutional problems in relation to women. Having supplied the colleges with relevant data through publication of our *Report to the Chancellor* (1972), we further hope that they will clearly assess the status of women within their individual colleges and will, on their own initiative, write and implement affirmative action plans that comply with regulations. And we hope that the CUNY colleges will meet this challenge without being forced to do so by show cause notices, sanctions, or penalties.

The basic argument is that affirmative action cannot be done well unless it is understood in all its complexities by those who are charged to design and implement affirmative action plans. A solid data base requires the dual research perspective we have illustrated. Without such a perspective, it is virtually impossible to collect data that will prove or disprove the existence of sex discrimination.

In the case of CUNY, a major role that an ad hoc advisory committee played was that of helping to provide the requisite data base by designing and collecting information to measure areas in which women are likely to experience discrimination. Too often women have fought to get affirmative action plans written only to find that the plans do not speak to their needs, in part because the data collection and analysis proved to be unrelated to actual problems faced by women in academe.

Advisory committees rarely have implementary powers. In their advisory capacity they make recommendations but are not charged with enforcement. They must, therefore, exert every effort to ensure that resolutions (made from their data) can contribute a solid base for formulation of meaningful affirmative action goals and timetables. To this end, the data collected must be based on feminist and affirmative action concerns and must clearly show where operating policies function to hinder certain groups or classes of employees.

Through appropriate and thoroughgoing data collection and analysis, an advisory committee can help lay the foundation for policy changes, rather than tokenism, as the necessary and proper means to overcome the discriminatory patterns of the system. Although what is statistically acceptable may be debated, the policies that impede women—for that matter, all minority groups—can be eliminated.

Part Six

CONTEXTS FOR DECISION

"Justice as Fairness"
Between Men and Women

IN THIS CONFERENCE ON "Women in Higher Education," I have chosen, for my part, to address the subject from the standpoint of the male. There are a number of reasons for this choice. One is simply that other papers of high competence have already spoken directly to the needs, aspirations, and current position of women. The quality and variety of the contributions attest the rapid growth in the strength and skill of the movement for fairness to women at every level of higher education.

It is probably a matter for some rejoicing that the movement for fairness to women has now advanced to a high level of sophisticated action, argument, and regulation. Earl Cheit tells me it is an axiom of sociology that it is a sure sign of progress when discussion shifts from the ideological to the technical. Nevertheless, it may be fitting to step back and try to consider first principles again, and, because the leaders in this movement have nearly all been women, it may be reasonable to attempt such a restatement from a male starting point.

My second reason for considering the male view is simple: I have some direct knowledge of the topic. Not only have I been a male for some time, but also my own direct experience of higher education came in the twenty-five years between 1936 and 1961, and during that time—whether as undergraduate, graduate student, or administrator—my professional encounters with women were extraordinarily few. It was only as a teacher that I encountered any significant number of women on a professional basis, and it is obvious that in the 1950s the interests and attitudes of most undergraduate women—and many graduates too—were not the same as they are today. I will cite, in passing, the rather comfortable and even smug speeches that both Harvard and Radcliffe administrators used to make then on the advantages of their complex and ambiguous association. It is as plain as day, in retrospect, that the treatment of women in Cambridge in the 1950s was deeply unfair, but few people, men or women, seemed aware of it.

My most serious reason for discussing male views is that I think it is not male chauvinism to say that males are at least half the problem. And here I mean them not as part of a power structure either in government or in the university, nor even as insecure bundles of protective prejudice.

It is obvious that one could urge prudential and political grounds for attention to this topic. Most of the decision points of higher education are still controlled by males (although it is an open question whether any one man occupies a post as critical and commanding as that of Mrs. Edith Green as chairperson of the House Special Subcommittee on Education). Seen from the point of view of the reformer, the practices and prejudices of males are the principal obstacle to change. In almost every subject discussed at this meeting, it is errors of omission and commission by male professionals that have had most to do with the unsatisfactory shape of present affairs. But if I were to remark about males simply in these terms, I should be doing little more than repeating those discussions from a reversed perspective. My emphasis is on males as one-half of the group of human beings who are required by the new currents of our time to think through their own positions on the relative roles and responsibilities of women and men.

There are many ways of addressing the question of relative roles and responsibilities as males do and should see it—historic, sociological, psychological, psychoanalytic, and economic—but the approach that seems to me at once the most straightforward and interesting is to ask what a reasonable person should regard as fair in these matters. To put it another way, as Alan Pifer did in a notable address a year ago, most of the changes now needed in higher education, as elsewhere in our society, are needed as a matter of justice. To put it still a third way, I think these two ways of saying it are the same, because I find myself wholly convinced by the argument of John Rawls that the right way to think about justice between human beings is to think, in his phrase, of "justice as fairness." In his remarkable book *A Theory of Justice*, Professor Rawls has given new life and strength to the grand old notion of the social contract, and I myself have found that the

consideration of some of his determining propositions is most helpful in thinking about what men should think about the roles of men
and women.

"Justice as Fairness"

The core of John Rawls' argument is that the right way to think
about a just society is to ask what basic social and economic arrangements reasonable people would accept as fair if they were
planning to enter upon a social contract without knowing in advance what their own position would be in the society so designed.
They know a good deal about human nature and about the ways
and means of economic and social behavior, but they do not know
whether they themselves will be black or white, rich or poor, old
or young, male or female. What basic rules would they adopt in
this position? The answer which Rawls gives is deceptively simple,
and in fairness to him I state his principles in his own language:

> *First Principle*
> Each person is to have an equal right to the most extensive total
> system of equal liberties compatible with a similar system of liberty
> for all.
>
> *Second Principle*
> Social and economic inequalities are to be arranged so that they are
> both:
> (*a*) to the greatest benefit of the least advantaged. . . .
> (*b*) attached to offices and positions open to all under conditions of
> fair equality of opportunity.[1]

The first principle here comes first and the second comes second,
in the sense that where the two conflict, it is the principle of
liberty that must be respected. This point in itself has critical importance to the relations between men and women in that, if we
accept it, we must take a categorical position against any arrangements not genuinely required by human nature which restrict the
liberty of either sex. But for our purposes the second principle is
even more interesting. What Rawls says about social and economic
inequality, in effect, is that it is justified only if it genuinely serves

---

1. John Rawls, *A Theory of Justice* (Cambridge, Mass.: Harvard University
Press, Belknap Press, 1971), p. 302. My indebtedness to Professor Rawls is so
great in what follows that the least I can do is to combine a word of appreciative
thanks to him with a blanket absolution from any responsibility for what I have
done with his ideas.

the interest of the least advantaged members of the society. As a simple example, it can be argued that it is important for the chief surgeon of a medical unit to be spared the heavy physical labor that is a necessary part of complete medical care. It does not destroy this argument to recognize that in a highly tendentious form it is sometimes used to justify extraordinary disparities of wealth as essential to a successful system of economic enterprise. Tested severely, as I believe Rawls intends, all forms of inequality must face a heavy burden of proof: that they are genuinely to the advantage of those at the bottom of the scale.

An especially interesting element in the process by which this initial social contract is formed is what Rawls calls the "veil of ignorance": the parties to the initial contract do not know what their own roles will be. So if we apply the theory now to the relations of men and women, what we must ask our reasonable person to decide is what is fair in these relations, without advance knowledge of whether in the upshot that person will be male or female. This is a question that the male animal does not often ask. What happens if he does?

The first thing that happens is that he has to ask himself about the role of women in a wholly new way. He has to ask what rights and opportunities seem to him so clearly a part of being a free person that he would insist at the outset on their being a part of the social contract for persons of both sexes, since otherwise there is a fifty-fifty chance that he would find himself without them when the veil of ignorance is lifted. If we follow Rawls, as I do, we will put liberty first, and in modern society much would follow from that simple requirement. Liberty in our world surely means freedom of expression, freedom of protest, freedom of association, and freedom from political fear. And I think a person choosing under the "veil of ignorance" would be very careful before accepting any rule that no one should ever embarrass a spouse by free speech.

But again it is the wider implications that are even more interesting. Should not every person have a reasonable right to choice among different kinds of work? Should not every person have a right to an equal role in such relations of partnership as the life of siblings or of married couples? Should not every person be free, within the limits of the resources and opportunities in society as a whole, to test his or her talents and possibilities by whatever kinds of challenge are available to any other person? And while it is true that persons of opposite sex are by that very fact different in a way which is quite fundamental, is there any reason to assume, in the initial contract, or in the marriage contract, or at any other time, that this difference should be allowed to place general and large-scale limits upon the choices of persons of either sex?

In my view, to ask these questions is to answer them. I do not believe that any of us, faced with an even chance of being born in one sex or the other, would vote ahead of time for any avoidable inequality between the two. And the consequence of this proposition, if you accept it, is that every institutionalized differentiation or inequality is open for reexamination.

So far, in one sense, we have done nothing more than provide some basis in moral philosophy for the awakening of consciousness among men. But we must take the argument at least two steps further. First, we must ask a somewhat different question, about the rights to which women may be entitled as women, and, second, we must ask whether in the relation between the sexes there may be kinds of inequality that are justified because they meet the stern test set by Rawls: that they truly serve the interest of the less advantaged party. These questions are not so simple.

The Rights of Women as Women

The first of these questions is so hard that I am glad that my present self-imposed assignment requires me only to show that the question is real. There is no doubt whatever that by the nature of things women can bear children, while men cannot. There is almost as little doubt that this fundamental fact has consequences which are not simply physiological; no difference so great, in any part of human existence, is totally limited in meaning to itself alone. There is an enormous amount of uncertainty, a vast library of myth, and a trash heap of simple nonsense about what this basic difference does and does not signify. But it does not signify nothing. In the process of reproduction the female has a *physical* capacity of the most intimate and ultimate importance, against which the indispensable but episodic *physical* role of the male is inconsequential.

I do not know at all what choices any person would actually make about this capability, from behind the veil of ignorance. I do not know what I would say—and still less what John Rawls would say—about the degree to which we must take for granted what we observe of the present customs of mankind with respect to motherhood. There is, I think, good reason to be doubtful about much of what is readily associated with that role. Indeed the veil of ignorance may also serve to protect us from any automatic belief in things as they are. But still it seems to me, as a matter of logical choice in what Rawls calls the "initial position" before the contract is made, that the capacity for motherhood is so remarkable and so important that it should carry with it a right to choose to make that role as large as is fair to others. If there are things that only a mother can contribute or even that a mother can contribute best, then it seems likely that one of the things one would choose, in advance, is that if one turns out to be a woman and has this capability, one must have the right to exercise it.

Here I am talking not about obligation but about right. The mores of our own and of most other modern societies deal not with the rights but with the obligations of mothers (and fathers too—but I am coming back to them). I do not choose to deal in obligations now, for obligations require a closer showing of need and of reciprocal dependence than I can attempt here. The meaning of rights is quite demanding enough for now, and in the context of today's avant-garde arguments it is already enough to assert the *right* of motherhood.

We live in a time in which the excesses of self-centered and possessive motherhood are not only a banality of popular fiction but also an observed reality in the most sober social inquiry. It follows that I should distinguish sharply between the right to be a mother and the nonright to abuse that status. All I need ask for the moment is that two propositions be accepted: first, there is such a thing as a good mother, and, second, a woman has a right to choose to make that task her first priority. I think that these propositions are evident both in the reality of life as we observe it and in the less embattled process of rational discussion before the social contract is signed. Moreover, I believe that the right to be a mother is not parallel to and congruent with the equally obvious fact of fatherhood. Fathers clearly have essential rights and obligations too, but they really are not quite the same.

So if we return to the initial position and consider what it means for the social contract to recognize the right of motherhood, I think we are forced to recognize the high probability that rational persons, acting under the veil of ignorance, would seek to assure for the female a pair of options that have no precise parallel in the case of the male: one, the option to be a free person with all the opportunities of any other person, male or female; the other, the option to be a mother and to give that choice whatever priority one wishes, consistent with fairness to others.

In one sense, even this simple assertion is open to criticism. In another sense, it seems self-evident, if only on the ground that as a matter of statistical fact the choice of fulfillment through mother-hood, whether excessive or not, is still the first priority of so many millions of females—here and around the world—that those who would deny them the right to make this choice face a most grievous burden of proof.

But let me leave this area where any male must move with much uncertainty and restate my point in what may be less contentious terms. As far as rational analysis can tell us today, and with the exception of certain physical skills like those of speed and strength in competitive athletics, a female is, or can be, just as good as a male in every field of human activity. It *may* not be so—folklore may not be wrong—but there is no evidence that you or I could rely on in framing a fair social contract. So it follows, on the fifty-fifty chance that we'll be women, that we must insist on equal access to all careers, to every profession, and to all the positions of special influence and authority that are covered in John Rawls' rule 2(*b*): that such positions must be "open to all under conditions of fair equality of opportunity."

We have also asserted an equally cardinal right to choose the role of motherhood and to give that role the priority it needs. We have asserted (though without adequate proof) that the common sense view of motherhood as more than fatherhood is right. And we have asserted (or, more accurately, assumed) that we would claim for any woman the right to choose either one of these roles—career or family.

THE RIGHT OF CHOICE

But so far we have not confronted the question that is probably central to the lives of a great many of those who happen to find themselves young women today. What does all this ratiocination tell us, deliberately barren of detail as it is; what does it offer as an answer to the woman who rejects the notion that she must choose one good thing or the other, who is unimpressed by the argument—logically powerful though it may be—that, with all their pains, these choices are wider than those of a mere male? What do we say of the female who knows she has it in her to work well in the open market and also be a mother, in the best and most demanding sense of the role, and who says, as she faces this choice, "I'll take both"—what do we say to her?

The right to make this choice seems to me clear. Certainly it is a premise of this meeting that there can be no rigorous requirement upon women to choose either scholarship or family. That may have been the way of thinking of some academic women in the nineteenth century, but as many as half of the panels of this meeting have dealt in one way or another with our contemporary effort to reconcile both kinds of women's rights. Yet even when we have done all that has been left undone for this purpose, I think it will be true that hard choices will remain. There is no reform which can allow to any person—male or female—more than twenty-four hours a day. We all know individuals of both sexes who have managed to achieve high success in more than one kind of activity; we also know that for most of us, most of the time, effectiveness and achievement are heavily dependent upon quantities of time and effort expended. So I will hazard the guess that after we have done all that we can to remove obvious unfairness and to equalize that part of the work of home and family that is readily shared without regard to sex, the women of the future will still have three different choices to face: the world of work, the world of the family, and the world in which both are combined. And from behind the veil of ignorance, choosing in the initial position, it seems to me, fairness will require that insofar as the resources of society and her own abilities permit, a woman must have the basic right to make any of these three choices. Any given woman at any given time may believe that only one of these choices is right, but it seems to me a fundamental part of liberty that whatever course any one male or female may think best, all of us must recognize the right of others to choose differently. Many of the claims for reform which have been under discussion in this meeting are centered, I think rightly, on the need to widen opportunity for the woman who would be at once professional and maternal. But the opening of this door does not require or justify the closing of the other two.

But before I leave this matter of the married professional woman, let me underline that I am not trying to duck the question of change in the daily responsibilities of the professional who is also a husband and father. It seems to me as obvious as it is important that the male professional in the two-career family should recognize and accept the principle of equal obligation in all of those parts of home and family life where the work can in fact be shared without respect to sex. When I assert that there can be a special importance in the role of the mother, I am as far as can be from suggesting that motherhood requires sole responsibility for household chores or for family shopping or even for feeding and clothing the young. Once we accept a woman's right to choose both marriage and career, the husband who is a part of that choice will himself incur an important set of obligations. The exact shape and limits of those obligations will be as varied as the individuals and the careers involved. But if we go back once more to the initial position, I think that, from behind the veil of ignorance, when you face the problem of the two-career family without knowing which member of that family you will be, your likeliest choice will be for equal obligation and responsibility in all parts of the life of the family, just as far as basic differences of sex permit.

We come now to the last, the most complex and perhaps the most frequent case of all. It is the case defined by John Rawls' second principle of justice, and let me repeat the critical part of that principle: social and economic inequities are justifiable only insofar as they are to the greater benefit of the least advantaged. This principle is applied by Rawls only to public and social institutions, and it is at my own risk that I now attempt to apply it to the family. But it is evident that most families are not two-career families, that in most marriages one partner has a primary responsibility for career and for income, while the other takes the lead with home and family. And unless we are to assert that such arrangements are inherently wrong and unjust, we must suppose that, when they are justified, it is because this arrangement in the end is to the advantage of both parties and specifically to the advantage of whichever one is thought to be at a relative disadvantage.

What is most often wrong in the current patterns of this kind of family is that the professional or bread-winning member takes too much for granted. And it is in this case, even more than in others, that the male has much to learn by placing himself once again in the initial position, behind the veil of ignorance. We badly need a redefinition and reassessment of roles and responsibilities in the one-career family, and much of what is most unfair in our current social arrangements derives from a failure to examine with an open eye the parts of accepted custom which are out of date today—and perhaps always were. We all remember Molière's Bourgeois Gentilhomme and his delighted discovery that he had been speaking prose all his life. Our society is full of fair-minded, kind, upright, and generous men who are making the slightly less appetizing finding that they have spent their lives as male chauvinist pigs. And again I emphasize that I have chosen this general topic because I know something about it myself. But I have not raised this matter merely to make a plea in confession and avoidance. I want to point out instead that both males and females have a right to choose the one-career family, assuming the conditions of the choice are genuinely fair between them. Moreover, in a partnership of this kind the interest of the family as a whole may indeed be served as well or better than by other possible choices. The concept of the spouse as helpmeet is in no way obsolete. Indeed it is the accepted and expected pattern still in most of the executive and professional parts of our society. It is exceedingly improbable that this kind of partnership is out of date, and what is more important for my present purpose is that there is nothing in any theory of justice which allows us to prevent a male and female from making this shared choice.

So we have not two choices for each sex—career and noncareer —but three, the career, the family, or the combination. The principles of justice require us to accept the right of both male and female to make any one of these choices, and the consequent right in marriage to choose a partner whose perferences are compatible. Indeed, one lesson of this analysis is the extraordinary importance of understanding between spouses on exactly this question, and one of the great tests of married people for years to come will be their capacity to adapt to preferences that change. The new consciousness of women is not a trivial fad and it will not go away.

I do not believe that it will sweep from the field more traditional concepts of the organization of the family precisely because there is more than one way for both males and females to treat each other fairly, both in and out of marriage. But what I do expect is that, beyond the struggle for elementary fairness, there is a process of recognition and of reconciliation among different styles of life and marriage which no one, either male or female, has yet fully explored. It is possible, for example, to construct quite a powerful argument on each side of the question whether the professional in a one-career family is at an advantage or a disadvantage as against an opposite number in a two-career situation. We may wish it were not so, but there is a measure of competition in all forms of professional and executive effort, and we simply do not know the degree to which there may be some major difficulty in reconciling rights and opportunities among professionals who make such very different family choices.

In the widest sense, therefore, what we may face is a reassessment and a reconstruction of our sense of the differing and yet compatible forms which the family can take in a fair and open future. What I have tried to suggest here, as a kind of prologue to that inquiry, is that one necessary element in the process must be the constant recollection that only an accident of chromosomes stands between any male and life as a woman. Persistent contemplation of this fact, and of the consequent need to consider what is fair as if one did not know which sex would be one's own, is a powerful stimulus to thought—or so it seems to me.

MASON W. GROSS

Issues of Equality and Equity

FOR ITS ANNUAL MEETING IN 1972, the American Council on Education has chosen as its theme "Women in Higher Education." The function of this paper is to present the context of the troubled times in which the demands of women for equality in our colleges and universities constitute only one set of such demands. If the status of women were the only problem facing our institutions today, a solution might be worked out relatively easily. Instead we have manifold demands for equality, equal opportunity, greater participation, and even new orientation, and each set of demands has been countered by strong protests from those who see their vested interest as being threatened. Furthermore, these conflicts have been staged against a background of increasing costs, a frustrating war, and radically changing life styles. In the center is the college or university president, who must not only hope to achieve some kind of answer to the demands so that his institution can maintain a degree of stability, but must also try to figure out how, over the long run, these changes will affect the character and objectives of the institution.

Note the three key terms above: equality, equality of opportunity, and greater participation. Which of these is the key demand varies with the demanding group. For women, the central term is equality, and equality is demanded in employment, pay, opportunity for advancement, and, in general, absolute equality of status. For minority groups, the demand is for equal opportunity, mainly for admission, financial aid, faculty appointment and advancement, and status. For undergraduates, the demand is for greater participation in decision making at all levels, to give them in these respects a position of almost equal responsibility with faculty and governing boards. Faculty also want greater participation in decision making vis-à-vis the president and the governing board. Alumni, too, seek a greater voice in such matters as selection of the president, athletic policy, and scholarship awards.

Of these various demands, the most comprehensive is participation in decision making. Women will probably not achieve the equality they seek without first achieving greater participation. Minority students, since obtaining more nearly equal opportunity, demand representation at the highest levels of decision making. Faculty and students, in demanding greater participation, are concerned to preserve what they view as their rights against the demands for equality by the other groups. Participation is sought by still others: state governments, in the case of public institutions; municipal governments, who demand something in return for institutional tax exemption.

Most of these demands are put forward as rights, but the justification for them as rights varies. Women demand equality as a right, by which they basically mean that men have no right to deny them equality. Minority groups demand educational opportunity as a right, deriving this from the necessity for education in today's world. Faculties claim greater participation in decision making as a right because they alone have the professional competence necessary to such decision making. Students demand participation in decision making as a right because their futures may be seriously affected by the decisions.

These demands, by their very nature, come into conflict with each other, to generate a further problem: Who decides amongst the various demands? Faculty, students, and the general public traditionally assumed the president's absolute power of decision, but more recently students have discovered the governing board, and faculty have claimed more power for themselves. In all cases, the president's role has recently appeared more as mediator than as sole source of decisions.

What are the various kinds of demands heard today in connection with decision making, and what are the responses to these demands?

STUDENT DEMANDS

I have said that the students significantly demand a more powerful voice in decision making. This demand is by no means a historical novelty, but it has become more insistent in the last few years, for several reasons. The traditional concept of *in loco parentis* is gone, and the students demand to be treated as mature adults. They now have the vote and are gradually acquiring other rights and privileges that were originally reserved for twenty-one-year-olds. In addition, they want a greater voice in determining their education. They want the faculty to grant them membership, and preferably voting membership, on the committees that determine the curriculum and degree requirements. They want to join in the evaluation of the faculty and to be considered on matters of appointment, reappointment, and promotion. In some cases they have even questioned academic tenure, because they see tenure as nullifying the effects of their evaluations of faculty performance. They also seek, and sometimes get, membership, but not necessarily voting membership, on governing boards. In public institutions, they demand, and often win, the right to be heard by the governor and the legislature when they feel the university is being badly treated. At the level of the governing board, they demand that the university sign no contracts with the government, especially secret ones that have implications for warfare. They protest against investing university funds in companies whose profits come from military sources and companies that do business with segregated countries such as South Africa and Rhodesia. Sometimes their spokesmen represent formal decisions passed by regular student government groups. At other times they seem to feel that, being students themselves, they automatically represent student opinion.

Inevitably, these student attitudes arouse defensive opposition. The board perceives itself as having a specific responsibility for the financial welfare of the institution and, therefore, as having a right to conduct those affairs without interference from anyone. They also consider they are the bridge between the university and the general public and, therefore, must determine the role of the university in relation to the national defense or foreign policy. Student protests thus far seem to have had some effect in changing policies but not enough to alter the basic position.

Student protests in curricular affairs have apparently been more effective. Not long ago the undergraduate course of study consisted in large part of required courses or at least required areas of study. Attacks on these requirements seemed to threaten faculty empires and, therefore, faculty rights. (The abolition of the two-year foreign language requirement in some colleges is a case in point.) It is hard to say why these attacks have attained their degree of success.

The faculty prerogative in determining prerequisites in the field of the major has on the whole been maintained, but the area of general education has been considerably loosened up.

FACULTY DEMANDS

The student attack on tenure raises a serious matter for the faculty. On the one hand, faculties cling to the concept as their most basic and inalienable right and constantly seek to shorten the probationary period. In this they are supported by the full force of the American Association of University Professors. Student questioning of this right has not reached significant proportions, but outside agencies, such as some superboards of education for public institutions, have made questioning noises. If academic tenure becomes seriously threatened, a major battle seems certain to ensue.

On the other hand, there are instances where governing boards and presidents, not to mention department chairmen, are being sued by disappointed faculty members who failed to receive anticipated tenure appointments. At issue is the question whether either malice or academic freedom was involved. Should the aggrieved parties win these suits, the concept of tenure as a right would probably be greatly strengthened.

Faculties today are becoming more outspoken about what they believe to be other rights besides academic freedom and tenure, particularly about their right to greater participation in decision making. One example is their insistence on greater participation in the selection of the president and other top administrators. Traditionally, the most important task of the governing board was said to be choosing the president, with the clear assumption that this was their right. Today the boards still insist that this is their duty, but they use advisory committees—of faculty, students, and alumni—to the extent that they can hardly reject or ignore a committee veto or strong recommendation. If the faculty is not considered in the appointment of a new dean, it is fair to predict that he will have many difficulties ahead of him.

Like the students, the faculties also are seeking positions, even without vote, on the governing boards and on important board committees. They are trying to ensure that no important decisions on academic policy are arrived at without prior approval by a faculty senate or other appropriate body, and a bone of contention is whether such a body should be composed exclusively of faculty or should also include students or administrative officers, or both.

Faculties also maintain the right to determine the qualifications for academic degrees, and normally this activity is accepted as their prerogative, without question. Occasionally, however, there is trouble, for example, now, in many colleges, over ROTC. A board may argue that ROTC must be maintained as a public service. The faculty will counter that courses given by the military do not meet academic standards and cannot be counted toward a degree. Students enter the argument by insisting that military forces have no business on an academic campus. On many campuses this problem has not been resolved, and is being kept alive by the continuation of the war. But aside from the emotion aroused by the military aspect of the matter, the basic question is: Who has the right to make the final decision?

In recent years faculties have been turning increasingly to some form of unionization to secure their rights, particularly in regard to salaries. At independent institutions, the usual means employed has been collective bargaining, with the AAUP providing the faculties with most of their data. On public campuses the matter is more complicated, because the faculties feel that they must bargain with the state authorities who, in the last analysis, provide the money to meet the payroll. In such circumstances the governing board sees its responsibilities as being bypassed and its autonomy threatened. This dispute is likely to continue for some time.

Similarly on many public campuses, the nonacademic staff has been unionized, and there have been serious strikes. Here the board finds itself in a confusing position. It is no longer able to operate the university—its obligation—and it is powerless to settle the strike because it does not control the supply of funds.

THE ADMISSION PROBLEMS

Another touchy area is admissions. In an established institution whose overall mission is understood and accepted, the answer is relatively clear: the faculty, which determines the curriculum and degree standards, also determines amongst the applicants who shall be admitted and who must be rejected. Admissions has always been a subject of argument. Some colleges have been accused of being anti-Semitic or otherwise improperly discriminatory. The validity of admission tests has been questioned. Potential athletes have been granted admission despite lower than normal academic credentials. Nonetheless, it has been generally agreed that the responsibility belongs to the faculty, guided by their understanding of the institution's mission.

Recently, however, two types of decisions have been made that struck faculties as assuming their prerogative. In one type, colleges that have been exclusively for men or women have elected to become coeducational. The initiative for change may come from either the faculty or the board. The question is: Who has the power to make the final decision? In 1971, the Rutgers College faculty, supported by the students but with the vocal alumni more reluctant, voted to change from all men to coeducational. The board, pointing out that the university as a whole contained one women's college and four coeducational undergraduate colleges, declined to approve the change on the ground that all the alternatives should remain available. Soon thereafter the sentiment within the college became clearly almost unanimous, in favor of coeducation, and the board changed its vote, to go along. The point is: at no time was there any suggestion that the faculty had the right, on this important issue of admissions, to go ahead on its own.

MINORITY DEMANDS

In the other type of case, some colleges were faced by demands to do more for the educationally and economically underprivileged. Again, Rutgers University is an example. The division of Rutgers in Newark had only about 2 percent blacks among its undergraduates, whereas the city itself was approximately 60 percent black or Puerto Rican. The enrollment proportion did not reflect any anti-black policy of the admissions committee; rather, few blacks applied for admission, and many who did apply were far below normal admissions standards. The black students in the college protested, insisting that passive reception of applications was not enough. Rather, they said, an aggressive recruiting procedure should seek out students who really were motivated to go to college, but either had been advised against applying or couldn't raise even the bus fare to commute.

There was a three-day sit-in, and members of the faculty and administration spent hours considering the matter. At its next meeting, the board voted to increase the class size by admitting as many motivated graduates from the Newark high schools as could be recommended by community groups, to find the necessary funds, and to provide preparatory courses as needed to meet the gaps in their high school education. Similar policies for high school graduates were adopted at the other two principal locations of the university—Camden and New Brunswick–Piscataway.

The admissions policy adopted by the board differed somewhat from the one the faculty had been considering. The faculty, therefore, resented to some degree, not necessarily the policy, but the board's having changed, by itself, an important university policy. To the board, however, the change was much more than one of admissions policy; it represented a new concept of the responsibility of the State University to the people of the state, particularly those who were both economically and educationally underprivileged. Since the adoption of the new policy, the faculty has accepted the responsibility of revising earlier procedures to make the policy more effective.

In many ways, changing admissions policies extensively was only the beginning of new troubles. Inasmuch as most state universities cannot begin to satisfy all the applications they receive, particularly in their professional schools, rejected students or their parents began to protest and even to take their cases to court. They claimed, and probably could prove, that students with lower levels of demonstrated academic accomplishment had been admitted whereas they were rejected. If standard admissions procedures—practiced in this country ever since the serious competition for admission to college began—were to be the absolute rule, then their cases were unanswerable. But if it can be shown that students from inadequate schools simply cannot meet the competition of students from good schools, then the traditional formula is, it would seem, most unjust. And if a state needs professional people among its minority groups, then again a new standard needs to be developed.

So long as the percentage of black students admitted to any college was relatively small, there were few problems about their careers as students. They apparently sought as full integration as possible, and quite often turned out to be outstanding members of the academic community. Black students apparently accepted their own presence in a white man's college and for the most part played their roles in accordance with white man's rules. But as their numbers increased, they began to demand recognition of themselves as black students rather than as guests of the white man. They began to reject much of the curriculum as irrelevant to them and to demand various types of black studies. They demanded that more of the faculty and nonacademic staff be black and in positions of responsibility and authority. They tended to reject integrated housing and to demand a degree of segregated housing that would violate regulations laid down by the U.S. Department of Health, Education, and Welfare. Essentially, they rejected the whole notion that, because of the charity or generosity of the white man, they had been admitted to his college: they were there by right, and they demanded that these rights be recognized.

One problem, probably predictable, is beginning to appear at Rutgers and elsewhere. In admitting students with educationally inadequate preparation, courses designed to give them a more adequate background for college education were instituted. Such courses would not normally carry credits toward a bachelor's degree. Now the pressure is building up to grant credit on the ground that students in college have been taking the courses. Some students refuse to take them, and in the regular courses they more or less dare the instructor to flunk them. These problems have not been solved.

I have been talking about black students, because they are the largest minority group with whom most colleges deal. Similar problems occur with other minority groups—Puerto Ricans, Mexican-Americans, American Indians, and others, depending in large part on the section of the country. In all cases the demands are phrased in terms of rights.

WOMEN'S DEMANDS

One obviously large group making demands and asserting rights, which I deliberately have not considered, is women. The problems here are many and will be dealt with in other papers prepared for this conference. Some problems are special to this group; others are much like the ones I have been discussing. Women have admissions problems: at some of the newly coeducational colleges, the quota for women is all too small, initially at least, as it is also in admissions to graduate schools. Mostly, with the blacks, they demand greater equality of rank and status in the academic hierarchy. They can point out that no woman has been president of a state university (the blacks have achieved at least one). These and similar problems will be dealt with in other papers.

IMPLICATIONS FOR REORIENTATION

Now I propose to consider the question: What next? In the past decade American colleges and universities have been confronted with an unprecedented set of demands, and have responded by inaugurating a tremendous number of changes. Are these changes capable of being assimilated into the traditional college structure, or are they, in effect, bringing about more radical transformations than were originally intended? The most important development has been the number of people involved. The second—already mentioned—is the greatly increased costs. The third is the increasing demand that the university concern itself more with the world as it is today, rather than *sub specie aeternitatis*.

One still frequently hears people talking about higher education as a privilege. The implication clearly is that, while secondary education has become a necessity and therefore a right, further education can make no such claim, and, therefore, the student who wants to go on should expect to bear a large portion of the cost. In 1900, about 5 percent of the college-age population went to college, and they could reasonably be regarded as a privileged group. But when the President of the United States expresses the hope that by 1976 two-thirds of the college-age population will be enrolled in some form of post-high-school institution, the whole concept of the privileged few disappears. The recent flowering of the two-year community colleges at great public expense reflects a changing attitude toward the importance of higher education, and minority students are advised that more education is the only way to escape from the ghetto. In some parts of the United States any high school graduate, and even some who have not graduated, can look forward to admission to some further program of education. If the notion of privilege survives at all, it is only in connection with admission to some particular institution.

In the days when college could be considered a privilege, it meant the opportunity to study the program of courses offered. Assuredly, that program was not conceived with any short-range conception of utility or necessity in mind. It is hard to imagine any eloquent argument establishing one's right to study Xenophon or Tacitus. By 1900, the American curriculum had evolved considerably, but practical utility was still not a source of major concern. The possession of a diploma probably had greater practical value than all the knowledge presumably attested to by its acquisition.

The American colleges then enrolled at least two types of students. One group, probably relatively small, consisted of those who were scholarly and intellectual by nature, who had a genuine love for many of their subjects and would probably shape their careers around them. Those in the second group were supposedly to become the leaders in American society in the years ahead. They would represent the Western cultural tradition and carry it forward. Colleges boasted of the kind of person they turned out—a Harvard man, a Yale man, and so on. And institutional quality might well have been discovered in the way they performed on the football field or in the fraternity. Without question, they thought of themselves as the privileged few.

The curriculum to which these privileged students were exposed is clearly not what the relatively underprivileged are hoping for today but may well find. There is still, to be sure, that percentage of students who are genuinely scholarly by nature, and want a program of intellectual toughness, without demanding any standard of utility. But the greater number have been sold on the idea of practical utility, and will continue to demand that it be demonstrated. Many colleges, particularly some of the newer ones, now boast of the ways in which they are of immediate usefulness to their home communities.

It is worth noting that many black students now in college give evidence of this same difference in objective. On the one hand, some of their most prestigious advisers advocate that they concentrate on useful subjects such as mathematics and economics in the interests of practical advancement. But many of the students demand black studies and black culture, which reflects the earlier American, humanistic interest in preserving the traditional Western culture, regardless of utility.

Obviously, both the fantastic rate of scientific development in the past generation and the growth of technology based on the sciences have encouraged belief in the need for, and the immense value of, the kind of knowledge to be found in our colleges. This kind of knowledge is presumably communicated by good teaching, and thus the quality of teaching moves to the fore. Also, these three developments may arouse the suspicion that older teachers are already out of date but are unreasonably kept in their jobs by academic tenure. The sciences often lend themselves to a kind of teaching which, with audiovisual aids, can be given to very large classes, at least to a degree not possible for classes in poetry or philosophy. The performance of the student can be judged by objective examinations, and the personality of the student need not be known at all. The nature of such teaching has undoubtedly encouraged the feeling, widespread amongst students, that they, as individuals, do not count, and has produced bitter resentment.

The rapidly rising costs, mentioned earlier, have had a major influence in changing educational patterns. Large classes are one way to keep expenses down, especially when routine tasks can be delegated to graduate students, who are at the bottom of the economic ladder. Salaries, both academic and nonacademic, are only one element in the pattern of rising costs, but with unionization on the increase, they will remain a factor. As student-faculty ratios continue to go up in order to offset high costs, student complaints seem certain to grow more insistent, and the lack of personal relations between teacher and students may well bring on the kind of crisis that recently swept through the University of Paris. There is also the danger that rising tuition charges will come into open conflict with the increasing belief in higher education as a right, not to be denied for economic reasons.

In an attempt to justify these costs, most public institutions, and also some private ones, have endeavored to show that they are contributing to the welfare of their communities. Here the students often take the lead in trying to determine the ways in which this help shall be given. Recently the focal point of much of their attention has been the problem of pollution, which, as they see it, calls not so much for long-range research as for immediate action. Similarly, when some new action is announced in the war in Vietnam, students proceed to occupy a university building, presumably in order to force the university to do something about a deplorable war. They reject with contempt the concept of the ivory tower and emphasize the primary importance of today's crises, in which they demand that the university involve itself. They demand, in other words, that the university establish itself as relevant to the world in which they are now living.

Our colleges and universities have not as yet, in my opinion, come up with an answer to this kind of demand. The situation confronting them is new in the history of academia but it is a logical consequence of the new relationship institutions of higher education bear to society. They are considered useful institutions and, as such, they need continually greater and greater financial aid. In times of crisis they have an opportunity to demonstrate their utility, and are called upon to do so. In the present situation, just how this is to be done has not as yet become clear.

All this may seem a long way from the topic with which this paper began—the demands for greater equality and greater participation in decision making. In all the demands, however, there is the importance of *now*. We must now revise our admissions procedures to admit many more students; we must now indicate how we plan to include more representatives of the minorities and of women at all levels in the university structure; we must now revise our course of study to establish greater relevancy to current social problems.

The emphasis is on the immediate, which traditionally has not been a principal concern in the academic world. Yesterday is gone and can be forgotten, and tomorrow won't come unless today is satisfactorily managed. Values are transitory; there are no absolutes. We must find pragmatic solutions.

In summary, the demands with which colleges and universities are being faced today will actually result in indeed drastic changes. Insistence on the right to higher education has already brought about changes in admission policies which will result in an ever greater undergraduate population. One inevitable result is a pervasive atmosphere of impersonality and less concern for individual growth. The great increase in costs will bring about a rising demand for demonstrable utility. The demand for greater community service and greater involvement in current affairs will tend to bring about a change in the evaluation of the work done in the traditional academic modes.

These changes, coming about in recognition of rights, will also affect the nature and responsibilities of governing boards. For state institutions, it seems inevitable that the state government will increase their involvement in the administration of the universities, and for all colleges and universities the composition of the boards will alter drastically, and the power of the boards will have to be shared widely.

I do not evaluate these changes as of now. Universities have been described as devoted to "the life of the mind." Whether this concept can survive is the principal challenge today.

CATHARINE R. STIMPSON

Conflict, Probable; Coalition, Possible: Feminism and the Black Movement

As a child, I learned a strict rule about polite conversation: Race, sex, politics, and religion were taboo. They might be brought up within the family or at school, but never in company. As I grew older, I learned two reasons for the taboo: First, the subjects were so volatile that their introduction transmogrified conversation into controversy or polemic. Second, too many people spoke nothing but nonsense about them. Opinion was inflated into dogma, bias into bibliography, and personal fallacy into public fiat.

My discussion here violates my childhood taboos for its subjects are race, sex, and politics, to all of which many people now ascribe the infallibility of faith. My perspective is that of a middle-class, white, professional woman now working in New York. I am a feminist. That is, I am part of a public movement that seeks to guarantee to all women full political and economic rights, that profoundly questions the ideology and institutions that assign some virtues and talents to men and others to women on the basis of gender alone, that challenges patriarchal modes of social organization, and that believes that the liberation of women will increase the well-being of all.

I do not speak for all feminists. Feminism is neither a monolithic force for which one person might speak, nor, at this moment, a majority force to which most American women subscribe. I do not know what black women or blacks say to each other about feminism, about those black women who are feminists, about black feminism, or about black women in general. My evidence comes from what some black women have said in public or in print.

My thesis is that serious tensions exist between feminism and the black movement, as movements, and between white and black women, as persons. Not only have white feminists often ignored such tensions, but also they have presumed that a natural allegiance

261

among women of all classes and all races will well up, given the chance to do so. The following discussion will outline some of these conflicts, which the unscrupulous easily exploit, and suggest some modest coalitions that might be put together. (Universities may be referred to more often than other types of institutions because I know them better, rather than because they seem better or worse in these matters.)

My subjects are more labyrinthine for a white feminist than one might suspect. She knows that in 1972 more white women have believed in "efforts to strengthen or change women's status in society" than did so in 1971. The 1972 Virginia Slims American Women's Opinion Poll, conducted by Louis Harris and Associates, found that 48 percent of American women "favored" such efforts; 36 percent opposed them; 16 percent were unsure.[1] A year earlier, only 40 percent of American women "favored" such efforts; 42 percent were opposed; 18 percent were unsure. Yet the feminist also knows that most American women dislike feminism as an overt, self-conscious, political movement that supports, channels, and initiates such efforts. Of the women surveyed in 1972, 71 percent agreed with the statement that "If women don't speak up for themselves and confront men on their real problems, nothing will be done about these problems," but 60 percent also agreed that "Women who picket and participate in protests are setting a bad example for their children. Their behavior is undignified and unworthy." The feminist may represent subterranean currents, but she cannot count on their rising to the surface in her support.

Ironically, more white men, whom the feminist accuses of membership in an oppressive class, may support her than black men, whom she may see as an ally in her struggle. In 1972, half of the white men interviewed in the Virginia Slims poll favored the "efforts to strengthen or change women's status in society," but only 47 percent of the black men did so. On the other hand, 50 percent of the black men were "sympathetic" to the "efforts of women's liberation groups," in contrast to only 41 percent of the white men. The white feminist understands that more black women than white accept her rough analysis that being a woman in

1. The data in this section are from *The 1972 Virginia Slims American Women's Opinion Poll*, pp. 2, 4, 6. See Gloria Steinem, "Women Voters Can't Be Trusted," *Ms.*, pp. 47–51, 131, for an analysis of the poll.

America is to be neither the celestial angel nor the pretty wife that myth describes. In 1972, 62 percent of black women favored the efforts to strengthen or change women's status and 67 percent were "sympathetic" to the "efforts of women's liberation groups." Yet black women distrust her.

Surely such contradictions are a symptom of social change.

BLACK WOMEN'S PERCEPTIONS

Despite their radical dissimilarities of experience and of response to their experience, there is an attractive logic in comparing white women as a class and blacks as a class in North America. (It should be noted that my comments apply less well to Latin or Chicano women and to Asian women, each a group that has inherited a unique culture.) White women and blacks share the unhappy consequences of not being white men in a society that white men have dominated. One sign of that domination is the fact that in 1969 white English-speaking men held 96 percent of the jobs paying more than $15,000 a year, 89 percent of those jobs in the public sector, 98 percent in the private.[2] Though white women and blacks have been excluded from public positions of power, they have hardly been deprived of a life sentence at hard labor. Scholarship and the arts have ignored, distorted, or maligned them. Either Divine Intelligence or Natural Destiny, but never human cruelty and error, has been held responsible for their peculiarities, roles, and putative inferiority. In an interesting congruence, those regions most aggressively hostile to blacks have been those most aggressively conservative about women. Of the ten states most reluctant to ratify the Nineteenth Amendment, giving women the vote, nine were below the Mason-Dixon line. The comparison between white women and blacks has been as common among both Americans and foreign observers as it is apt. For example, Mary McLeod Bethune, the magnificent black educator, wrote, "the history of women and the history of Negroes are, in the essential features of their struggle for status, quite parallel."[3]

2. John Kenneth Galbraith, Edwin Kuh, and Lester C. Thurow, "The Galbraith Plan to Promote the Minorities," *New York Times Magazine*, Aug. 22, 1971, p. 35.

3. From an incomplete, undated typescript, "Notes for the Address before the Women's Club," in Gerda Lerner, *Black Women in White America: A Documentary History* (New York: Pantheon Books, 1972), p. xxxv. Lerner's collection

If both women and blacks have been members of an inferior class, even outcasts, then black women have been doubly damned. In the nineteenth century, Sojourner Truth was but one of several black women militants who also worked with the women's rights movements to remove both curses. In the twentieth century, Frances Beale has written, "Let me state here and now that the Black woman can justly be described as a 'slave of a slave.' "[4] The Honorable Shirley Chisholm has said, "I have pointed out time and time again that the harshest discrimination that I have encountered *in the political arena* is anti-feminism—from both males and brainwashed 'Uncle Tom' females."[5] More and more, in the work of such scholars as Robert Staples, Jacquelyne J. Jackson, and Joyce A. Ladner, the notion of the mean black matriarch is being exposed as a deceptive, even cruel illusion. Consequently, it is unsurprising that black women reveal favor of efforts to strengthen or change women's status in society, noted above, or, as Inez Smith Reid describes it, an "empathy for certain specific goals of women's liberation which touch on the functioning of the total American system."[6]

Yet, the distrust that many black women feel for feminism, a distrust that apparently overlaps a general doubt about all white women, remains. A black student leader, who came to the Barnard Women's Center for the first time, not spontaneously, but as a polite response to an invitation, asked bluntly, "Is this Women's Lib?" Reid reports that the black women she interviewed also believed that their interests were "almost diametrically opposed to those of the women's liberation movement."[7] The tone of such

---

is extremely valuable. Other helpful works are: "The Black Woman," an issue of *Black Scholar* 3, no. 4 (December 1971); Toni Cade, ed., *The Black Woman: An Anthology* (New York: New American Library, Signet Book, 1970), 256 pp.; Joyce A. Ladner, *Tomorrow's Tomorrow* (Garden City, N.Y.: Doubleday & Co., 1971), 304 pp.; Inez Smith Reid, *'Together' Black Women* (New York: Emerson Hall, 1972), 383 pp.

4. "Double Jeopardy: To Be Black and Female," in Cade, *The Black Woman*, p. 92. The application of the term "double jeopardy" to black women is not uncommon.

5. "Race, Revolution, and Women," *Black Scholar* 3, no. 4 (December 1971): 20. Italics are hers.

6. *'Together' Black Women*, p. 54. Reid, the executive director of the Black Women's Community Development Foundation, is professor of political science at Barnard College.

7. Ibid., p. 53.

comments ranges from casual indifference to skepticism to hostility.

The reasons for such a rejection are complex. The first pictures of the New Feminism were apparently unappealing to most black women. Its concerns seemed at once remote and trivial. Toni Morrison, the black writer, has said: "The early image of Women's Lib was of an elitist organization made up of upper-middle-class women with the concerns of that class (the percentage of women in professional schools, etc.) and not paying much attention to the problems of most black women, which are not in getting into the labor force but in being upgraded in it, not in getting into medical school but in getting adult education, not in how to exercise freedom from 'the head of the household' but in how to *be* head of the household."[8]

Indeed, many black women, if only because of the pressures of history, if only because of the fissure between what American society was willing to grant and what any person needs in order to live, are already "liberated." Most black women have already earned the self-sufficiency that the white feminist is seeking. Most black women have already nurtured, without much fanfare, the realism, stamina, toughness, and commitment the white feminist proclaims as virtues. As Morrison comments, "Black women have always considered themselves superior to white women. Not racially superior, just superior in terms of their ability to function healthily in the world."[9]

Not only do many black women provide examples of autonomy and heroism that anyone might imitate to his or her profit, but also they have learned how to survive a demographic trend that the white woman has only begun to encounter: the ratio of men to women within a particular racial community. As Professor Jacquelyne J. Jackson has shown, black women have outnumbered black men in America since 1850; white women have outnumbered white men since sometime after 1940. A result has been that

8. Morrison, "What the Black Woman Thinks about Women's Lib," *New York Times Magazine*, Aug. 22, 1971, p. 15.

9. Ibid., p. 64. Morrison's comment is taken out of its immediate context. Her subject is "the growing rage of black women over unions of black men and white women," a source of tension between black women as a group and white women as a group, which may then wash over the white feminists, a minority group within white women as a whole, who may even disapprove of black male–white female unions if they imitate old patterns of domination-submission.

"blacks have had a 'headstart' on whites in developing alternative familial patterns."[10] Black adaptability may become a white gain, a familiar American pattern.

The sense of feminism as a distant event is consistent with, even a part of, another response that white feminists have received to their movement. Many black women and the few black men (Frederick Douglass is one) who have sympathized with the women's movement have told white audiences again and again that race equality is a more urgent need in America than sex equality, that the oppression of blacks has been more brutal than the repression of women, that the sexual exploitation of black women by white men has been far more degrading than the sexual exploitation of white women by white men, especially in communities where black women are more accessible, more vulnerable, than white women. Thus, the black struggle must have priority in the allocation of energy, zeal, and money.

In 1869, at a convention of the Equal Rights Association, Francis Harper, a black orator, abolitionist, and feminist, said, "Being black is more precarious and demanding than being a woman; being black means that every white, including every white working-class woman, can discriminate against you."[11] In 1925, Elsie Johnson McDougald, a Harlem educator and social worker, wrote, "In this matter of sex equality, Negro women have contributed few outstanding militants. Their feminist efforts are directed chiefly towards the realization of the equality of the races, the sex struggle assuming a subordinate place."[12] In 1971, Ladner, the black sociologist, concluded, "Black women do not perceive their enemy to be Black men, but rather the enemy is considered to be the oppressive forces in the larger society which subjugate Black men, women, and children. A preoccupation with the equalization of roles between Black men and women is almost

10. "But Where Are the Men?" *Black Scholar* 3, no. 4 (December 1971): 30–41. The essay appeared in modified form and title, "Where Are the Black Men?" *Ebony*, March 1972, pp. 99–102, 104, 106. Professor Pauli Murray has also noted the effects of the ratio of black men to black women.

11. Elizabeth Cady Stanton, Susan B. Anthony, and Matilda Joslyn Gage, *The History of Woman Suffrage* (2d ed.; Rochester, N.Y.: Charles Mann, 1889), II, 391. The convention was irreparably divided between those who supported suffrage for black men, even at the price of suffrage for women, and those who supported suffrage for women, even at the price of making black men wait. The latter were a minority.

12. Cited in Lerner, *Black Women in White America*, p. 171.

irrelevant when one places it within the context of total priorities related to the survival of the race."[13]

Moreover, if women are black, they are likely to be poor as well. Approximately 30 percent of black families live below the poverty line, but less than 10 percent of all white families in America join them there. To eat may seem more vital than to be a woman in equal partnership with men.

WHITE WOMEN'S TRADITIONAL PERCEPTIONS

Though I believe the general discrimination against women to be more pervasive, more poisonous, and more ancient than any other form of discrimination, I accept the black analysis for America. This view is supported by history: the women's movement has followed the black movement in time, and the women's movement, unlike the black movement, has been discontinuous in time. The black movement evidently has responded to more violent, dramatic, and sustained pressures. The black movement was probably a necessary, if not a sufficient, cause of the great nineteenth-century feminist movement. Some of the women's most passionate and courageous leaders served apprenticeships as abolitionists. They learned an analysis of oppression, an ideology of human rights and liberation, and strategies. Rebelling against the social and psychological strictures on public women, they gained self-confidence. Ironically, the way many male abolitionists treated women impelled the women toward defense of their own rights. For example, the formidable Lucretia Mott and Elizabeth Cady Stanton were forced to sit behind a curtain at a World Anti-Slavery Convention in London in 1840, simply because they were women. That night they resolved that after they returned home, they would hold a meeting on women's rights. Eight years later, at Seneca Falls, New York, they did. To a lesser degree, but similarly, the civil rights movement of the 1960s helped generate the New Feminism.[14]

13. *Tomorrow's Tomorrow*, p. 283. Ladner also uses the term "double jeopardy" to describe "the twin burden of being *Black* and *female*."
14. For substantive detail see Catherine R. Stimpson, "Thy Neighbor's Wife, Thy Neighbor's Servants," in *Woman in Sexist Society*, ed. Vivian Gornick and Barbara K. Moran (New York: Basic Books, 1971), pp. 452–79 (Paperback, Signet [New York: New American Library, 1972]). For another comment about the black movement by white feminists, see Juliet Mitchell, *Woman's Estate* (New York: Pantheon, 1971), pp. 22–24; Shulamith Firestone, *The Dialectic of Sex* (New York: William Morrow, 1970), pp. 119–41.

Despite the myth of their moral superiority, white women have not been innocent bystanders at the scene of American racism. Consciously or unconsciously, voluntarily or involuntarily, they have shared in the fear, distrust, and contempt for black persons; they have benefited from black labor; and they have supported the institutions and laws that have reinforced racism. Even today, 50 percent of American women believe that black progress is too fast; 32 percent, that its pace is acceptable; and only 8 percent, that the pace is too slow; 10 percent are unsure.[15]

A charged symbol of the power that white women have exercised over black women is that white women hire black as domestic workers. This does not say that no white woman has ever been a domestic, or that only white women have maids. Yet in 1969 one out of every five black women at work was a domestic. In popular mythology, the figure of an employer is Miss Ann, who is white; the figure of the cook-laundress-nurse-maid, especially in white mythology, is Aunt Jemima, who is black. The two represent, not simply a difference in power, not simply a difference in race, but a difference in economic class. Feminists have done too little to answer the charge that if more white women abandon the ambiguous pleasures of housework, more black women will be pressed into service. The use of black women as domestics extends to the office as well.

The contradictions that the white feminist confronts when she sees other women doing her dirty work are acutely felt and morally baffling. In the spring of 1972, I was part of a women's coalition at Columbia University. One of our most critical projects was to help thirty university maids (twenty-nine of them black or Puerto Rican) keep their jobs. In brief, the women's coalition charged that the job termination notices, which were given only to women, who were being paid less than male janitors though they said their work was roughly the same, added up to sex discrimination. The university claimed that a budget deficit and the need to reduce that deficit compelled its action. Let me point out the picture of a white professor carrying picket signs and raising money over a microphone for maids. On the one hand, she is supporting some marvelous, strong women who want to keep their jobs and

15. *1972 Virginia Slims Poll*, p. 90. The figures are more promising than those reported from the 1971 survey.

take care of their families. Many of the maids were the sole support of their children. On the other hand, the white professor is showing her solidarity for hands that dust the library stacks from which she takes her books, hands that empty the wastebasket into which she and her colleagues throw unread book advertisements.[16]

Some white women protest that even if white women took on the part of mistress to the master, it was a part they neither wholly chose nor wholly enjoyed. Moreover, such women go on, white women have always been more sensitive to racism than white men. In effect, they have occupied a halfway house between the control room of a society and its ghettos. So doing, they have lacked the power to excise the malignancies they have dimly diagnosed. Although they themselves have not always suffered, they know enough of painful submission and of submitting to pain to sympathize with blacks. This analysis has some merit. Yet it seems frail in comparison to the white woman's record of bigotry, tardiness of protest, and acceptance of privilege. White women did form the Association of Southern Women for the Prevention of Lynching in 1930, but Ida B. Wells Barnett, the black writer, teacher, and organizer, had been fighting against lynching—often at personal cost—for thirty-eight years, and black women often had to prod the association members. The U.S. death rate for white women is now 70.9 per 100,000; the death rate for nonwhite women is 200.7 per 100,000.[17]

It would be folly to exempt white feminists from charges of white racism. The feminist movement also has an unappetizing history of complicity with racists. A suffragist argument was an appeal to white men to give white women the vote in order to

16. In an important essay, Angela Y. Davis notes that black slave women did both field and domestic work and worked both for white masters and in the slave quarters. She suggests that the domestic work black women did in the slave quarters was, paradoxically, a foundation for "some degree of autonomy...in the infinite anguish of ministering to the needs of the men and children around her (who were not necessarily members of her immediate family), she was performing the *only* labor of the slave community which could not be directly and immediately claimed by the oppressor. There was no compensation for work in the fields; it served no useful purpose for the slaves. Domestic labor was the only meaningful labor for the slave community as a whole (discounting as negligible the exceptional situations where slaves received some pay for their work)" ("Reflections on the Black Woman's Role in the Community of Slaves," *Black Scholar* 3, no. 4 (December 1971): 7).

17. *New York Times* report of a U.S. Public Health Survey, Nov. 21, 1971, p. 58.

sustain a monolithic white supremacy over blacks as well as an Anglo-Saxon supremacy over European and Oriental immigrants.[18] In 1867, Henry D. Blackwell, a male feminist, suggested such a strategy in an open letter to Southern legislatures. Not all suffragists liked the strategy, but few vociferously denounced it, and suffragists used it until the vote was won. As for the women's colleges, which were founded because men's colleges refused to admit women, by 1910 not Bryn Mawr nor Mills nor Barnard had a black graduate. Smith and Radcliffe each had four.

CONTINUING CONFLICTS

Contemporary white feminists, like their ante bellum predecessors, deplore racism. Most contemporary Americans say they do. Indeed, a phenomenon of the women's movement has been that some white feminists refer to themselves and other women as "niggers." The best-known use of the analogy is in the song "Woman Is the Nigger of the World," by John Lennon, an Englishman, and Yoko Ono, a Japanese woman. The rhetorical claiming of kinship, which other white radicals have also done, has been a strident irritant. It has gratuitously permitted the feminist to moor herself to the black struggle without having paid the price of being black. It has perpetuated the liberal stereotype of the black as sacrificial victim. So doing, the white feminist has implied that black women and blacks share her sense of worthlessness. The assumption is both arrogant and dubious. Ladner, for example, writes of the black girls she knew in the Saint Louis housing project that was the setting of her book: "A very small number of girls did not speak favorably of being Black, but none wished to be white. The overwhelming majority of them seemed proud of their race, as a factor of life which, although problematic at times, was still real and did not need to be changed."[19]

The white feminist may, through the false romanticism of thinking of herself as black, even slide away from uncomfortably recognizing herself as a sister of the white woman who might abhor much the feminist respects, who might have had a wretched edu-

---

18. A feminist works on a broad variety of women's rights issues; a suffragist concentrated on getting the vote. After the Civil War, suffragists dominated the feminist movement.

19. *Tomorrow's Tomorrow*, p. 82.

cation, who might be paying off a mortgage on a tract house, and who might mutter that busing is a Communist conspiracy.

Perhaps such a perception is as poignantly ironic as it is politically useless. The genuine victim, transcending her victimizers, has achieved self-respect. The partial victim, unable fully to transcend victimizing forces—often literally wedded to them—falls into anxiety, self-doubt, and self-contempt. Such a white feminist is unable to claim either the spoils of triumph or the triumph of knowing herself to be superior to the spoilers.

I believe that the false romanticism is being purged. Few white feminists today seriously compare themselves to blacks. Some still manipulate the analogy between a white woman and a black in order to convince the skeptical that women as women have a rough time in America. Affirmative action plans also group blacks and women together as classes to which attention must be paid. Most white feminists I know are anxious to prove themselves worthy of black support. They hope for as much moral and political unity with the black movement and with black women as possible. They regret black repudiation. In fact, some white women, particularly among students, are so fearful of being called "racist" that they willy-nilly overthrow the baggage of personality in order to meet what they believe to be black demands. The prevailing mode of racism among white feminists toward black women no longer veers toward either overt hostility or callous apathy, but toward condescension. In gestures, words, and pamphlets, blacks are invited to share in white power and glory.

I also suggest that some white feminists are now frankly confused about blacks and black women. A leader of the Women's Political Caucus in an eastern industrial state is disturbed because women, saying they represent the National Welfare Rights Organization, have disrupted meetings. She wonders if her concern reflects a lingering racism, or a class response that may have little to do with racism, or, if her meetings are being disrupted, motives obscure to her or even invalid in the judgment of most reasonable persons.

As acting director of the Barnard College Women's Center, I, too, had an uncomfortable time with a group of black, Latin, and Asian women. The students, who had never before shown any interest in the Women's Center, became the student representatives to the temporary governing board. I found their procedures highly dubious and challenged them. They, in turn, found my procedures both highly questionable and "racist." I believe—perhaps at the risk of both oversimplification and special pleading—two other conflicts were also apparent: (1) There was the conflict between notions of cooperation, which I advocated, and control, which the students wanted, saying that cooperation was simply a word for my control of them. If they lacked control, cooperation would be a dirty joke. White students also argued this point. (2) There was also conflict between one method of internal government, which I was following, and another, which the particular black, Latin, and Asian students were advocating. I took actions that I found both legal and necessary if the Women's Center was to survive. Yet one wonders if one would have moved so quickly, so formally, if the students in question had been white.

Even if white women and the feminists among them had an impeccable history, even if a miraculous leap from confusion were made, feminism and the black movement might still be incompatible. Their internal structures and the general context in which their members live are quite different. Feminism creates moral, political, and psychological bonds among women. I find irrational the fears of both blacks and whites that such bonds might be sexual. Not only is the charge that a feminist must be a lesbian unfounded, but I reject the theory that homosexuals are perverse, evil, or sick. Feminism asks that women question their homes, families, and intimacies. Wives look hard at both husbands and at the institution of marriage. Women look hard both at men and at the accepted definitions of femininity and masculinity. The feminist who is a separatist, which means separating men and women, must create social units that are artificial, new, and without popular appeal—women's communes are an example. Any serious feminist, separatist or no, must rethink the old social units.

The black movement, however, embraces moral, political, social, economic, psychological, and sexual bonds among men, women, and children. It includes, and often celebrates, homes, families, and intimacies. The black who is a separatist, advocating separating, not sexes, but races, need not create new basic social units. In brief, a women's movement, if it is to be politically radical, must be emotionally radical as well. A black movement, if it is to be politically radical, may still be emotionally traditional within its own traditions. Moreover, if a black woman challenges the black community, she is challenging a place of safety within an obviously dangerous white community. If a white woman challenges the white community, she is challenging the place of safety within her own life that has suddenly been perceived as a source of danger.

Perhaps Professor Reid summarized my themes when she summarized two themes that the women in her book expressed about women's liberation: "fear of cooptation or subordination of Black liberation goals through a merger of interests with women's liberation . . . fear of undermining relationships between Black men and Black women."[20]

Still another source of conflict remains: the competition among black men, black women, and white women for the political positions, jobs (including university jobs), and prestige that white men now have. Should Shirley Chisholm, Frances T. "Sissy" Farenthold, or Julian Bond be the first nonwhite or nonmale to be President of the United States? Attributes of race and sex give the competition its intensity and local texture. A white man, looking for his own replacement, may find it easier to hire a black man, rather than a white woman. However, the deep structure of the struggle to replace incumbents is probably the same no matter where it occurs or what parties are involved.

Descriptions I have of the competition are scattered and informal. Most white feminists I know agree that black women, having suffered "double jeopardy," now deserve "double reparations." A correspondent in the West Coast women's movement writes that the Berkeley City Council has experienced divisions between the two radical black men and the one radical white woman which are too sharp for anything constructive to happen. The competition for "civic crumbs" and for the title of "most oppressed" makes it hard "to work for common goals." Another report concerns a committee monitoring implementation of affirmative action where a black man has sided with white men against white women.

One always hears stories. The most hopeful come from institutions where every concerned group has participated fully in drafting affirmative action plans or their equivalents. The most depress-

---

20. *'Together' Black Women*, p. 53.

ing come from institutions where one group or another—the more obvious feminists, the custodial staff—has been excluded from the drafting as well as enforcement process of affirmative action plans or their equivalents. It is unrealistic to the point of Panglossian self-delusion to expect black men, black women, and white women to keep a cheerful, common front if the power and the justice, which they all seek, sift down bit by bit, or if they must be pulled away slowly, bit by bit, before they are carried in new hands. It may also be unrealistic to expect everyone to find such a cheerful, common front in his or her own immediate self-interest.

SOME DIMENSIONS FOR COALITIONS

Stubborn hopefulness, theory, and some actual occurrences convince me that some coalitions are possible between black and white women on issues that clearly affect both as women (for example, decent maternity care). Some coalitions are also possible between all blacks and white women on issues that clearly affect both groups as outsiders (for example, an administration that resists the very notion of affirmative action). Certainly a rough consensus that the times are out of joint, and have been for some years, drifts through the political air.

I submit that the success of coalitions depends on the satisfaction of at least two conditions. First, the white feminist, largely middle class so far, must correct the public impression that she is concerned only with her own well-being. As she has thought through and made known her own sense of oppression, she has appeared solipsistic. To be fair, the media treatment of white feminism has thrown a weird, misleading picture on the national screen. She must reinvigorate a practice adopted by the great figures of the women's movement before the Civil War: the eloquent articulation of an ideology of universal human rights and of a politics of universal civil rights. She must project the vision that animates so many of us, that of the women's movement as a part of a vast attack on injustice, a vast drift toward human dignity and freedom. She must clarify her perception of the profound connections between private sexuality and public behavior and institutions. Finally, she might remember that people who shrink from the label "feminist" may still work diligently for women.

Next, coalitions should have certain characteristics. They should be local, so that members know each other and the issue well. They should be built around a sharply defined "common task and mutual goal,"[21] so that work toward an obvious end will simultaneously stimulate moral fervor, gratify self-interest, loosen the tight knots in which history has tied us, and diffuse hostility, suspicion, and divisive arguments about tactics. They should plan to become obsolete when the common task is more or less done, so that the members may avoid delusions of grandeur, illusions of stability, and demands for loyalty that may conflict with allegiance to a larger struggle. Finally, coalitions must include people from as many groups, classes, and races as the issue demands. For example, the Columbia Women's Affirmative Action Coalition has several constituencies—students, administrators, staff, faculty—which meet both separately and together. In organizing coalitions, the risks that white women in lower-echelon or marginal jobs take must be remembered.

Universities are fertile grounds for coalitions. The citizens of most universities are among the groups most responsive to women's issues—the young, the educated, the single, the divorced or separated, and the black.[22] Yet a university coalition of women, if it reflects the university as a whole, will probably symbolize the divisions that now breed much of the tension between the black movement and feminism. My guess is that the faculty women will be mostly whites and more of the staff women will be blacks. The hierarchy of American life will be again revealed: a white woman in the middle, probably subordinate to a white man; a black woman near the bottom, probably subordinate to both.

Some figures from Columbia University, with its varied employment picture, are suggestive. My informal impression is that, as of March 1972, Columbia had 3,131 faculty members of all ranks: 2,477 men and 654 women. Of the women, 522 were white, 69 black, 41 Oriental, 17 with Spanish surnames, no American Indians, and five "other." It had 442 officials and managers: 296 men and 146 women. Of the women, 112 were white, 27 black, three Oriental, four with Spanish surnames, and no American Indians.

21. The phrase is that of Yolande Ford, a member of the chancellor's staff and director of the Human Relations Program at the University of Maryland, College Park, in a telephone conversation with the author, Aug. 29, 1972.
22. See *Virginia Slims Poll*, pp. 2, 4.

The institution also had 2,575 office and clerical workers: 590 men and 1,985 women. Of the women, 1,305 were white, 450 black, 60 Oriental, 160 with Spanish surnames, and two American Indians. (I have not tried to reconcile the discrepancy between total and breakdown of women office and clerical workers.)

The most promising areas for coalitions are "employment and educational equity for all people."[23] Employment and education are clean issues. Discrimination in each can easily be documented. Equity in each improves material well-being and materially improves the range of each person's choices. A number of legal tools exist to compel equity if equity must be compelled.[24] Other plausible issues for women include: more good day care centers under community control; more security, benefits, and dignity for domestic workers; and strict enforcement of laws against rape, for women of all races, no matter what the race of the man who rapes them, as well as a more humane administration of those laws to guarantee humane treatment of victims.

I once thought that the repeal, or at least the reform, of abortion laws might be a coalition issue. Some black women, such as Florynce Kennedy, the attorney, have worked hard toward repeal of the abortion laws, but abortion has not yet become a coalition issue. Indeed, attitudes about abortion replicate some of the complexities of the relationship between feminism and the black move-

23. The phrase is again Ms. Ford's. A good source of material about discrimination in education and employment against all women is *Discrimination Against Women: Hearings Before the Special Subcommittee on Education of the Committee on Education and Labor,* House of Representatives, 91st Congress, 2d Sess., on § 805, H.R. 16098, Pts. 1–2 (Washington: Government Printing Office, 1971), 615 pp., 1261 pp. Commonly known as the "Green Hearings," for the Hon. Edith Green, who chaired them, they included testimony from both black and white women. I am editing a version for R. R. Bowker Co., forthcoming.

24. *New York Times,* Aug. 22, 1972, p. 45, lists the tools for which the women's movement has worked: (1) Equal Rights Amendment (ERA); (2) title VII of the Civil Rights Act of 1964, which banned sex as well as race discrimination; (3) strengthened powers for the Equal Employment Opportunity Commission (EEOC); (4) Revised Order 4, issued December 1971 by the U.S. Department of Labor, which applies to "companies having at least 50 employees and doing at least $50,000 in Federal Government business a year"; the order also requires affirmative action plans if necessary; (5) extension of the Equal Pay Act, enforced by the U.S. Department of Labor, affecting an estimated 15 million people, requiring equal pay for substantially similar work; (6) new rules of the EEOC, giving more rights to pregnant women, making them eligible for work and for sick pay. The ERA was a goal of the women's rights movement for decades, but many of the other legislative breakthroughs have built on the work of the black movement and other civil rights groups.

ment. White feminists have made abortion a primary issue. The black response has been mixed. Some blacks thought of abortion as another mode of white control of blacks, even of the white destruction of blacks, through a Herod-like attack on the innocent. Hearing this, white feminists amended their demand for abortion to "Abortion on demand, but no forced sterilization." No feminist had ever equated abortion and sterilization anyway; for her, the right to have an abortion was an aspect of the principle that a woman should have the control of her own body.

Other blacks suspected abortions because they were dangerous. Feminists answered that if abortions were legal, they would and should be safe. Still other blacks were convinced that abortions were unethical, even murder. For them, the white feminist may have an argument, but she has no answer, any more than she does for the white person who shares such a conviction. Now, however, some black women and white feminists may be nearer an understanding. The ground of agreement is the right of each woman to freedom of choice in matters of childbearing. Perhaps an indication is a resolution of the National Black Women's Conference in February 1972. Placing abortion in the larger context of family planning, it said: "In recognition that proportionately more black and other minority group women die from butchered abortions we move that: *a*) present abortion laws be changed to allow for inexpensive medically safe abortions, upon request only, *b*) no 'rider' be attached requiring mandatory sterilization, particularly for those women involved in the welfare system, *c*) mandatory counseling be given before a black woman submits to an abortion, and *d*) mandatory post-operative examinations be performed and supportive services be given."[25]

BASIC HUMAN RIGHTS

During the Angela Davis trial a *New York Times Magazine* (June 27, 1971) cover photograph showed in the foreground a table with some books and papers in file folders. In the middle,

25. National Black Women's Conference, Pittsburgh, Feb. 17–20, 1972 (Mimeo.), p. 8. Though I respect Ladner's work immensely, I take sharp exception to some of her remarks about abortion. Listing symptoms of the bankruptcy of American life, she gives the generation gap, drug abuse, pollution, absentee middle-class fathers, and "liberalized abortion laws," as if they were equivalent in evil (*Tomorrow's Tomorrow*, p. 274).

dominating the picture, seated behind the table, was Angela Davis, serious, contemplative, wary, perhaps even contemptuous, her hair in a magnificent Afro. Behind her, looking in the opposite direction, the left part of her jaw hidden behind Davis's hair, was a white woman, her face longer and grimmer than Davis's face. She was in uniform. She was obviously a prison matron or a guard.

The picture could be interpreted as an obscene icon: the black woman on trial, the white woman watching her. I refuse to say that this particular white woman is evil. She was probably simply doing her job and not getting very much money for it. However, white feminists might try to persuade such a white woman that she should work, but should not do that particular work. White feminists might try to persuade such a white woman to see the malice and oppressiveness embodied in the news photo. Only if white feminists reach deep into the white community will they be able to go beyond coalitions with black women or blacks to transform a national citizenry into a national conscience.

The task, enormously difficult, will take years. Performing it, white feminists might most gracefully help create the equitable society we now lack, a society scoured of the lush crust of privilege that sex has brought to so many and race has brought to so many others, among them women. If they can succeed in this task, white women may become more like black women in strength. While they are doing it, an extraordinary spirit might be born. Toni Morrison went to a meeting of white feminists and black activists. Something, she said, might be going on. The "women were talking about human rights rather than sexual rights—something other than a family quarrel, and the air is shivery with possibilities."[26]

26. "What the Black Woman Thinks about Women's Lib," p. 66.

MABEL M. SMYTHE

Feminism and Black Liberation

WHEN WE LOOK at liberation movements in historical perspective, some basic principles seem to emerge, along with common problems, common needs, and common experience.

In all American movements to liberate a segment of the population, the American creed is a potential asset. It sets a moral ideal that is offended by conditions calling for liberation; thus, the failure or refusal to accord equality and justice is seen as a violation of the code.

At the same time, the existence of an ideal of equality encourages people to hide from themselves the reality that the ideal is being breached. Thus many "decent" people have had difficulty in perceiving that black citizens were miserable with their poverty and lack of opportunity, or that women had just cause for dissatisfaction with their traditionally assigned roles. As a result, "consciousness-raising" must necessarily precede the process of liberation, making people aware of the evil to be overcome before enrolling them in activities designed to achieve that end. In this sense, women's liberation and the civil rights movement have traveled the same road.

Liberation movements vary in prestige; they take their status from those engaging in them. In American society, on the color scale, whites have more status than blacks. Among whites, men have higher status. Among social classes, the poor and disadvantaged have lowest status (and less to lose). There is a tendency for higher status groups to coopt and exploit quickly and completely and gains made by any group on a lower level. "Higher echelon groups," says Dr. Charles A. Pinderhughes, "are less repressed, have more status and resources, and encounter less resistance. Thus liberation of women has advanced further and faster than has liberation of blacks."[1]

1. Reply to letter of inquiry from the author, dated June 12, 1972.

This tendency to make progress in accordance with status is shown in the women's movement by the concentration of their advances among the more educated and by their symbolic advances on the executive level. The working-class woman sees less change in her lot than does the talented woman leader, and colleges and universities are the setting of a disproportionate share of the gains, as compared to the factory, the farm, or the household. Similarly, the early gains in the civil rights movement against racism were won in the arenas of higher education, use of railroad sleeping and dining cars, and access to places of public accommodation—none of which was relevant to the life of the black working class.

A difference in the strength of the feminist movement among blacks and whites results from two influences: (1) the simultaneous and competing demands of two areas of liberation have left many black women feeling that their first duty is to black liberation, in itself a demanding and challenging involvement; (2) since black men have been even more repressed by whites than have black women, because of the special nature of white sexual hang-ups regarding the former, black women have often seen their unequal treatment by black men as a kind of compensation—a *quid pro quo* —which makes them view the problem less as male chauvinism than as white racism. My small acquaintance with the movement for Indian liberation suggests a similar situation there.

Yet black women and Indian women, as well, are far from oblivious of the missed opportunities, the lower salaries, the narrower career openings, the higher requirements for promotions. They sometimes feel that their role is the most difficult and their status the most vulnerable of all, partly out of their need to help their men achieve a liberation which can free them to accept the equality of their feminine partners. The problem they face is complex and difficult, and it is small wonder that for the time being many black women are leaving women's liberation to their white sisters.

Given the ambivalence of some black women about the feminist movement, it is nevertheless pertinent to note the parallels between the two movements. The same symbols are important in both: (1) the concern for titles (*Ms.* for feminists; the dignity of *Mr.*, *Mrs.*, or *Miss*—or *Ms.*, for that matter—for blacks); (2) the stretching of limits on access to high-level jobs; (3) the use of courtesies (a negative symbol to feminists; a positive one to blacks after a history of indignities). There is danger to both of being bought off by the symbolic advances that leave relatively untouched the realities underneath the images; leaders are especially susceptible to the trap. The two also share the certain prospect that change depends on their convincing the oppressors that their interests too will be served by progress.

It is now the vogue to try to combine black and female counts so that tokenism can be kept to a minimum, and black and other nonwhite women who serve as professors, executives, directors, trustees, or political appointees are counted twice. (It is no accident that Patricia Roberts Harris is perhaps the top-ranking woman in the country in service as director of major corporations; and she could be appointed to at least double the number of posts if she had not learned in self-defense to say no.) It will require fast footwork and a good deal of cooperation if the two movements are to offer each other the support that could strengthen both, instead of this opportunity to cancel each other out. It must not be expected that either set of rights should give way to the other; both are important, and both must be fulfilled.

The relationships of the feminist movement to racially based movements reveal overwhelmingly similar histories. We can see also, if we look closely, opportunities for those who have the highest status and resources (and who thus encounter least resistance) to wield their influence with vigor on behalf of those whose clout is negligible; the most solid and enduring gains must also be the most fundamental. When we liberate the least of our sisters and our ethnic groups, we ensure improved status and expanded opportunities for all who enjoy relatively greater privileges.

JULIAN H. LEVI

Issues of Accountability

IN A RECENT REPORT, Harold Howe II commented that "about every five years, education in the United States finds a new rallying cry." That practice is a little like the parlor game of cliché, in which players are scored according to their cliché's triteness.

This is the year of accountability: "Accountability is an idea whose time has come." It may be helpful to consider the occasion for this current vogue and then, first, question the subject matter of the accounting, and, second, question to whom the accounting should be made.

It is in no sense surprising that the various publics who view themselves as contributors to higher education, either by voluntary act or forced support through taxation, now inquire about the results they have "purchased." Some reasons for the pressure of their interest are immediately apparent from the sheer immensity of the increases in higher education's enrollments and expenditures and the amount of public support that goes into the enterprise.

In 1939–40, the total undergraduate enrollment in four-year institutions, junior colleges, and graduate schools was 1,494,200. The comparable figure for fall 1970 was 7,920,000, and the projected figure for fall 1971 was 8,475,000.[1] And in 1939–40, expenditures of public and private institutions of higher education for educational and noneducational purposes totaled $762.4 million; in 1964–65, the comparable total was $15.7 billions; for 1971–72 it was estimated at $28.4 billions.[2] Between 1960 and 1971, federal funding to institutions of higher education increased from $1.2 billion to $5.4 billions per annum.[3] In fiscal 1971, the estimated federal obligation to universities and colleges for research and development

1. *A Fact Book on Higher Education* (Washington: American Council on Education), March 1972, p. 2.
2. Ibid., Second issue, 1971, p. 71.106.
3. U.S. Office of Education, *Digest of Educational Statistics, 1963* (Washington: Government Printing Office), p. 73; ibid., *1970*, p. 19.

was $2.4 billions.[4] The total of voluntary support to colleges and universities in 1970–71 has been estimated by the Council for Financial Aid to Education at $1.9 billion, of which public colleges and universities would receive 22 percent.[5]

On the bases of size and financing alone, it is little wonder that accountability has become an issue.

EDUCATION: SORTER AND CERTIFIER

Financial accountability is, however, but one facet of the matter. Planners of educational programs describe the education system as a sorting system. For example, the New York State Commission on the Quality, Cost and Financing of Elementary and Secondary Education considers that a stated objective might be "to provide each student with a marketable skill," and then asks: "But one should first decide whether the sorting system is working properly. Are qualified students failing to prepare themselves for four-year college? Are some students who plan to enter four-year college really desirous of entering the work force by some other route? So we need to develop a choice and channeling policy for occupational education."[6]

The claims for the financial rewards of education are many and variously documented. For example, a study of the Federal College Housing Loan Program stated in its introduction: "The average college graduate earns a lifetime income of more than $600,000; the average high school graduate only $370,000."[7] The college student's investment in his education was, then, calculated as producing an income 67 percent greater than that of a high school graduate. Inevitably, a university catalogue directed toward the adult student would assert that: "Working toward a degree means

4. National Science Foundation, *Federal Funds for Research, Development, and Other Scientific Activities, Fiscal Years 1970, 1971, and 1972*, NSF 71-35 (Washington: Government Printing Office, 1971), p. 81.

5. *Voluntary Support of Education, 1970–71* (New York: Council for Financial Aid to Education, 1972).

6. *Report of the New York State Commission on the Quality, Cost and Financing of Elementary and Secondary Education* [Fleischmann Report] (Advance Copy; New York: The Commission, January 1972), p. 2.65.

7. Albert L. Kraus, "U.S. Financing at Colleges Is Producing Empty Rooms," *Weekly Bond Buyer*, May 8, 1972, Sec. 1, p. 2. See also "Lifetime and Mean Income of Males 25 Years Old and Over, by Years of School Completed: 1949 to 1968," U.S. Bureau of the Census, *Statistical Abstract of the United States: 1971* (Washington: Government Printing Office, 1971), p. 111.

greater earning potential over a lifetime. . . . Working toward a degree can bring advancement on the job."[8] The college then becomes the sorter, certifier, and keeper of the gate, and the college diploma is regarded as the admission card to the realm of higher income, a career, and the good life.

In the light of these pretensions, demands for public control might well be expected, power over admissions, employment, promotion, and tenure policies of institutions of higher education. As one response to these demands, the federal government seeks affirmative action plans from institutions which receive certain measures of federal support. However, as the *New York Times* of April 2, 1972, reported, "a basic difficulty is that nobody seems to have a clear definition of 'goals and timetables.' " The same newspaper story quotes the director of the Office for Civil Rights, Department of Health, Education, and Welfare, as saying: "Nobody knows precisely what a plan should contain. In the commercial context, you can measure the number of people available for a particular position on the basis of information available by race, job, salary level, and geography. There is no similar mechanism for the university."

How, then, does an institution account? The director "strongly denies" that "goals and timetables" are "just a euphemism for quotas." A quota, he says, "means a level of employment is set in a given period of time and a failure to meet a quota would constitute a violation of the employer's commitment. . . . A goal is a target of expected employment, also set by the employer, using his own best judgment of what he can recruit. A failure to meet that goal would not in itself constitute a violation. The standard to be used is good faith effort, not quotas."

The *New York Times*, June 21, 1972, reported the City University of New York was "warned" by the federal Office for Civil Rights "that it must provide certain employment information, including data on the sex and race of all staff members, or face the loss of $13 million in Government research contracts," and "the university was being put on 'clear notice' that continued noncooperation would lead to proceedings for failure to comply," although the director "did not expect that 'drastic enforcement'—the cancellation of federal contracts—would be necessary." The velvet on the glove wears thin despite the assurance that the object was

8. "The Adult Student," *University of Wisconsin—Green Bay.*

only "good faith efforts" toward achieving goals for recruiting women and minority group members.

Hence, the university administration and faculty search and tenure committees are told that their deliberations will be watched by a modest observer, whose adverse judgment of their "good faith effort" could, in this instance, impose loss of a $13 million federal contract with their institution. This, of course, is accountability with some vengeance, not to mention accountability to a functionary who presumably does not claim and, in fact, could not in good faith claim any background or experience in the selection or recruitment of university faculty. Yet that very ignorance could explain the tendency to develop and apply overall percentages to a problem incapable of such analysis.

If education is to be the classifier and the sorter, is there then the right to group by ability? The same New York State Commission on the Quality, Cost and Financing of Elementary and Secondary Education finds ability grouping contaminated, undemocratic, and discriminatory:

> In addition to racial and ethnic isolation in counties, districts and schools, "tracking," which results in further isolation of students *within* schools, is an acknowledged practice in New York City. While the educational merits of ability grouping for all children must be carefully weighed, authorities familiar with New York City schools assert that ability grouping is highly correlated with race and ethnicity.
>
> . . . psychological damage of tracking is profound. The children in the "stupid" classes find it hard even in adulthood to shake the fear that the school was right and that they are really stupid. They, in turn, reject the school and seek other ways of regaining self-esteem. The self-fulfilling prophecy is realized: A child is identified as having a learning deficiency, teachers accept the diagnosis and treat the child as deficient; the child lives up to their negative expectation, whether or not the deficiency, in fact, existed in the first place.[9]

So the sorter may sort, but the consequences of that sorting cast so long a shadow that merit judgments are easily suspect.

THE UNDECLARED WAR: AN ANGRY PUBLIC DEMANDS AN ACCOUNTING

In recent years came the agony of the undeclared war. What followed the disorders of protest on so many campuses can be illus-

9. *Report of the New York State Commission*, p. 4.34.

trated in the Congress, where competition developed between members over who could propose the greatest penalty and forfeiture against the disorderly students. And the cry came from the campus:

> When I began teaching English twenty years ago, I saw myself as taking up the weapons of reason against a world committed to emotionalism, illogical appeals, and rhetorical trickery—a world full of vicious advertisers and propagandists who were determined to corrupt the young minds I was determined to save. Now, as a professor of rhetoric and dean of a liberal arts college, I may seem still to present myself in the same melodramatic light: the valiant champion of rationality against the forces of darkness. But bravely as I may try to hold my pose, both the world and the reasonings of men look more complicated than they did twenty years ago. Even as I turn my weapons on the enemies of reason, you will catch me revealing that I am not quite sure who they are, or whether I am qualified to challenge them.[10]

Colleges and universities act under an illusion if they think they can assert sole rights of governance and accountability and if they assume that the essential public power is thus invested in them. Higher education, both public and private, learned bitter lessons in those years: institutional governance requires loyalty and consent of both affirmer and dissenter; the university disciplinary proceeding cannot be the substitute for the public court, the sheriff and the constable, and the public police power.

Much that had enabled higher education to account according to its own lights evolved from belief that man's intellect was key to his progress and even survival. More recently, man is seen as far more complex: childhood failures in adjustment cripple man's intellectual development; subconscious, often unrecognized social and cultural constraints affect and filter his perceptions. Thus conventional wisdom is questioned; the old verities are regarded as inadequate.

Blackmur, writing in 1955, recognized both a cause and some effects on the higher learning and in the society:

> No amount of reflection has deflected me from the conclusion that the special problem of the humanities in our generation . . . is to struggle against the growth of . . . the new illiteracy and the new intellec-

10. Wayne Booth, *Now Don't Try to Reason with Me* (Chicago: University of Chicago Press, 1970), p. 5.

tual proletariat together with the curious side consequence of these, the new and increasing distrust of the audience by public and quasi-public institutions. All three of these are the results of the appearance, in combination, of mass societies and universal education. . . . we deal not with ignorance but with deformities of knowledge. . . . The old illiteracy was inability to read; as the old literacy involved the habit of reading. The new illiteracy represents those who have been given the tool of reading . . . without being given either the means or skill to read well or the material that ought to be read. The habit of reading in the new illiteracy is not limited to, but is everywhere supplied by, a press almost as illiterate as itself. It is in this way that opinion, instead of knowledge, has come to determine action; the inflammable opinion of the new illiterate is mistaken for the will of the people, so that arson becomes a chief political instrument.[11]

THE QUASI-PUBLIC UTILITY CONCEPT

The issues are taken to the ultimate in the suggestions that the combined impact of external pressures will push higher education closer to the status of a quasi-public utility. The notion is explained by Mortimer as resting on two assumptions: "First, institutions of higher education tend to protect their own vested interests to the detriment of the broader public interest. There is, therefore, a basic conflict of interest between the public and individual institutions. Second, higher education is a commodity or service, similar to electricity and telephones, to be provided to the public at a regulated cost."[12]

The essential characteristic in law of a public utility, quasi or not, is monopoly of an essential service—the railroad, the electric company, the telephone company, or even the sole grain elevator in the agricultural community. Those who assert, either out of belief or arrogance, that higher education as keeper of the gate has the monopoly over admission to the presumed good life, or those who suggest that colleges and universities are ideally fitted to perform a great variety of desirable public services—whether improvement in viniculture, mass medical care, or community development—they also, of course, lay the foundation of a public utility. *A satisfying organizational symmetry may be achieved at the incidental cost of higher education itself.*

11. Richard P. Blackmur, "Toward a Modus Vivendi," *The Lion and the Honeycomb* (New York: Harcourt, Brace & World), pp. 6–7.
12. Kenneth P. Mortimer, *Accountability in Higher Education* (Washington: American Association for Higher Education, February 1972), p. 48.

The force of these various considerations now centers in the problems that colleges and universities encounter in scientific areas. First of all, government support of science is pervasive. The costs of the new technology are generally quite beyond the capacity of the institutional academic budget and thus federal support is sought. Much of that support, however, arrives with strings attached. The recent Mansfield amendment is illustrative. At one time the Department of Defense provided considerable support for basic research. Senator Mansfield's amendment forbidding such expenditures unless they related to a military function or operation generated interest and support from quite disparate groups: (1) Those opposed to the Vietnam policy deplored any relationship between colleges and universities and the Department of Defense. The express restriction in the senator's amendment, for instance, thus provided some faculty and students, in their eyes, reason to invade scientific laboratories and offices where DOD work was being performed. It is their claim that such work is dedicated to the destruction of human life and does not belong on campus. (2) Those opposed to federal support of higher education in any form welcomed the Mansfield amendment as one opportunity to reduce federal support. (3) Cynics acknowledged that the amendment presented an opportunity for a ceremonial washing of hands in which the colleges and universities would be purified from evil entanglement while, it was claimed, appropriations to the National Science Foundation for support of pure science would be increased to cover any slack. Subsequent events demonstrated the degree to which thus far the suggestion of substitute support was cynicism or optimism.

The disparate reactions all evidence a crisis of confidence, which Bevan has described for science in terms applicable as well to higher education:

> We Americans have always regarded ourselves as essentially unique in our commitment to a bright tomorrow. We have steadfastly believed that we can, with appropriate effort, achieve whatever we wish, and over the years science has been seen as a handmaiden to that achievement. In this tradition and flushed by its successes during World War II, the American scientific community turned to the problems of a world at peace and assured their countrymen that, with sufficient funding, anything was possible.
>
> Funding was indeed provided—and in unprecedented amounts. By the mid-1960's, the annual total had in a dozen years grown from $2.8 to

$12.6 billion and was continuing to grow at the rate of 12 percent per year; meanwhile, the leaders of the scientific community were asserting that 15 percent per year was closer to the necessary rate. Then the troubles began. Scientists had based their justification for the large-scale support of science by public resources on the criterion of utility, but had failed to take into account the principle of public accountability and thus had failed to reconcile the traditional laissez-faire philosophy of research with a need for strategies that relate basic studies to socially useful outcomes. More than this, the scientific community had built a closed world of grants and contracts, publications, professional meetings, and committee business that inevitably excluded such matters as public concern and welfare. Thus, when their hand was called on specific national problems—curing cancer, curbing the physical deterioration of the environment, reducing crime rates—they were caught by surprise.

This failure to perceive fully the implications of public support of science has meant many things. Among other things, it has meant that scientists simply have failed to understand the importance of making clear to the nonscientific public the long time lag that usually occurs between the formulation of a scientific concept and its practical application. The average scientist, let alone the average layman, does not readily recall that 100 years separated Babbage's idea of a computing engine and the modern electronic computer, that 40 years were required to get from Oberth's analysis of space propulsion to Sputnik, or that a similar period elapsed between Einstein's paper on stimulated emission and the first laser.[13]

THE COLLEGE AS CHURCH

Yet another cause for disquiet has been described by Wayne Booth in an eloquent address "The College as Church," before a group of Danforth Associates in August 1966, in which he quoted a faculty member:

> What you don't seem to realize is that the students' passion comes from a sense of betrayal by an object of love. Most of these students have no church, no institution whatever into which they could invest their faith or to which they could in full self-respect give their lives. They have, many of them, fallen into the arms of the university as the only institution on earth with any integrity left, the only institution in which truly human qualities and values have a chance for preservation. They *expect* the university to care about intellectual integrity and about human dignity. When they think she has failed them, they fight back in anger.[14]

13. William Bevan, "The Welfare of Science in an Era of Change," *Science* 176 (1972): 990.
14. *Now Don't Try to Reason with Me*, p. 175.

Thus, as the *New York Times* reported, on April 14, 1972, higher education, in its investment and management of endowment funds, is not to be like any other prudent investor; it is, rather, to be an activist "ethical investor," passing judgments on corporate practices that appear to inflict significant "social injury." Social injury is defined as "particularly including a violation or frustration of domestic or international legal norms meant to protect against deprivations of health, safety, or basic freedoms"[15]—a standard most prudent investors, without fanfare and in cold self-interest, would regard as appropriate. The stated new policy may, in fact, be pretense rather than substance. Nevertheless, the ecclesiastical glow remains. If the moral task force which is dispatched by the ethical investor to faraway places will require corporate chaperonage and monitoring, the chairman of the board may well conclude that the company ought not afford the honor of the educational investor.

MR. SURREY PROPOSES AN ACCOUNTING

At one point J. K. Galbraith exhorted educational institutions to take the very practical step of regaining control of their own budgets:

> For many years this control has been undergoing steady erosion. Funds are accepted from the Federal government and, in lesser measure, directly from industrial firms, for research, for teaching and for scholarships for specified purposes or areas. . . . The nineteenth-century entrepreneur who, from his position on the university board, intervened to suppress heresy and insist on proper respect for Christian principles and acquisitive capitalism, exercised only the most trivial influence as compared with the power thus deployed.[16]

At the same time Surrey attacks colleges and universities for supporting the current tax treatment of gifts of appreciated property, saying:

> It is thus clear that our colleges, insofar as such support through "gifts" is concerned, are really receiving nearly all of the support from the government with the "donors" providing very little of their own funds and instead "voting" through the deduction these appropriations of government funds to the colleges.

15. John G. Simon, Charles W. Powers, and Jon P. Gunnemann, *The Ethical Investor* (New Haven, Conn.: Yale University Press, 1972).
16. *The New Industrial State* (Boston: Houghton Mifflin, 1967), pp. 372–73.

> ... government funds are allocated, without questions being asked, to the institution designated by the taxpayers involved.[17]

Hence, Surrey concludes, the federal government should make the decision rather than the private donors: what colleges and universities should be supported, and for what programs, and in what amounts, and under what circumstances. But look at what is threatened in one circumstance.

Some colleges and universities have, by now, been adequately instructed concerning to whom and about what matters they are to give accounting in return for receipt of federal support. In recent years, a few colleges and universities have dropped their ROTC programs. Last year, the chairman of the House Armed Services Committee called on the Department of Defense to impose restrictions on those individual colleges and universities by prohibiting the spending of federal money at such institutions. When the voluntary restrictions were not sufficiently observed, the result was a provision (Section 602) inserted by the House Armed Services Committee in the military procurement bill for Fiscal Year 1973 (H.R. 15495) which prohibits the use of DOD funds at any institution of higher learning which, as a matter of policy, bars military recruiters from its campus or has directed the disestablishment of ROTC units despite the desire of the Armed Services to continue them.

The bill was passed by the House of Representatives on June 27, 1972,[18] but at this writing has not been approved by the Senate.

The universities that have disestablished ROTC units are, with one exception, private (the excepted institution was once private) and thus, historically, have drawn their support from private donors who, Galbraith concluded, exercised only the most trivial influence as compared with the federal government.

For purposes of the present analysis, it is not necessary to agree or disagree with institutions that adopted policies of excluding ROTC units or not permitting military recruitment on campus. It should be sufficient to note that a university faculty may reasonably conclude that academic credit should not be given at their

17. Stanley S. Surrey, "Federal Income Tax Reform: The Varied Approaches Necessary to Replace Tax Expenditures with Direct Governmental Assistance," *Harvard Law Review* 84 (1970): 388–89, 391.

18. See *Congressional Record*, June 27, 1972, pp. H 6130–66.

university for an ROTC course taught where neither the instructor nor course content is subject to university academic choice and approval.

If Surrey's views were adopted in practice, the chairman and influential members of congressional committees, as well as federal executive and administrative bureau chiefs, would become de facto surrogate administrators of higher education. The surrender of academic freedom, deplored and noted by Galbraith, can be avoided only when financial support is available from a plurality of independent sources. The principle is equally applicable to public higher education.

HIGHER EDUCATION—SOCIAL ENGINEER

In early 1972, James S. Coleman, principal author of *Equality of Educational Opportunity*—the Coleman Report—reflected on that document and its uses. His revealing statement began by noting: "The long range impact of the report will probably be to strengthen the move toward evaluating schools in terms of their results rather than their inputs. The idea of evaluating school preformance in terms of student performance is fairly commonplace now, but was less so when the report came out. I think the report helped to strengthen an existing trend. Inputs have been traditional measures of school on the basis of achievement outputs."[19]

This evaluation, of course, is quite different from accountability as it is usually regarded in other enterprises. Although one commercial product is advertised as tasting terrible, most people judge the cook by how things taste. The annual stockholders' meeting receives a profit and loss account in which corporate management states, in effect, how many people have been employed and at what cost, how much in goods and services has been sold and delivered, but finally, and most significantly, whether the operations achieved the purpose of the corporation: Was there a profit or a loss?

Accounting by input says only that the school board, the trustees, and the general public will be told, in elementary and secondary education, for example, that so many teachers were employed, working at so many attendance units, instructing a stated

19. "Coleman on the Coleman Report," *Educational Review*, March 1972, p. 13. The original report, issued in 1966, is a publication of the National Center for Educational Statistics, U.S. Office of Education (Washington: Government Printing Office).

number of children, and carrying out a described number of programs. Few superintendents or boards of education will report that the reading level is equal to, or less than, some standard—in effect, what skills or learning were acquired during the year.

Accordingly, accountability in the expenditure of billions of dollars under title I of the Elementary and Secondary Education Act is almost exclusively in terms of financial application of funds, and, incidentally, not well done. Specifically, the accounting comes down to whether the federal dollars were spent in schools attended primarily by children of poor families, as described in the act, and whether the funds were used for types of activities permitted by U.S. Office of Education regulations. The regulations nowhere provide for base-line studies that would enable an investigator to determine the level of educational attainment prior to the disbursement of federal funds. Testing during the administration of the program has been scant, and the results often are stated in terms not of reading ability and comprehension but, rather, of reading readiness.

Nor is the situation different under titles III and IV of the same Elementary and Secondary Education Act, pursuant to which higher education receives financing to help solve problems in primary and secondary education. The research efforts often produce curriculum materials of various kinds, but classroom performance and achievement and effective teaching are seldom tested.

The process of learning is, of course, not well understood. Many would contend that, like horses, pupils can be led to water but cannot be made to drink. As Coleman puts it: "School superintendents and educators have been reluctant to measure schools by how well the students do. Whether or not they admit it, they feel the primary variation in student performance is not what the schools are doing but what the child comes to school with. Research techniques had not been capable of sorting out the effect of various school inputs."[20]

What follows is a fascinating exposition of accountability in social science research in higher education. The results of the Coleman Report showed, according to the author, "that certain kinds of attendance patterns provide higher achievement for children from lower socio-economic levels." As Coleman acknowledges, the courts, in examining school attendance patterns, looked

20. Ibid., p. 15.

upon this conclusion—and the report—as "some kind of evidence on which they can base a decision." This consequence, according to Coleman commenting on Coleman, now produces dismay: "But I don't think that a judicial decision on whether certain school systems are obeying or disobeying the constitution ought to be based on that evidence." At the same time the author contends the report is "appropriate for legislators and school boards in encouraging the kind of student body mix which can provide achievement benefits," and says social science research is often not used because "it's not commissioned by a policy-making body."

The late Carl Byoir, pioneer public relations man, was equally cynical. Most of his recommendations, he said, told his clients what they already knew, but he charged them a great deal of money so that they would be obliged to take his recommendations seriously. Most legislators and school boards would be reluctant to accept the assumption that the evidence submitted to them as a basis for making policy was of lesser quality than required by a court. Therefore, unless the Byoirism applies, the source of financing the report ought not to matter.

The New York State Commission report cited earlier[21] throws further light on the problem. At one point the report notes:

> The state has made a massive investment in reducing class size in order to raise quality. Unfortunately, however, pupil-to-professional educator ratios vary widely from school district to school district. Personnel resources are not being applied equally throughout the state....
>
> Average teachers' salaries in New York are the highest in the nation, with the exception of Alaska, where pay scales reflect a substantially higher cost of living. In 1970, a New York State teacher received an average salary of $11,100; the national average for the same year was $9,265. This average does not include pension or fringe benefits, which are generous in New York and probably enhance the already favored position of the New York teacher. [P. 1.12]

Now, what has all this accomplished?

> The most striking fact that emerged from our studies of school performance in New York State is the high correlation shown between school success and the socio-economic origin of its pupils. This is

21. *Report of the New York State Commission on the Quality, Cost and Financing of Elementary and Secondary Education*; specific citations are given at close of quotations.

true at all levels of the performance scale. Students whose parents have high incomes and are highly educated tend to do well on all measures of school success (length of time in school, test scores, post-secondary school attendance and occupational success); students on the bottom of the scale tend to do poorly in these same measures; and students from middle-level socio-economic backgrounds tends to perform somewhere in the middle.

The close parallel between school success and the child's socio-economic origin suggests that something is wrong with the way our educational system operates. The commission is well aware that innate learning ability varies widely from student to student, but it has seen no persuasive evidence that such innate ability correlates with family income, race, sex, parental occupation or ethnicity. In theory, therefore, differences in average group levels of performance should be insignificant. In fact, they are not: Equality in educational opportunity does not exist for the student of New York State. We conclude that in schools in which differences in the average performance levels of social class, racial and geographic groups exist, public policy should be directed toward their elimination. [Pp. 1.28–29]

Further:

> Despite the substantial increase in college enrollments, the relationship between a student's social class origins and his educational attainment, which is so crucial in elementary and secondary school, continues to be influential at the post-secondary level. This is a result of a multiple sorting process which has already occurred at lower educational levels. Further stratification takes place within the post-secondary system. [P. 1.48]

" 'Tis the Mill That Makes th' Wather Run"

The New York State Commission, drawing on data gathered by the Office of Research, American Council on Education, concluded that, for students, social class origin continued as a classifying and stratifying factor throughout their careers in higher education. The reasons for their conclusion become apparent from Tables 1–3. Further:

> The connection between parental education and income levels and students' post-secondary school activities is not new. In 1938 the *Regents Inquiry* noted variations by race and social class in high school graduation and college attendance. The 1938 study noted variations in school persistence levels and college attendance by family financial level, race, language spoken in the home and parental occupation. It concluded from these results that:

TABLE 1: *Trends in College-Going Rate, New York State, 1964 to 1970*

Entering Postsecondary Education in the Fall of	Percent of Graduates of Public High Schools Entering			Percent of Graduates of Nonpublic High Schools Entering			Percent of All Graduates Entering			
	Degree-Granting Institutions		Other Post-secondary	Degree-Granting Institutions		Other Post-secondary	Degree-Granting Institutions		Other Post-secondary	Total Post-secondary
	4-Year	2-Year		4-Year	2-Year		4-Year	2-Year		
1964............	37	14	7	55	12	7	41	13	7	61
1965............	36	16	8	56	13	7	38	15	7	60
1966............	32	18	8	53	19	7	35	18	8	61
1967............	35	19	7	56	17	7	39	19	7	65
1968............	37	21	7	56	18	7	40	20	7	67
1969............	37	22	7	57	19	6	41	22	6	69
1970............	38	25	5	58	21	5	42	24	5	71

Source: *Distribution of High School Graduates and College-Going Rate, New York State, Fall 1970* (Albany: New York State Education Department, Information Center on Education), in *Report of the New York State Commission on the Quality, Cost and Financing of Elementary and Secondary Education* (Advance Copy; New York: The Commission, January 1972), p. 1.49.

TABLE 2: *College Attendance by Parental Income and College Type, New York State Freshmen, 1969*

A: *Composition of Institutions by Parental Income*

Institutional Type	Less than $6,000	$6,000–$9,999	$10,000–$14,999	$15,000 Plus	Total*
Percent of total sample....	*12.3*	*31.3*	*29.6*	*26.8*	*100.0*
Private university.......	4.2	11.6	22.1	62.1	100.0
Public university........	4.4	13.2	22.3	60.1	100.0
Private 4-year college....	8.8	21.9	27.9	41.3	99.9
Public 4-year college.....	11.7	36.5	32.1	19.6	99.9
Private 2-year college....	13.5	29.5	31.5	25.6	100.1
Public 2-year college.....	16.8	38.0	29.7	15.5	100.0

B: *Percent of Income Classes in Types of Postsecondary Institutions*

Parental Income	Percentage Attending						
	Private Univ.	Public Univ.	Private 4-Year	Public 4-Year	Private 2-Year	Public 2-Year	Total*
Percent of college population in institutional type..	*4.6*	*4.7*	*17.7*	*31.0*	*11.9*	*30.2*	*100.1*
Less than $6,000....	1.6	1.6	12.7	29.6	13.0	41.4	99.9
$6,000–$9,999.......	1.7	1.9	12.4	36.1	11.2	36.7	100.0
$10,000–$14,999.....	3.5	3.5	16.7	33.5	12.6	30.3	100.1
$15,000 plus........	10.8	10.3	27.3	22.7	11.3	17.5	99.9

Source: American Council on Education, data supplied to the Commission. In *Report of the New York State Commission,* p. 1.51.

* Figures may not total exactly 100 percent because of rounding.

TABLE 3: *College Attendance by Father's Education and College Type, New York State Freshmen, 1969*

A: *Composition of Institutions by Father's Income*

Institutional Type	Less than High School	High School Degree	Some College	College Degree or More	Total*
Percent of total sample....	*27.2*	*32.8*	*16.4*	*23.7*	*100.1*
Private university.......	9.3	20.6	18.9	51.2	100.0
Public university........	9.4	20.1	18.8	51.6	99.9
Private 4-year college....	18.2	26.1	17.7	38.0	100.0
Public 4-year college.....	27.0	35.4	17.3	20.3	100.0
Private 2-year college....	34.2	32.6	15.1	18.1	100.0
Public 2-year college.....	35.3	38.0	14.5	12.3	100.1

B: *Percent of Educational Classes in Types of Postsecondary Institutions*

Father's Education Attainment	Percentage Attending						
	Private Univ.	Public Univ.	Private 4-Year	Public 4-Year	Private 2-Year	Public 2-Year	Total*
Percent of college population in institutional type..	*4.8*	*4.6*	*17.8*	*30.2*	*11.9*	*30.6*	*99.9*
Less than high school	1.7	1.7	11.9	30.1	15.0	39.7	100.1
High school degree..	3.0	2.8	14.2	32.6	11.9	35.5	100.0
Some college........	5.6	5.3	19.2	31.9	11.0	27.1	100.1
College degree or more............	10.4	10.1	28.5	26.0	9.1	15.9	100.0

Source: American Council on Education, data supplied to the Commission. In *Report of the New York State Commission,* p. 1.52.

* Figures may not total exactly 100 percent because of rounding.

"These differences possess far more than statistical significance; they are challenging our whole educational and social plan, for they show clearly that retention in school has varied with the assets or the advantages of pupils. While encouraging variations occur occasionally, the great mass of adolescent boys and girls seem destined to maintain in their generation the economic hierarchy established for the preceding one. It is incumbent upon the school, however, as the only agency in society actively in touch with all boys and girls, to make certain that the accident of birth has not robbed able young people of the opportunity to rise above home limitations."

The study also noted that low-economic status tended to be associated with low-scholastic achievement, but this did not account for all the variation in school performance: "of all the pupils indicating choice that will involve no college study, from a fifth to a fourth are superior in intelligence to the average student specifying some professional goal."

A New York State Education Department study, *Crucial Questions about Higher Education*, revealed that the same problems existed 17 years later. In 1955, 48 per cent of those planning to continue their education were children of men who had some post-secondary education; 24 per cent were the children of college graduates. Only 13 per cent of the youth not continuing their education were the children of college graduates.

A comparison between all high school graduates continuing their education full-time and all graduates whose I.Q.'s were 110 or higher showed that "family income exerts a greater influence upon the decision to pursue higher education than does the ability of high school graduates as indicated by I.Q."

In 1938 and 1955, family characteristics were highly correlated with college-going patterns for New York State students. In 1969, students from high-income families were more likely to attend four-year private colleges, and go to school out-of-state. During the past 30 years, only slight progress has been made in severing the connection between socio-economic status and post-secondary school attendance." [Pp. 1.50–54]

Thus the cynic might well inquire whether the claim that college education increases income is in fact result or coincidence arising from the type of population attracted and accommodated. The thought is not altogether new, as evidence Peter Finley Dunne:

"D' ye think th' colledges has much to do with th' progress iv th' wurruld?" asked Mr. Hennessy.

"D' ye think," said Mr. Dooley, " 'tis th' mill that makes th' wather run?" ["The Future of China"]

"THE MEN OF MEASURED MERRIMENT"

Accountability in American higher education also includes the New World version of the English Royal Commission—the study task force that is appointed and financed by the private foundation, the mirabile dictu commission. Work of this kind is not new and is often useful. The 1910 Flexner Report on medical education is probably the classic model, even though the imprimatur of a commission is lacking.

There is an inevitable ritual about the organization and composition of such a body which, though private in authority and appointment, must achieve the aura of officialdom.

Thus, membership will include among others:

> A British scholar, or better yet a British college master, to recall the Royal Commission parallel.
>
> The equivalent of the archbishop of Canterbury.
>
> Representatives of special groups such as blacks, women, etc. On occasion a double-threat player appears who qualifies in more than one classification.
>
> A "public man," preferably a former high public official whose public career lends esteem but small likelihood that he can contribute future responsibility, power, and resulting criticism.
>
> "Enlightened industrial leaders."
>
> Altogether with an assortment of university presidents, often emeriti and now relieved of day-to-day, troublesome responsibilities.

Despite the formula of commission organization and composition and the assurance with which pronouncements are made and issues decided, the brute truth is that the New World Commission, like many people in higher education itself, has the opportunity to persuade and little else. Moreover, the commission must know that what it says, by and large, will be cited as authority for previously held positions rather than any changing of minds. Such, of course, is the fate of most expert witnesses who are divorced from power-to-decide and responsibility-to-account.

Thus, the current work of the Carnegie Commission on Higher Education, dealing with suggested levels of federal support of higher education, will be cited by lobbyists for higher education and completely disregarded by members of congressional appropriation committees. At the same time, the work of the commission in *More Effective Use of Resources*[22] will be used by opponents of full funding as evidence of profligate and inefficient administration that ought to disqualify higher education from public assistance until it first cleanses its own house.

Attempts to generalize about higher education inevitably lead to serious inaccuracies; for example: "The administration, however, raises the money. The people who spend the money [the faculty] do not raise it, and the people who raise it have only modest influence over how it is spent" (pp. 21–22) is simply wrong. Any consideration of practices in funding research demonstrates the contrary.

Rarely is any commission able to rise above the lowest common denominator of its staff. The individual members of the Carnegie Commission would never make the patronizing comment that "We support continued faculty responsibility for the essentials of academic life" (p. 22).

At times the rhetoric hides the assumptions. Thus it is suggested that, in planning budgets, institutions "concentrate more on outputs and less exclusively on inputs, and particularly more on 'value added'" (p. 23). What is the output of higher education? The Carnegie Commission offers to this writer an opportunity for an unpardonable pun in the recommendation that "Counselling can help reduce the reluctant attenders, as can limits on the years permitted as a graduate student, as can more frequent exit portals as provided by the Associates of Arts and Master of Philosophy degrees" (p. 16). These functions are outputs, in fact put outs, but is this what higher education is all about?

The failures of secondary and primary education in this country, particularly in the central city, impose on the educational system responsibilities for massive retreading. The high school diploma may be evidence of "social promotion" rather than ability to read, and there is the extra essential, for the welfare of all society, that further opportunity be offered. *But is this further opportunity an obligation of higher education?* Often the wisest institutional deci-

---

22. *The More Effective Use of Resources: An Imperative for Higher Education*, A Report and Recommendations by the Carnegie Commission on Higher Education (New York: McGraw-Hill, 1972); specific citations are given at close of quotations.

sion is the most modest. The decision of the University of Michigan that its mission did not permit a proliferation of campuses over the state built no empires but did preserve the soul of the institution.

Generalizations do not apply with accuracy. The Carnegie Commission recommendation on graduate programs is a case in point:

> A more general problem, exemplifying a danger of overreaction to factors tending to depress enrollment, is the recent trend toward deliberate curtailment of graduate enrollment at some of the leading research universities, including Harvard, Princeton, Yale, the University of California at Berkeley, and the University of Wisconsin at Madison. [P. 95]

Thus,

> The Commission recommends that leading research universities refrain from cutbacks in graduate programs except on a carefully considered, selective basis. We also recommend that institutions with less emphasis on research consider curtailment or elimination, on a selective basis, of Ph.D. programs that are not of high quality or that are too small to be operated economically. We urge great caution in the development of new Ph.D. programs in particular fields at existing doctoral-granting institutions and do not believe that there is a need for any new Ph.D.-granting institutions, although some or even many institutions will be introducing the D.A. degree. [P. 97]

Never have decisions to curtail graduate enrollment at "leading research universities" been taken lightly. These determinations have come, no doubt, only after searching examination of institutional strengths, weaknesses, needs, and resources, all as measured against the university's view of its own mission and responsibility. Generalizations from the bleachers, however well located and occupied, are really quite unimportant.

The strength of many of the great state universities is evidenced, not by the state's Higher Education Organizational Chart, but rather by the ability of these institutions to attract and hold great and productive faculty and students over long periods of time. Merited private endowment and support have been generated so that these institutions could have the flexibility to undertake the extraordinary efforts not permitted under state funding. Often this support, though not large in proportion to total budget, made the difference between mediocrity and greatness, and the board of regents that permitted the dissipation of funds to a statewide system failed their responsibilities to a past generation who cared about the future.

The Carnegie Commission is not alone in trying to quantify. Other groups, some genuinely governmental, now seek to determine comparative costs of education, classroom instruction, and all the rest, divided among departments, schools, and institutions. The Carnegie Commission concedes that comparisons cannot be made of universities and colleges of widely varying type, but it then suggests that at least comparisons between generally similar places could be helpful.

The comparative measurements would be most helpful where the matters compared are comparable—particularly among auxiliary services. But how can one truly compare academic instructional costs without assuming that one hour of instruction is the equivalent of another? If the purpose of higher education is forced feeding of information, the assumption might be tolerable, but if the purpose is to teach men and women to think, and think creatively to the end that knowledge be advanced, the measurements and the comparisons fail.

THE CREATIVE SCHOLAR

The creative teacher will fool the computer. Designers of the Plato computerized system of instruction believe that the system cannot be "committed to any single educational approach but could usefully augment any teaching strategy," and that strategy depends on the interest, insight, and ability of the teacher.[23]

A recent letter of Albert Szent-Györgyi is worthy of quotation:

> Wilhelm Ostwald divided scientists into the classical and the romantic. One could call them also systematic and intuitive. John R. Platt calls them Apollonian and Dionysian. These classifications reflect extremes of two different attitudes of the mind that can be found equally in art, painting, sculpture, music, or dance. One could probably discover them in other alleys of life. In science the Apollonian tends to develop established lines to perfection, while the Dionysian rather relies on intuition and is more likely to open new, unexpected alleys for research. Nobody knows what "intuition" really is. My

23. Allen L. Hammond, "Computer Assisted Instruction," *Science* 176 (1972): 1112.

guess is that it is a sort of subconscious reasoning, only the end result of which becomes conscious.

These are not merely academic problems. They have most important corollaries and consequences. The future of mankind depends on the progress of science, and the progress of science depends on the support it can find. Support mostly takes the form of grants, and the present methods of distributing grants unduly favor the Apollonian. Applying for a grant begins with writing a project. The Apollonian clearly sees the future lines of his research and has no difficulty writing a clear project. Not so the Dionysian, who knows only the direction in which he wants to go out into the unknown; he has no idea what he is going to find there and how he is going to find it. Defining the unknown or writing down the subconscious is a contradiction in absurdum. In his work, the Dionysian relies, to a great extent, on accidental observation. His observations are not completely "accidental," because they involve not merely seeing things but also grasping their possible meaning. A great deal of conscious or subconscious thinking must precede a Dionysian's observations. There is an old saying that a discovery is an accident finding a prepared mind. The Dionysian is often not only unable to tell what he is going to find, he may even be at a loss to tell how he made his discovery.

A discovery must be, by definition, at variance with existing knowledge. During my lifetime, I made two. Both were rejected offhand by the popes of the field. Had I predicted these discoveries in my applications, and had those authorities been my judges, it is evident what their decisions would have been.[24]

Ernst Mayr, in "The Nature of the Darwinian Revolution," speculates why the theory of evolution was so long delayed in promulgation and acceptance:

> A scientific revolution is supposedly characterized by the replacement of an old explanatory model by an incompatible new one. In the case of the theory of evolution, the concept of an instantaneously created world was replaced by that of a slowly evolving world, with man being part of the evolutionary stream. Why did the full acceptance of the new explanation take so long? The reason is that this short description is incomplete, and therefore misleading, as far as the Darwinian revolution is concerned.
>
> The long time span is due to the fact that not simply the acceptance of one new theory was involved, as in some other scientific revolutions, but of an entirely new conceptual world, consisting of numerous separate concepts and beliefs. And not only were scientific theories involved, but also a whole set of metascientific credos....

24. *Science* 176 (1972): 966.

> It is now clear why the Darwinian revolution is so different from all other scientific revolutions. It required not merely the replacement of one scientific theory by a new one, but, in fact, the rejection of at least six widely held basic beliefs [together with some methodological innovations].[25]

Mayr's paper is, of course, much more than an essay in the history of science. It is, rather, a penetrating and unusual analysis of man's intellectual processes and efforts, truly belonging in any liberal arts curriculum. Szent-Györgyi and Mayr, it is submitted, are really what higher education at its best is all about.

The tasks of reparation for previous failures of the educational system; a custodianship assumed by some people to be a desirable feature of the late teen-age and young adult years; the process of information certification, even in later years, through the "open university"—all these may all be desirable societal objectives. But they need not, in fact ought not, be committed exclusively to higher education. Colleges and universities are only one of the paths through which maturity may be achieved.

The time has long since gone when higher education was needed to act as custodian or, for that matter, protector. Whenever higher education assumes that role in today's circumstances, two things are bound to happen: One group of people is certain to demand why the dean cannot compel students to cut their hair and to act and dress decently and respectfully. Another group will contend that the university must protect the members of its community from responsibility for excesses because youth is the time for deep feelings and experiences, and only in the maelstrom of emotion can truth be found. However colleges and universities may vary in their views of mission, the end product cannot be emotion as a substitute for intellect.

Thus at one law school, so it is reported, a professor of criminal law recommended to his students that, to understand criminal law, they must first be arrested and spend a night in the local jail. The difficulty with the approach is that the function is misconceived. Law students at some point in their future careers may be obliged to enter a courtroom or a negotiation where the freedom, perhaps even the life, of the client is at stake or, in civil matters, the financial security and future of the client and his family may be in the balance. Few people would contend in these circumstances that,

25. Ibid., p. 981.

for the lawyer to function properly, he need have been a bankrupt or a prisoner so that he could understand the pain, indignity, and humiliation of his client.

LESS RATHER THAN MORE

Higher education, then, must claim less rather than more. It must say to supporters and detractors alike that the enterprise of higher education itself is an act of faith, not a guaranty. No college or university can contract with anyone that on graduation day it will deliver an output—as the phrase goes—of certified educated bodies. It could far more honestly say that in the course of human history the ideas and concepts that have changed man's view of himself and his universe, as Darwinism did, come but at rare intervals; that the process of education at the creative level is not one where accounting can ever be immediate.

Thus the accounting required of higher education is quite different from that often proposed. Whenever colleges and universities become the equivalent of high schools or vocational academies, then the standards of the educationist are indeed fitting. Or whenever the college or university is understood only as an organization of competing selfishness rather than one of principle, then the viewpoint and techniques of labor conciliation may seem proper. These responses are never appropriate from those who understand that higher education, despite all its frailties and inefficiencies, is a testament and legacy to the power and promise of the inquiring mind. The accounting then required is far more rigorous: loyalty to a mission provided by a generous past and fidelity to a demanding future.

Women in Higher Education: An Unsatisfactory Accounting

CAROLYN SHAW BELL

MR. LEVI'S REMARKS are entitled "Issues of Accountability." Let me begin with the issue of Mr. Levi's accountability to this conference, whose topic is "Women in Higher Education." What has he given us by way of a contribution to this subject?

His paper includes a rehash of disputes surrounding the Coleman Report, which of course dealt with schools, not higher education. He presents a superficial account of several controversies over the proper role of the university: Should it engage in secret defense research contracts? Should it manage investments with consideration given to social policy? Should it respond to student unrest, or to an overtaxed public? None of these bears directly on the subject of women in academe. His two paragraphs referring to federal law about discrimination by race and sex badly distort the content of that law. Mr. Levi does not help us understand the situation of institutions of higher learning with respect to women. He offers no prediction of what colleges and universities will do to give account of themselves, no insight into how their decision-makers formulate questions about women in higher education, nor any analysis of organizational or administrative characteristics that might affect the status of academic women. Yet Mr. Levi can easily defend himself against this charge of irresponsibility, of irrelevance to matters that count at this conference, for he takes the lofty position that those who truly appreciate the nature of higher education realize that it is above accountability, that it need not defend or justify itself, because, after all, education is a Good Thing.

Well, it won't do. This sort of hortatory rhetoric no longer impresses us. To all the high-flown language about the inquiring mind, about education's generous past and demanding future, people may give the deadly serious response, "*Whose* inquiring mind? Whose past? Whose future?" And in simple fact, women are people. We have inquiring minds; we are not content with the past record; we expect more from the future. Need I add that we are quite capable of amassing power not only to demand an accounting but also to demand change?

Any responsible contributor to a conference dealing with women in higher education would treat the topic of accountability in terms of its implications for women. There are at least three ways in which the word *accountability* can be used: to give an accounting *of*, to be accountable or responsible *to*, and to stand up and be counted *for*.

The last, of course, implies a moral or ethical stance, the straightforward question of what is right. Is it right for those discussing higher education to speak of its functions in teaching men *and women* to think, and then for them to claim that women are not thinking when they find male-dominated universities and colleges less than satisfactory? Is it right to speak of a "generous" past which, for centuries, has seen women in this country and the world denied an education? Is it right to prescribe what belongs in a liberal arts curriculum while refusing to prescribe also that women be allowed to study that curriculum? Is it right to expect faith and loyalty to institutions which forced women to set up their own separate system of education so that they could learn to think? Indeed, let the decision-makers in higher education stand up and be counted. The first issue in accountability, for women concerned about what is going on, is to find out who is *for* us, who is for our inquiring minds, who believes that we can think.

Next, the question of being responsible or accountable *to*. Mr. Levi dismisses the demands of government or the public or investigating commissions for such an accounting because, he thinks, such bodies lack expertise and understanding. But surely students have a right to responsible action from their teachers. Anyone engaged in higher learning must accept some accountability to students, at least to cope with questions raised by the inquiring minds exposed to higher learning. How then will universities and colleges answer their women students? If we are qualified to be admitted to your institutions, if your faculties find us qualified to graduate from your institutions, if we fulfill not only your requirements but also your highest expectations for learning, why are we not qualified to be part of your faculties? What did we leave undone? What did you not tell us?

Mr. Levi, like many others, tells us that numbers are suspect, that the quantitative approach cannot be trusted to deal with equality, that colleges and universities hire individuals, not quotas, and—but you know what comes next. Sad but true, the best qualified individual most frequently turns out to be a man. Well, Mr. Levi, numbers do count, as the institutions of higher education themselves have proved, in their so-called generous past, when they maintained a strict and small percentage of Jews in the student body, a token representation of blacks among the students, and zero percentages of free-thinkers, oddballs, malcontents, and women on the faculty.

Finally, to be accountable *for*. As an economist, I am tempted to chide Mr. Levi gently for using dollars to measure the cost of education or its returns in the form of higher income. These miss the point, as economists know. What colleges and universities are spending is not money, but human resources. What higher education deals with is human energy, human skills, human effort, and human accomplishments. If we don't devote these to education in our existing institutions of higher learning, we can use them elsewhere, and the alternatives encompass both war and peace. How can we decide what resources to use where unless we have an accountability for these resources—the stuff of human lives— by our colleges and universities? I suggest that in our demanding future we will insist that institutions of higher learning be accountable for the human resources entrusted to their activities. The male establishment, in our demanding future, will no longer be able to evade the issues.

ROBERT M. O'NEIL

Autonomy and Mythology: The Need for Neutral Principles

FOR ONE SECTOR OF THE AMERICAN ACADEMIC COMMUNITY, the issue of autonomy was centrally implicated in the nonrenewal-nonreappointment cases decided recently by the Supreme Court.[1] Numerous organizations and associations—the American Council on Education among them—appeared as amici curiae to caution against judicial intervention in such personnel matters. Court review of nonrenewal decisions would, they maintained, severely hamper internal university decision making, dilute the tenure system, and substitute external decision for campus judgment on vital academic policy questions.

There is at least a superficial validity to the claim that court review of such matters invades institutional autonomy. Yet the American Association of University Professors and other faculty organizations—vigilant guardians of campus autonomy in most contexts—took precisely the opposite view. From the faculty perspective, the extent of judicial review reflected in these cases provided an essential safeguard for other vital academic interests. Recognizing the tension between autonomy on the one hand and due process for nontenured faculty on the other, AAUP, the National Education Association, and the American Federation of Teachers resolved the dilemma in favor of the latter concept. Their judgment is not that autonomy of colleges and universities should be lightly sacrificed; rather, the faculty organizations believe that even institutional autonomy must occasionally yield in order to secure other vital interests. The dilemma is critical but must be resolved if real cases are to be decided.

Few cases involving infringement of university autonomy are easily classified. There are the relatively obvious instances of crude

1. Board of Regents of State Colleges v. Roth, No. 71-162, June 29, 1972; Perry v. Sindermann, No. 70-36, June 29, 1972.

309

political interference—demands by a governor or legislative committee for the summary dismissal of a controversial professor—where almost everyone would agree that autonomy has been illegitimately breached. But when the same action is ordered by a governing board, the answer is less clear. The *result* is no less reprehensible when the board acts in this way; indeed, it is probably more so because the board should know better and should protect rather than undermine academic integrity. From the perspective of the faculty, the students, and the campus administration, summary dismissal by a governing board is just as grave a threat to autonomy as gubernatorial intrusion. But has the institutional autonomy of the *university* been impaired by the board action? The answer is less clear because ultimate responsibility and authority for the governance of the university reside in the very board that has taken the controversial action. Indeed, board members will sometimes justify such summary action on the ground that hesitation on their part would subject the university to more grievous wounds at the hands of the legislature or the voters. Thus board action might be seen as a defense of, rather than an attack upon, the university's autonomy.

ACADEMIC FREEDOM AND INSTITUTIONAL AUTONOMY

Several other examples will suggest the difficulty of classifying cases in terms of invasion/noninvasion of institutional independence. When the governor intervenes to force the firing of a professor, all will agree that autonomy has been sacrificed. But what of the case in which a faculty member is terminated according to institutional procedures or policies that fall short of AAUP regulations? If an AAUP Committee A investigation is authorized, a report published, and censure voted by the association's annual meeting, has there not been external interference? The AAUP's investigation and censure mechanism would be largely ineffective if this were not the situation—if an adverse judgment followed by blacklisting in the *AAUP Bulletin* did not weaken the censured university's capacity to recruit faculty.

Objectively, then, AAUP investigation poses a threat to university autonomy. Yet few responsible university officials would indict the association and its machinery for this reason. External interference it may be, but of a wholly different kind. There is the critical difference of procedures, of course. No adverse AAUP action is taken without careful procedures having been pursued by the ad hoc committee, the full Committee A, and the association's annual meeting, with ample opportunity along the way for institutional review and critique of the draft report. Moreover, AAUP does not intervene formally until options for informal accommodation have been exhausted. The critical difference between AAUP and the callous governor lies in the realm of purpose: the justification of AAUP surveillance is the protection of the very principles of academic freedom which the governor's intervention violates. External interference may, in short, be necessary at times to protect and preserve internal integrity and fairness.

In some other areas, the distinctions between interference and noninterference are relatively clear, though the lines are less precise. Take legislative appropriations, for example. When the California legislature withholds funds for faculty salary increases because they believe professors are overpaid and underworked, or because they are angered by campus political activity, an invasion of university autonomy is readily identified. Equally clear was the threat to campus governance when the California legislature struck half the budget for the Academic Senate, especially when the responsible committee chairman asked on the floor: "What does the Academic Senate do but make themselves obnoxious? Why don't they fund themselves out of their own dues?"[2] These cases are obvious. But what of parallel action taken by an equally piqued legislature in passing a reduced lump-sum budget appropriation where (without a rider actually forbidding faculty salary increases or abolishing the academic senate) the same result could not be achieved directly? Reductions in appropriations might well cause lump-sum recipients to claim invasion of autonomy. In the last two examples, loss of budgetary options is not the same as loss of autonomy. It is not enough for legislators to *wish* they could constrain campus choice; they must actually succeed in doing so before we can say external interference exists.

In such cases—all save the crude political interference in personnel matters—different views exist about the effect on autonomy. Many would agree that such actions threaten institutional inde-

2. Quoted in *Los Angeles Times*, May 27, 1970, p. 1.

pendence, but would differ about the legitimacy of such threats. Just as the American Association of State Colleges and Universities and AAUP ended up on opposite sides of the nonrenewal-nonreappointment cases despite a shared commitment to institutional independence, similar differences exist with regard to many of the other matters reviewed here. Thus, it is misleading to label an action as a "threat to autonomy" as though the phrase were self-explanatory. Some threats to institutional autonomy are valid, even essential, to serve vital interests of the academic community; other intrusions are pernicious and illegitimate and must be checked. The hard task is to distinguish between the two.

A FRAMEWORK OF GENERAL PRINCIPLES

A set of neutral principles is needed to differentiate between legitimate and illegitimate intervention. The purpose of this paper is to offer five criteria that will not resolve all cases but at least may improve analysis. First, the criteria.

Displacement of professional judgment

1. *An external threat is illegitimate if it substitutes inexpert or uninformed judgment for expert, professional judgment on academic matters.* Several illustrations will suggest the application of this precept. One example is faculty teaching loads. The legislatures of New York, Michigan, and Florida took one route, attempting to prescribe in statutory form the minimum numbers of classroom contact hours per week for faculty members. Application of this crudest and least sensitive measure of faculty effort not only effectively preempted internal judgment on a vital personnel policy but also came at a time when institutional administrations were seeking their own ways to effect economies, improve efficiency, and increase contact between senior professors and undergraduate students.

The Ohio legislature took a quite different route. Early introduction of the Michigan formula evoked criticism from the Ohio AAUP Conference and the chancellor of the Board of Regents. The General Assembly eventually required instead that the faculties of the state colleges and universities generate the number of classroom credit hours required by the formulas of the Board of Regents. The difference is crucial: Apart from the preferable use of credit hours rather than contact hours, the Ohio law, instead of mandating a figure in the statute, left the specification of work load to the regents. If anyone is to prescribe such a formula, a governing board is far preferable to a legislature.

In another area, the Ohio General Assembly was less sensitive. A year earlier, Ohio House bill 1219 provided that the suspension and dismissal of faculty members and students following arrest for certain specified offenses would be judged by a referee appointed by the Board of Regents. Under the law, if a person who has been suspended by the referee is convicted of the offense, he forfeits his employment without further hearings. Because the referee is an attorney without any institutional connection, it is possible for highly complex and sensitive personnel decisions to be relegated to an external forum. Even the dismissal of a tenured professor could occur without internal faculty or administrative review. Thus the perils of external review and the possible displacement of internal procedures are substantial.

The hazards of displacement are also shown by the rash of court cases in spring and summer 1970. In the aftermath of the killings at Kent State University and the U.S. military incursion into Cambodia, many critical and sensitive decisions were shifted from the campus to the courtroom. Judges, often with little knowledge of academic traditions or needs, ordered some campuses to close and others to reopen. New York's highest court held that all law students must take written final examinations in order to be eligible for the bar, even though many classes had already been dismissed and final grades given. A New York trial court ordered members of the Queens College faculty to offer special instruction during the summer for classes "reconstituted" in May 1970. Many damage and injunction suits ensued, all with clear intent of displacing campus judgment by the process of inexpert judicial review.[3]

Absence of due process or fair procedures

2. *An external threat is illegitimate if it denies due process or fair procedure in the making of vital academic judgments.* It is in this area that a vital difference exists between the summary dismissal of a faculty member by gubernatorial edict and the thorough process

3. See generally Robert M. O'Neil, "Judicial Overkill," *Change*, September-October 1970, pp. 39–42.

of AAUP investigation. Cynical governors are not the only offenders, however. A similar objection can be made to legislation adopted without adequate notice to the academic community, thus denying any meaningful opportunity for participation or comment.

Cases in point are two New York bills, adopted late in the 1971 session. The first (vetoed by the governor) would have imposed faculty work load formulas, and the second virtually abolished sabbatical leaves for public employees. Both bills were rushed through committee and onto the floor in a matter of hours, with no warning to the educational community in the state. Where opportunity for comment and response is provided, the results have been markedly different, as in Ohio, where the work load bill was vastly improved, and in Illinois, where a similar proposal was actually defeated through vigorous lobbying.

The procedures of other external bodies may be similarly vulnerable. The enforcement of certain policies by the National Collegiate Athletic Association—policies with implications for university life far beyond the football field—may be procedurally deficient.[4] On similar grounds, the procedures of other state and local agencies might be challenged; state finance or auditing offices, for example, sometimes adopt rules and regulations that vitally affect academic life without first giving notice or opportunity for comment. On the *merits*, such action may be entirely valid; few would deny that a state auditor or finance director may ensure that appropriated funds are spent for the intended purposes. But the absence of fair procedures may also deprive a justifiable result of its substantive legitimacy.

Isolation of particular cases out of context

3. *An external threat in an area of legitimate concern may become illegitimate by singling out a particular case or individual rather than addressing general policies.* Although intervention in specific cases may at times be appropriate, the legitimacy of an external inquiry may often be forfeited by its very selectivity.

A prime example comes from the area of admissions policies and administration. There has been increasing resort to the courts

---

4. A recent suit filed on behalf of two disqualified University of California football players has challenged NCAA procedures and won a significant preliminary victory in the state courts.

through suits challenging the rejection of particular student applications. A state trial court recently held that a woman applicant had been improperly excluded from the Arizona State University College of Law, a decision reached after the judge had made an independent review of her file and was convinced that she was competent to do law school work.[5] No analysis was made of the hundreds of other persons accepted and rejected for the same class, or even of the criteria generally employed by the admissions committee of the faculty. More recently, a state superior court ordered the University of Washington School of Law to admit an Anglo applicant because his paper record seemed to the judge better than that of some thirty black and Chicano students accepted for the same class. Again, no attempt was made to appraise the matter in context; indeed, the court conceded that the plaintiff ranked in the fourth quartile of rejected applicants and thus would almost certainly never have been accepted had there been no preferential program.[6]

The error in such cases is not judicial intervention per se. There are times—the rejection of James Meredith by the University of Mississippi being a prime example—when a court must be ready to review the admissions policies of a public institution, despite the complexity of the process and the obvious perils of intrusion. A court should, however, limit its inquiry to the fairness and legality of the policies and procedures employed in making the admissions judgment. In the Meredith case, one could readily perceive that the University of Mississippi had drawn an unconstitutional color line.[7] Meredith might or might not be entitled to admission; that was ordinarily a question for the faculty to decide. Since the faculty refused even to consider the merits of the issue, it was appropriate for the court to decree his admission. But in the Arizona and Washington cases, scrutiny of the admissions policies and procedures would disclose them to be fair—as the Arizona Supreme Court in fact held in reversing the trial court—and would thus preclude judicial review of the application of those policies to individual files. Were the court to find constitutional fault with the

---

5. The Arizona Supreme Court reversed this unreported trial court decision. See Arizona Board of Regents v. Superior Court, 102 Ariz. 430, 477 P.2d 520 (1970).

6. DeFunis v. Odegaard, No. 42198, pending in the Washington Supreme Court.

7. Meredith v. Fair, 298 F.2d 696 (5th Cir. 1962).

policies or procedures, the appropriate remedy would be their remand to the responsible faculty committee for further consideration under valid guidelines.

Similar selectivity has tainted several recent actions of the Regents of the University of California. The regents had delegated to the Committee on Courses of the Academic Senate pervasive authority over course content. When the regents discovered that Eldridge Cleaver was scheduled to deliver several lectures in Social Analysis 139X, they withdrew the delegated power just long enough to deny academic credit for that course. Some months later, the regents withdrew from the UCLA chancellor the recently delegated power over nontenured faculty appointments just long enough to deny renewal to Angela Davis. In both instances, the delegation itself was neither inevitable nor immutable. Had the regents wanted to reassert authority over *all* such cases, that would have been a quite different matter—though both actions would still have been vulnerable on other grounds. The critical fault, however, was the *selective* and *ad hominem* (or *ad feminam* in one case) nature of the withdrawal to achieve a precise and specific regental objective while preserving the general policy.

Use of unnecessarily intrusive means

4. *An external threat may be illegitimate if it employs means more intrusive than are essential to the task.* This criterion derives directly from a constitutional law analogy. The courts have long held—in regard to loyalty oaths, security investigations, and the like—that even where the end is legitimate, a government agency must employ those means that are least dangerous to constitutional liberties. A showing that less intrusive means exist may deny the government resort to the more drastic approach.[8]

There are many situations in which less restrictive or intrusive means would achieve a valid governmental objective. In faculty work load, for example, the legislative aim may be to improve the efficiency of institutions of higher education or to increase the contact between senior faculty and undergraduate students. But there are many ways to realize either goal without requiring professors to punch time clocks. Faculty self-regulation is a vital component of responsible academic administration. Legislative mandat-

8. See Shelton v. Tucker, 364 U.S. 479, 488 (1960).

ing of work loads is likely, in fact, to be counterproductive because of its insensitive and intrusive character. Only where no viable alternatives exist should such restrictive approaches be utilized.

Political or other improper motive

5. *An external threat which is formally valid may be illegitimate if motivated by goals unrelated to higher education.* This final criterion seems obvious. The difference between crude political interference and self-regulation is explained by the terms themselves, if in no other way. The objective of any inquiry by an academic group, whether outside or inside the institution, is presumably to protect academic interests, whereas the purpose of legislative or gubernatorial interference in campus matters is often merely to win popular acclaim. The former objective is central to the integrity of higher education; the latter is not only irrelevant but also antithetical.

Once again, of course, these are the beguilingly easy cases. Most legislative actions are harder to appraise. Each legislator may in fact have a different reason for voting a particular way. Consider, for example, the curious case of an Oklahoma speaker ban bill cosponsored in 1970 by two lawmakers on the extreme opposite ends of the political spectrum. Support came from a man on the right because he was annoyed by radical protests on a state-supported campus; his ally on the left, one of two blacks in the legislature, was seeking ways to punish a campus administration he believed had unfairly excluded minority students. (Despite this unholy alliance, the bill ultimately failed.)

Moreover, each lawmaker may have goals that are partly pedagogical and therefore valid; partly parsimonious and therefore questionable; partly political and for that reason illegitimate. At the critical moment when the vote is cast, it is impossible to say which concern dominates. In most states, the absence of legislative history makes motive problematic.

Even where the goals are clearly stated, a judgment about their legitimacy may still be difficult. Consider the increasing use of government aid to influence subtly the policies of private colleges and universities—in New York, through the Bundy Act, to force the filing of student conduct rules by all campuses, and to shape curriculum of certain Catholic institutions; in New Jersey, to induce private colleges to "educate more New Jersey students, with a particular emphasis on students from low-income families," and so on. As the price for public support, pressures on the private sector are bound to increase and, with them, the attenuation between clearly valid educational concerns and other goals more remote but not obviously "political."

Of course the private institutions are theoretically free to avoid these subtle pressures by rejecting public funds. For a few potential recipients, refusal of funds is a viable option. Most private colleges and universities, however, face financial needs so severe that available aid must be accepted even if conditioned in ways that threaten autonomy. The claim that restrictions on public aid do not coerce conduct is rather like an argument—long since rejected in constitutional law—that an applicant for a government job who does not wish to sign a loyalty oath is always free to work elsewhere.

This analysis suggests that, in reviewing external threats to higher education, motive is an elusive, if important, criterion of legitimacy. Between the clear extremes, assessment of motive or purpose is complex and often confusing. Perhaps such assessment should be used only when motive is clear or when the resort to other criteria fails to resolve close cases.

THE PRINCIPLES APPLIED: THE CASE OF AFFIRMATIVE ACTION

This five-factor formula for judging threats to university autonomy is obviously not self-executing. One practical illustration is in order. No case study seems more suitable than the current federal affirmative action policies designed to ensure expanded faculty representation of women and racial minorities. Affirmative action provides a good microcosm for several reasons. First, of course, it is intensely controversial; the academic community is sharply divided over several facets of both policy and implementation. Second, many details of affirmative action are still being worked out, both in Washington and on the campuses, so that timely analysis may yet shape relations between the academic community and external agencies. Third, affirmative action poses for the academic community an acute dilemma: On the one hand, it is clear that something must be done, and done quickly, in this area. On the other hand, it is less clear that the current situation warrants extensive review and surveillance by governmental agencies.

Alan Pifer, president of the Carnegie Corporation, has recently and forcefully posed the dilemma:

> Personally, I regret that it has become necessary, because of intransigence, or at least a lack of perceptiveness, on the part of higher education, for government to take coercive action [under federal law]. Measures such as these seem to me to constitute an invasion of campus autonomy and an abridgement of academic freedom. On the other hand, government has a basic obligation to protect the rights of its citizens—yes, even women—and without the threat of coercion it seems unlikely higher education would have budged an inch on the issue. Certainly it had every chance to do so and failed.[9]

Motivation

Undeniably affirmative action policies and programs do threaten university autonomy.[10] But are such threats illegitimate? Resort to the five factors outlined earlier may suggest a tentative answer. First, let us consider motive or purpose, since it is most easily appraised. Although the government's rationale for the affirmative action program is not strictly educational, it is surely consistent with the basic premises of liberal and responsible higher education. Faculties on which women, blacks, and Spanish-Americans are acutely underrepresented—as they typically are in our predominantly white universities—cannot effectively provide broad and meaningful education for a democratic society. Even if the exclusion has not resulted from deliberate discrimination, the resulting imbalance is no longer tolerable. Some compensatory measures are now necessary. Apparently the catalyst must come from outside the academy, because we have failed to take adequate corrective measures on our own. As Columbia President William J. McGill acknowledged last summer, "We can have no quarrel with the principle of affirmative action, or with its objectives."[11]

The critical questions about affirmative action arise in regard to implementation. Had the federal government simply warned

9. Speech before the Southern Association of Colleges and Schools, Nov. 29, 1971.

10. This discussion, it should be noted, deals with affirmative action policies and their implementation in necessarily general terms. No attempt has been made to review or appraise particular provisions of statutes or administrative regulations or guidelines. The technical aspects of affirmative action have been and will continue to be explored in other contexts. The present use of the affirmative action issue is illustrative rather than definitive.

11. Commencement address, University of Michigan, May 6, 1972.

higher education to expand opportunities for women and minorities by suggesting that student demonstrations or private lawsuits might follow failure to do so, there could be no charges of interference or invasion of autonomy. But the present compliance procedures far exceed admonition. They encompass demands for submission of data, review of past action and future commitments, continuing surveillance, withholding of federal funds, and possibly other sanctions for noncompliance. Hence all the ingredients of an illegitimate external threat appear to be present.

Locus of judgment

Moving beyond motive or purpose, we must determine whether the vital decisions about affirmative action lie in sufficiently sensitive or expert hands. In the early stages, there have been some disturbing indicia of governmental insensitivity. The terminology of the directives issued by the U.S. Department of Health, Education, and Welfare, for example—discordant to the academic ear—implies lumping professorial and clerical employees. HEW Office for Civil Rights directives have spoken of proportions of "the total labor force," and some OCR measures of affirmative action performance refer to "skills" in gauging academic competence and have analogized preparation for college teaching to "training which a contractor could reasonably undertake as a means of making all jobs open to [minorities]."[12] A university president or dean understandably winces at being called a "contractor" by a Washington agency, but we must get over this kind of squeamishness. Moreover, the director of the OCR has acknowledged that, given the national character of the academic marketplace, "there is no . . . mechanism [available to] the university," as in the construction trades, which determines local labor pools and hiring goals.

The critical issue, of course, is not tone or terminology of the directives. What we need to know is whether analysis of data and the review and surveillance of institutional performance and future commitment will be in the hands of people who know how different a faculty is from other occupational groupings. There is already some cause for optimism: a young woman historian on leave from the national AAUP office played a vital role in framing the new

12. *HEW and Civil Rights* (Washington: Office for Civil Rights, Department of Health, Education, and Welfare).

HEW compliance policies; her presence indicates a regard for academic freedom and a commitment to the involvement of professional experts in the process. Further stages should reflect comparable participation of the academic community to ensure sensitive and informed judgment.

Recent legislation poses a possible additional threat. From the time of its enactment in 1964 until spring 1972, the employment title of the Civil Rights Act exempted the educational activities of colleges and universities from the ban on job discrimination. Since the recent enactment of Public Law 92-26 (signed March 24, 1972), however, it is now possible for an aggrieved faculty member to bring a case to the Equal Employment Opportunity Commission, a federal agency with an exemplary record but no experience in academic matters. If the Commission fails to reach some resolution, the complainant may then bring suit in a federal court. Should the court find there has been intentional discrimination, it might order the employment or reinstatement of the plaintiff and might award up to two years' back pay. Given the rather spotty record of courts and government agencies in other sensitive academic matters, this recent extension of the fair employment law warrants some anxiety.[13]

Procedural fairness

Our third criterion is the fairness of the procedures used by an external body in judging academic matters. Under this rubric, the status of the affirmative action program is still problematical. On the one hand, actual termination of federal funds because of discrimination requires an elaborate procedure—so elaborate, in fact, that federal attempts to end discrimination in some public institutions in the South have been severely hampered. On the other hand, as Columbia University has discovered, new funds may be withheld from a recalcitrant or noncompliant contractor for long periods without any formal proceeding, specific charges, or opportunity for court review. It appears that "suspension" of this sort may continue for an indefinite term pending receipt of a contract com-

13. For general background on pertinent legal provisions and procedures, as of spring 1972, see "Sex Discrimination and Contract Compliance: Beyond the Legal Requirements," *A.C.E. Special Report* (Washington: American Council on Education, April 20, 1972).

pliance plan satisfactory to the agency. If this is the case, then the strong statutory guarantee of full due process under title vi of the 1964 act may be partly illusory.

Selectivity

Our fourth criterion is particularly apposite here. External intervention may become illegitimate, we suggested, when it removes a particular case from the institutional context and renders a selective judgment. Perhaps the greatest anxiety about the affirmative action program arises in this regard. It is one thing for a federal agency to find that a university has generally failed to employ sufficient numbers of women and minority faculty; it is quite another matter for that agency to decree that a *particular* woman or black or Chicano shall be hired, promoted, granted tenure, given a salary increase, or such. Even where the judgment of the agency is sensitive and expert on such matters, any external body should move with only the greatest caution to countermand the judgment of a faculty on academic personnel matters. If the agency determines that discrimination has occurred, that relevant evidence has not been considered (or irrelevant information improperly considered), that an unfair standard has been applied, or that the decision is otherwise tainted, the matter should be returned to the faculty for further consideration under proper standards. The later decision may, of course, again be reviewable to ensure compliance with the agency's mandate. But for an external body having coercive power to redetermine academic personnel questions may pose the gravest threat to academic freedom. The agency's role should be to appraise the fairness of the process by which the decision was reached, not to review de novo the merits of that decision.

Means and sanctions

Finally, there is the element of implementation: where an agency employs means more drastic than necessary to achieve a legitimate end, the result may be tainted. Affirmative action programs and policies raise three questions in this area. First, it would clearly be unsound for a government agency to mandate rigid quotas for employment of women and minorities—nor has the government done so—when goals and target ranges should suffice. Apart from serious constitutional objections to quotas, fixed and arbitrary percentages have in the past been most harmful to women and ethnic minorities. The nature of the academic profession makes flexibility in this regard particularly necessary. In a given year, the number of available women and minority persons meeting the institution's needs and requirements may far exceed the goal, whereas in other years it may fall below those levels. The long lead time created by tenure, dates of notification, promotion procedures, and the like require maximum flexibility in professional employment goals, as contrasted with goals for industrial or construction employment generally and for university employment of clerical and technical personnel.

Apart from the danger inherent in quotas, there are risks surrounding the sanctions for the enforcement of affirmative action. A temporary denial of federal funds may pose some problems for a building contractor or research corporation, whereas even a relatively short delay can cripple an academic program. Yet the affirmative action program appears to assume the propriety, if not the necessity, of holding back many millions of contract dollars pending submission of satisfactory compliance plans. Less severe sanctions must be developed, which will bring about compliance with valid federal regulations without bringing the institution to its knees. Moreover, there is the risk (nearly realized at Columbia) that an entire campus may be denied vital funding because of the recalcitrance of a few departments or units. Clearly there is need for sanctions that would be less harsh and more selective.

Finally, in the realm of means, something must be said about federal agency demands for personnel files in the course of compliance investigations. Given the extremely sensitive nature of file contents, it is small wonder that officials at Michigan and Berkeley granted access to those files with the greatest reluctance. Should personnel records become generally available to federal officials, without adequate safeguards of confidentiality, the very information that is sought could become unavailable in the future. For example, if senior faculty fear that written comments could be freely scrutinized by unknown federal officers, the transmission of collegial evaluations might increasingly become oral. Ways must therefore be found to gather and study essential information about university personnel decisions and policies without risking general access to sensitive files. Basic principles of academic freedom require safeguards for the confidentiality of these records.

A review of the five factors brings us back to the inescapable question: Does the federal affirmative action program represent an improper invasion of university autonomy? Any answer at this point must be strongly qualified. Given the validity of the governmental goals, institutional autonomy is not inevitably violated. The critical determination in each case will depend on the several factors we have reviewed here: the sensitivity and experience of the persons making the critical judgments; the fairness of the procedures used to determine compliance; the deference to academic judgment in particular cases; and the development of methods and sanctions that will safeguard vital institutional interests. As with any new governmental program, it is wisest to presume good faith and sensitivity at the outset. It is also appropriate to withhold judgment until we have considerably more experience.

Affirmative Action on the Campus: Like It or Not, Uncle Sam Is Here to Stay

BERNICE SANDLER

It is disappointing that Mr. O'Neil did not clarify the distinction between "academic freedom," which applies to individuals and their rights to publish, teach, and take positions on matters outside the classroom, and "institutional autonomy," which deals with the "freedom" of an organization to conduct its affairs without government interference. Moreover, there is the freedom of an individual to earn a living, a right that has been upheld by the courts as being constitutionally valid and guaranteed. How does it violate institutional autonomy or academic freedom to ask an end to preferences that have always existed: the preference for whites, the preference for males, the preference for graduates of the "better" schools, the preference for members of the "old boy" club?

What are institutions complaining about? Are they saying that the laws and regulations that require affirmative action are unfair and unjust and should be abolished? Or are they saying that the law is good and just, but that somehow academic institutions are "special," and should be exempt from the laws that the rest of society must follow?

Whether or not these laws are just, the courts have upheld them in case after case. They have upheld that affirmative action is necessary if discrimination is to end. The courts have distinguished between *affirmative action* on the one hand, and *preference* on the other, and they have upheld that numerical goals (not quotas) do *not* violate the Constitution or the legal prohibitions against preference. Surely the argument that the laws are unjust has found no support in our courts. And surely, when Professor O'Neil lists the ingredients of an "illegitimate external threat" as being demands for submission of data, review of past and future commitment, continuing review of employment practices, and the withholding of federal funds, he knows that these measures have all been upheld in the courts. If the law is just, then why should institutions be exempt from it? Every group offers special reasons why the law should not apply to them. Doctors talk about their "special" relationship to patients; lawyers talk about "privileged" information. No one likes having the government tell them what to do, especially in the area of discrimination.

The Congress has clearly mandated that equal opportunity should apply to the campus. The speed with which the Congress this year extended title VII specifically to cover educational institutions, the extension of the Equal Pay Act to cover faculty, and the prohibition of sex discrimination against students all indicate that Congress saw no reason to grant a special exemption for academe. (Women's groups had predicted these three measures would be passed between 1972 and 1975.)

Affirmative action is required to remedy the effects of past discrimination and to prevent the continuation of current discrimination. Most controversial are the numerical goals that are set in line with the number of qualified people available, *not* the number of women or minorities in the population. Goals are targets that an employer *tries* to achieve. He has to show that he has made a *good faith effort* to meet the goal: that he really tried to recruit, hire, and promote women and minorities, and he must document his efforts. If he fails to meet the goal, and if he can document his efforts, nothing happens, for the obligation to meet the goal is not absolute. There is no intention whatsoever to force employers to hire lesser qualified women or minorities.[1] If the best qualified

1. There is a not-so-covert assumption that women and minorities are, almost by definition, not "qualified."

person is white and male, that is who is hired. What employers need to do is twofold: (1) make a genuine effort to recruit women ("good faith" does not mean calling one's white male colleague, asking if he knows a good *man*, and then saying, "I'd have been glad to hire a qualified woman if I could have found one") and (2) apply criteria or standards set for men equally to women and minorities.

The words "academic freedom" and "institutional autonomy" have become smoke screens to obscure the basic issues. Women's groups claim the terms are being used in ways analogous to the cry of "states' rights" or "quality education." Institutions are upset because they have generally relied on the old-boy method of recruiting, the vast informal network of old school chums, colleagues, drinking buddies, etc., a network from which women and minorities have been largely excluded. The merit system has always been a closed merit system from which large portions of the available, qualified pool have been excluded. The government is not asking that the merit system be abolished, only that it be opened up to a larger pool of qualified persons. To recruit in a different manner means change, and change is never easy, particularly if it means women and minorities threaten the traditional power base.

Institutions are disturbed because administrators who have never had to justify employment decisions or to specify criteria for hiring and promotion are now being asked by the U.S. Department of Health, Education, and Welfare why Mr. X is a full professor and Ms. Y is a lecturer, particularly when X hasn't published since he wrote his thesis and is a terror to students, and Ms. Y is continually awarded the best teacher award and has a string of publications.

HEW, it should be noted, will not set criteria for hiring and promotion; rightly, they ask institutions or department heads to do this. What HEW does ask is *why* someone was hired or not hired, *and what the criteria were.* For those who have never had to justify an employment decision, the experience is quite threatening. Yet if an administrator cannot justify a hiring or salary decision, then either someone is in the wrong job or getting the wrong salary, or you have an incompetent administrator.

It is unfortunately true and tragic that some HEW personnel themselves have been misinformed about what numerical goals are. Any institution that feels it is being forced to hire unqualified women or minorities and to discriminate in reverse should indeed fight.

If institutions give preference[2] to less qualified women or minorities over better qualified white males, then such institutions are violating the very laws and regulations they are seeking to observe; such preference is clearly prohibited by law.[3] What is at stake is not the hiring of lesser qualified persons, but a very real economic threat: *for every woman or minority person that gets hired, one white male is not hired.* White males will now have to compete with women and minorities for the scarce job opportunities.

Professor O'Neil makes two other errors: He sets up the straw man of "confidentiality of records" when he must know that these records cannot be disclosed by HEW personnel; the records are protected from disclosure by the Freedom of Information Act. He discusses the application of title VI of the Civil Rights Act to federal procedures; yet that title has no jurisdiction whatsoever over employment nor does it relate to sex discrimination (covering only race, color, and national origin), nor does it have affirmative action requirements such as those contained in the Executive order.

Women are the fastest growing and potentially the largest advocacy group in academe. The demands for equal employment opportunity are not a passing fad, but will be with us until institutions truly practice the democratic ideals we all profess.

2. For a look at arguments *for* preference (as in admissions), see Robert M. O'Neil's "Preferential Admissions: Equalizing the Access of Minority Groups to Higher Education," *Yale Law Journal,* 80 (March 1971).

3. The only time preference may be given is when two applicants are equally qualified *and* there has been a history of discrimination or exclusion. In some cases where blacks were almost totally excluded from employment, the courts have ordered that a particular number of vacancies be filled by *qualified* blacks, or that the employer explain why he was unable to do so. In no instance have employers been forced by the courts to hire unqualified persons.

ROGER W. HEYNS

Renewal, Financing, Cooperation: Tasks for Today

I WANT TO TAKE this opportunity to make some observations about the nature and responsibilities of leadership in postsecondary education today, to offer some views on the present situation in higher education, and to outline what I consider the main tasks before us.

The function of leadership in higher education today is complex. Collective higher education has chosen, and quite properly, to avoid a centrally administered apparatus for its activities. It is committed to diversity in virtually every area: curriculum, organization, governance, and sources of support. As a consequence, higher education is not and does not look tidy. Opinions and practices continue to differ. On those issues on which consensus appears desirable, we must accept that the processes for achieving it are laborious and imperfect. I am not suggesting that the mechanisms for voluntary collective policy making should not be improved. Indeed, one of the principal objectives for the American Council on Education is to work with others to improve these mechanisms. But, to paraphrase John Gardner, we must have the grace to live with the consequences of our choices.

With this reminder of the extent to which we share the leadership task, let us turn to the situation of higher education today. The goals we choose and the style with which we pursue them are substantially affected by our views about the distance we have come, our assessment of current strengths and weaknesses, and an evaluation of our environment.

First, some observations about the recent past, the period of turmoil. On balance, I am more heartened by the accomplishments of education in the past decade than discouraged by its failures. Academic leadership has been beset by enormous challenges to its purposes, modes of governance, and procedures. Yet, our institutions have emerged stronger, more adaptive, and more sensitive.

In the last few years, they have made substantial progress toward achieving a better fit between their resources and their expenditures, painful though that process has been. There are many indications that institutions are responding to new obligations. For example, many graduate schools, particularly the largest and most firmly established, have made remarkable, perhaps even too drastic, responses to the current reduced demand for postgraduates. In every state there are new institutions responding to new educational responsibilities and established institutions experimenting with new pedagogical methods and revised curricula. Colleges and universities have come through a period of severe threat as, by and large, sturdy institutions with the internal strength to make the constructive changes that will continue the pattern of usefulness characteristic of the past.

Parenthetically, our institutions were not the only ones to learn from their difficulties. It has been insufficiently noted that society as a whole has learned to be more sensitive to value differences and discontents among its members. Many other institutions have also undertaken to complicate their decision-making processes. Acceptance of the need to share authority and responsibility with new constituencies is greater. In these and other ways, society has applied the lessons that the educational institutions mastered, often painfully.

With this evident adaptability and sensitivity to social needs comes a proper wariness of the fads and fashions of education beyond high school. Not only is there an awareness that educational institutions are creatures of society and must be relevant to it, but there is also an equally keen appreciation that the proper educational stance consists of more than a quick response to social wishes as currently defined.

Current Attitudes Toward Higher Education

Continuing this internal look: What about the attitudes of students and faculty? How do they feel about our collective enterprise?

Data collected by the Council's Office of Research and published by the Carnegie Commission on Higher Education show that a large proportion of undergraduates and graduate students are satisfied with their college experience. In 1971, *Newsweek* published the results of a study indicating that students hold overwhelmingly positive attitudes toward educational institutions and rate them more favorably than any other type of institution. Another Carnegie study shows that a substantial majority of faculty members are satisfied with their career choices and the way their institutions are treating them. This degree of satisfaction is probably higher than many other professions could show.

What about public attitudes? In spite of our problems, public opinion polls continue to show that the majority of citizens have retained, with startling constancy, a high regard for college and university education.

Another Carnegie study shows the same to be true for that very important group, the state legislators. By and large, they retain great faith in higher education and indicate a considerable and sophisticated understanding of our problems and an appreciation for our contributions. And they manifest their esteem in continued financial support. The data available from thirty-seven states on 1972 appropriations show an increase of 24 percent over appropriations for these same states two years earlier.

Although the appropriation level for the federal government for 1973 is still unclear, the Congress passed and the president signed amendments to the Higher Education Act of 1965 which are basically positive in their effects and reflect an enlarged commitment to the support of education beyond the high school. Although supporters of higher education in Congress disagreed among themselves and some of them with the collective leadership, those who followed the legislation closely noted that the basic attitude of these elected officials, whose understanding is so important, was positive.

Private support shows the same positive trend. In 1970–71, the latest year for which data are available, private giving reached an all time high.

Enrollment figures, while not unambiguous, are an important index of the extent to which higher education is seen as important by society. Recent figures show an increase of 40 percent over five years ago, and the projected increase for fall 1972 was 6 percent.

In short, the leadership of higher education is not incompetent, we are not leading a bankrupt system, and we do not live in a hostile world.

The basic condition, then, is favorable. And it is from this fundamental posture that we contemplate the future. I do not suggest that there are no problems in the above areas: public understanding of the nature of higher education is incomplete. There are dissatisfied students, at least some of whom drop out as a result of higher education's failure to respond to their needs. There are faculty members dissatisfied with the conditions under which they work. Almost all institutions need more money and, for some, the financial problems are so severe they face closing. Another source of complexity for the leadership lies in the need to convey to the public both our accomplishments and the unresolved issues. All are eager to assert the strength of the higher education community and to defend it against unwarranted and ill-informed attacks, but we do not want to be, or appear to be, self-satisfied or defensive. Yet, if we can legitimately feel an inner strength, as well as the conviction that we can and must do better, then the only posture that makes sense is a mature acceptance of both conditions.

A conscientious evaluation of the situation, with proper recognition of the positive signs, will reduce response time and increase receptivity to new ideas. Many, by underestimating past success and present health, and by overestimating the inhospitality of the environment, have developed a habit of maintaining a low profile. Nothing will fill the alleged leadership gap more promptly and effectively than for us to speak out thoughtfully on educational issues and options. Consensus, while desirable, is less important right now than participating vigorously in the public debate on educational policy. The need is less for a unified voice than for carefully elaborated options put forward by dedicated and informed educators.

Toward Continuous Self-Renewal

Three major tasks encompass almost all the specific problems before higher education:

The first is to develop within our institutions the mechanisms and the attitudes that nourish continuous self-renewal. Here again, I acknowledge a debt to John Gardner, who provided a series of essays on this subject. My reading of the past decade suggests that we have lacked sensitivity to the early manifestations of discontent, and that we have tended to look for large, even total, institutional responses. The slow response led to the compounding of problems. The orientation to large-scale solutions also slowed reaction by requiring the involvement and participation of people who didn't feel the need for change. Improvements in performance and in the satisfactions of higher education are more likely to come from small incremental gains than from quantum leaps. We habitually think we satisfy the need for change by discrete events; I propose a constant posture of self-assessment and review.

There are many mechanisms by which this sensitivity and posture toward small experiments and reforms can be achieved within institutions. To cite one possibility: two institutions with which I have been associated have found it useful to sequester a small fraction of the annual budget to support good ideas. The amount of change that can be stimulated and the number of ideas for improvement which can be generated by a small sum are remarkable. Other institutions have also found this same device useful. In any case, we should systematically develop a section in our budgets for research and development in practices and procedures. Industry knows and approves this concept. The above two institutions were able to get support from the business community. This fund, whether it is from a reallocation of present resources or from outside sources, becomes an in-house foundation, asserting institutional commitment to self-renewal as a continuous, rather than an episodic, process.

The U.S. Office of Education's program for the improvement of postsecondary education—one could possibly call it an embryonic national foundation—should become a substantial resource over time. It will be much more effective if we adopt the mode of governance and the institutional stance that support efforts at continuous self-renewal. Although we often describe ourselves as conservative, when it comes to the institutional behavior, each of us is aware that ideas abound for doing things better. The task is to make these impulses toward improvement effective, not once every five years, but somewhere in the institution all the time. We tend to deprecate change for its own sake. I think we underestimate the value of novelty, of altering habits as a means to create new interest and stronger motivation. Sometimes the best argument for change is that some group wants to try something new.

Toward a Theory of Financing Higher Education

The second large task is to develop a theory—a social contract, if you will—about financing higher education. We must achieve some general agreement about which sources of support should provide for particular educational functions. What are the educational responsibilities of the state? Which responsibilities are shared by the state and federal government? What is the proper proportion of cost to be borne by the students? What assistance should be provided for what kind of student? These questions are now being asked and, indeed, answered as a practical matter. These social contracts are now being developed in the cities, in the states, and in various parts of the federal government, all more or less independently. In many cases, we now make decisions about student contributions in a setting of negotiations with legislatures about the annual budget. Or we deal with the student charges in the context of an attempt to reduce the differential between public and private institutions, as part of a larger program to help private institutions. A complicating factor in any discussion of financing is the new wave of proposals for tax reform. The new school of tax economists is challenging the very concept of the charitable deduction. These economists would have all funds flow directly into the U.S. Treasury and then be redistributed through the appropriations process. If one believes that the peculiar strength of higher education in this country is rooted in the diversity of its support, one can only view with dismay efforts to make institutions almost completely dependent on governmental support.

I am certain that the first statement of a complete theory of financing will be unsatisfactory; I am equally certain that we must develop a theory quickly for everyone to examine and debate. The outlines of one can be seen: the panel discussion in the September 1972 *Change*, participated in by the chancellor of a state system, the president of a quasi-public university, and the president of a large private university, comes close to outlining one set of propositions about who should pay and for what.

Soon we will have other tentative statements on these matters. The Carnegie Commission has a paper in preparation, the Committee on Economic Development is to release another. Presumably, the National Commission on the Financing of Postsecondary Education will also have something to say. Our task, as educators, will be to lead the national discussion of these reports through carefully stated positions as individuals and efforts to develop a collective position reflecting the welfare of higher education and the nation. We must regard these matters from the viewpoint of the total endeavor, as well as from our respective institutional vantage points. If these decisions are to be made in political terms by legislative and executive leaders in government, nothing will be more effective than for educators to array themselves as narrow partisans.

The need to develop consensus about financing seems especially urgent if we are to avoid painful and harmful controversy between public and private institutions. The public-private relationship is becoming increasingly strained, largely as a result of preoccupation with controversy over single solutions. A proper distribution of support and a proper sharing of educational tasks call for consensus on a broad comprehensive theory of financing education beyond the high school.

TOWARD STRENGTHENING COOPERATION

The third task, closely related, is to develop and strengthen mechanisms for collective planning, coordination, and control. Involved is the whole range of regional and state commissions and councils, both statutory and voluntary, advisory and decision making. No one can seriously doubt that such mechanisms are needed if higher education is to utilize its resources effectively and respond intelligently to the requirements of society. Yet the history of the relationship to these commissions and councils is not flattering to higher education.

For a considerable period, we denied the need for these agencies. When they were finally forced upon us, we were often responsible for their lack of authority and financial weakness. We could, as a consequence, ignore them. Now, both of these deficiencies are disappearing, and our posture has changed to a kind of reluctant participation that is given its tone through an artistic mix of legitimate anxiety and paranoia. We must now wholeheartedly accept the inevitability and legitimacy of these agencies, and make a genuine commitment to work collectively to solve the problems they present to individual institutions. We must all help in determining what these problems are, where decisions should be made, and what data are needed both by the institutions and by the central system to make the decisions assigned to each. These are not moral issues, though one is often tempted to conclude that several new religions have developed. They are practical problems that can be resolved to retain the integrity of both the planning and systems control process and the effectiveness of the institution. There is no question that many decisions, long made on individual campuses, will now be made elsewhere. The issue is which decision areas to locate on campus, which to locate in a central system, and which to share.

Unfortunately, higher education now lives with the consequences of its attitudes toward the coordinating agencies. The delicate issues, complicated enough in themselves, are made more difficult by accumulated distrust, scars from previous battles, and a continuous combativeness. The personnel in the central office view the institutions as secretive, rigid, and obsessed with the rhetoric of autonomy. The institutions view the coordinator as obsessed with power, insensitive to the dynamics of campus life and institutional aspirations, and preoccupied with cost data. Fortunately, there are illustrations across the land that these stereotypes are dissipating. But progress toward building a satisfactory overall framework for institutional performance will be made only through commitment to unreluctant participation and to making the coordinating mechanisms strong and wise.

COUNCIL COMMITMENTS

Each of these tasks involves us all. Each, of course, will receive special attention from the Council. With respect to self-renewal, the Council is committed to organize a systematic follow-up of the recommendations of the many commissions, such as the Carnegie Commission, the Commission on Non-Traditional Study, and the Commission on Academic Tenure in Higher Education. The Council will develop mechanisms to facilitate the discussion of financing. And, finally, in an effort to improve the quality of the discussion of coordination, the Council will strengthen its relationships with the parties involved.

In the context of these three tasks, the Council and educational leadership generally will also deal with important but subsidiary problems: responding more adequately to women and ethnic minorities in terms of admissions, curriculum, and employment; preserving and, where necessary, increasing the diversity of higher education; maintaining standards of excellence and an appropriate amount of institutional autonomy; preserving the health and vitality of private institutions; and increasing public understanding of post-secondary education.

The leadership tasks of today involve little that is exotic or new and exciting; they constitute just plain hard work. Nevertheless, they are important enough to stimulate us and give us a sense of participation in significant social developments. We have a good track record through participation in raising the educational level of an unparalleled proportion of the population. We now confront the tasks of ensuring equal opportunity for all and of developing a lifetime partnership with all citizens. To achieve those encompassing goals, higher education must develop the capacity for continuous self-renewal, a social contract about finance, and sensitive, strong systems to coordinate individual efforts.

It is not for us to argue that if problems of finance, coordination, and institutional reform would go away, then a career in educational leadership would be a good one. These are the demands and this is the life. And it is a good life.

AMERICAN COUNCIL ON EDUCATION

Roger W. Heyns, *President*

The American Council on Education, founded in 1918, is a *council* of educational organizations and institutions. Its purpose is to advance education and educational methods through comprehensive voluntary and cooperative action on the part of American educational associations, organizations, and institutions.